HOMOSEXUALITY AND THE CHRISTIAN WAY OF LIFE

Edward A. Malloy

UNIVERSITY
PRESS OF
AMERICA

Copyright © 1981 by

University Press of America, Inc.

P.O. Box 19101, Washington, D.C. 20036

All rights reserved

Printed in the United States of America

ISBN: 0-8191-1795-1 (Perfect)

ISBN: 0-8191-1794-3 (Cloth)

Library of Congress Catalog Card Number: 81-40385

DEDICATED: CHARLES SHEEDY, C.S.C.
            PRIEST, FRIEND, TEACHER

iii

Contents

v

Preface

Few aspects of contemporary life in America are as charged with emotion as the topic of homosexuality. In an age when public self-revelation has become fashionable, a whole series of famous and not-so-famous people, both inside and outside the Christian Church, have 'come out of the closet.' The increased militancy of homosexual activists has, in some places, precipitated an equally fervent counter-attack from those who feel they are defending the integrity of the monogamous family unit. Gay spokespersons accuse their enemies of an unexamined assent to the pervasive 'homophobia' of Western culture. In response, defenders of the traditional ethic picture the majority of homosexuals as promiscuous, immature and chronically unfulfilled (far from the usual connotations of 'gay!).

This controversy in the broader culture has also reached into the daily life of the Christian churches. At the theological level, a number of recent studies have challenged the viability of the traditional prohibition of all overt homosexual behavior. At the pastoral level, homosexual Christians have raised the issue of full homosexual rights within the Church.

This book is a response to this controversy. It is intended for Christian believers who would like to become better acquainted with the ethical issues raised by the problem of homosexuality. I have structured the book in such a way that even those who disagree with my ethical conclusions might become more familiar with the complexity of factors that must be taken into account in arriving at a responsible ethical judgment.

The book is divided into two major sections. The first part is organized around the descriptive concept 'the Homosexual Way of Life.' In the seven chapters of this section I treat various issues raised in the social scientific literature on homosexuality. In the second part I turn to

the explicitly ethical discussion of homosexuality
as it has taken place in the Christian community.
First, I review the Scriptural and theological
material that have been used to support the traditional prohibition of overt homosexual behavior.
Secondly, I analyze the three main approaches to
the issue in current Christian discussion. Then I
develop an interpretation of 'the Christian Way of
Life' and use this concept as a criterion for
judging the ethical status of the Homosexual Way
of Life. Finally, I turn to several pastoral and
ecclesiological issues related to homosexuality
and offer my own opinion about how the Christian
community should deal with them.

In preparation for this book I have read a
wide variety of literature and have discussed the
matter with homosexuals and heterosexuals. However, the very nature of the topic makes it impossible to know for sure whether pertinent dimensions of the homosexual experience have been
neglected. Because homosexuals have traditionally
been a 'silent' minority, it is only recently that
some of the less public forms of homosexual life
have been studied. The greatest deficiency I
experienced in researching the book was the dearth
of written material on the world of the Lesbian or
female homosexual. Overall I have striven to take
into account as many different points of view as I
could.

This book might best be characterized as a
response to the revisionists. I want to suggest
that every discussion of disputed moral issues
goes through several stages. The first stage is
usually a challenge to the inherited tradition.
The second stage is a response from the defenders
of the tradition. The third stage is the development of a new consensus. Depending on the outcome
of the debate in the first two stages, this new
consensus may represent either a reaffirmation of
the tradition or a significant modification of it.
As I view the present controversy we are in the
second stage. It is my conviction that the revisionists have not made their case. But it will be

the function of the book as a whole to offer proof
of this claim.

Acknowledgements

Grateful acknowledgement is made to the following for permission to reprint copyrighted material:

The Westminister Press for extracts from Jonathan Loved David: Homosexuality in Biblical Times by Tom Horner, copyright © 1978 by Thomas M. Horner; From "Toward a Theology of Homosexuality," by John von Rohr, from Is Gay Good?: Ethics, Theology and Homosexuality, edited by W. Dwight Oberholtzer, copyright © MCMLXXI. Used with permission of the publisher.

W.W. Norton & Company, Inc. for extracts from Sexuality and Homosexuality by Arno Karlen, copyright © 1971 by Arno Karlen. Used with permission of the publisher.

Paulist Press for extracts from Sexual Morality: A Catholic Perspective by Philip Keane, copyright © 1977 by Philip Sullivan Keane; From Human Sexuality: New Directions in American Catholic Thought by Anthony Kosnick, et. al., copyright © 1977 by the Catholic Theological Society of America. Used with permission of the publisher.

Our Sunday Visitor for extracts from Counseling the Homosexual by John R. Cavanaugh, copyright © 1977 by Our Sunday Visitor, Inc. Used with permission of the publisher.

Theological Studies for an extract from "Notes on Moral Theology," by Richard McCormick, copyright © 1971 by Theological Studies. Used with permission of the editor.

Homiletic and Pastoral Review for an extract from "The Priest and Teen-Age Sexuality," by Richard McCormick, copyright © 1965 by the Homiletic and Pastoral Review. Used with permission of the editor.

PART ONE

The Homosexual Way of Life

.

1

Chapter 1

An Introduction to the Language

of Homosexuality

In his moving autobiography the Episcopalian priest and writer Malcolm Boyd describes his evolution from closeted homosexual to gay activist within the Church. "Ever so gradually, I moved from self-identification as 'homosexual' to 'gay.' As I did so, I also moved out of isolation into relationship-finally, into community."[1] From a much different frame of reference, Arnie Kantrowitz speaks of his participation in a similar process of sexual self-definition. Referring to his days of gay activism in New York City after the Christopher Street riots in 1969, he says,

> "We practiced all forms of relating, from compulsive chastity to glad promiscuity and every sexual stripe in between. Sex was everywhere...My body made love to everyone it could, proudly offering and receiving pleasure, restrained only by the limits of imagination. Though sex ran lovely riot through the Gay Activists Alliance, we were more than an orgy: we were a tribe with all the complex loves and political rivalries of a nation."[2]

These are but two perspectives among many but they highlight the dramatic change that often takes place when an individual begins to employ the language of the homosexual sub-culture to describe him or herself. In terms of moral understanding, the sexual activity itself is less significant than the concepts and images which are used to interpret it. At that point in a person's life when a particular mode of sexual relating is no longer seen as compulsive, nor as an isolated fragment of behavior, nor as a phase of growing up, but as a freely chosen way of self-expression, then a new situation has arisen. Such a person searches for an adequate means of expressing this new personal vision.

4

I am convinced that one of the major tasks of
the ethicist is to help people recognize how the
language they employ to describe themselves and
others is full of potential for both insight and
self-deception. As Herbert McCabe has reminded
us, it is only because we belong to communities
of discourse that we can portray our experience to
others with some hope of being understood.[3] The
meaning a word has springs from the common frame
of reference of those who make up a linguistic
community. But just as communities change and
develop, so the available stock of words and concepts shift in meaning or are replaced by more
satisfactory alternatives.

Our present dilemma is complicated further
because most of us participate in a plurality of
communities, each of which may have its own manner
of describing the same phenomenon. Think for
instance of the range of terms available to us to
describe the death of a friend. In polite society, we might say, "She passed away;' among Christians, 'She is now at peace with God;' to a lawyer, 'She died without leaving a will;' and to a
physician friend, 'She suffered a severe heart
attack at close to midnight.' Or reflect for a
moment on the importance of language in the controversy over abortion. Is an abortion the death
of a 'person,' or a 'human being,' or an 'individual,' or a 'fetus,' or a 'growth in a woman's
body?' Is it an 'act of homicide' or a 'surgical
procedure' or a 'termination?'

What should be obvious is that the conflicting language schemes available to us incorporate competing views of reality. Thus our very
choice of words is a means of conveying our value
commitments and ultimate convictions about the
nature and purpose of human life in society. As
Stanley Hauerwas suggests,

> "the basis and aim of the moral
> life is to see the truth, for only
> as we see correctly can we act in
> accordance with reality...Ethics

5

is the modest discipline which uses careful language, distinctions, and stories to break the intellectual bewitchment that would have us call lamps the sun and adultery love."[4]

In this spirit of inquiry, I will examine in this chapter the language which has been employed by homosexuals, as well as observers of the diverse homosexual scene, to describe the various forms of homosexual life and experience.

I. The Matter of Definition-What is a Homosexual?

In its popular usage, the word 'homosexual' refers to a person who is erotically attracted to a member of the same sex. It is derived from the Greek word for 'same' (homo) and not from the Latin word for 'man' (homo), as is sometimes believed. Thus there is no specification given whether the person being referred to is male or female. It is proper then to say male homosexual or female homosexual unless both types are under discussion. In fact, however, the word Lesbian (from the Greek island Lesbos where the poetess Sappho celebrated female homosexual love in her poetry) is normally employed when a female homosexual is the point of reference.

But these definitions according to common usage do not prove very helpful once the more difficult questions of categorization begin to be asked. For example, how can a homosexual be told apart from a heterosexual? Are there only two pure types or are there other mixed categories which encompass the majority of humans? Is one assigned an identity on the basis of a certain number of, or percentage of, homosexual acts or are desires and dream content sufficient? Can one be a homosexual in one stage of one's life and a heterosexual in another? Do homosexuals look or dress or act different from homosexuals? Can one falsely think oneself a homosexual because of

6

propaganda or peer influence? Once these and other questions begin to be asked, the problem of definition becomes more acute.

(a) The first factor that must be taken into account in any adequate definition of homosexuality is the relationship between feelings or emotions and overt behavior. Some commentators wish to concentrate almost exclusively on the level of feelings or erotic attraction. Martin Hoffman describes homosexuals as "those individuals who have a sexual attraction toward partners of the same sex, over at least a few years of their lives."[5] There is no mention of whether this identity has to be tested through acting out with same-sex partners. Presumably, the attraction is the key and could be sustained over the course of a life-time without any sexual interaction of an explicit sort. The vast majority of writers on the subject would adopt this same position. For them, homosexuality is more a matter of feeling than of action.

C.A. Tripp, on the other hand, places a greater stress on sexual activity.[6] Since he presupposes a subtle interplay of various influences in the sexual maturation process as the key to sexual identity, the ultimate test is finding a degree of contentment and pleasure in same sex erotic involement.

(b) The second factor of significance is the age and maturity level of the person being described. There is plenty of evidence that the experience of many men and women includes some episode or period of life when either homosexual behavior took place or a strong attraction to members of the same sex was present. Many of these individuals later make an adjustment to heterosexual patterns and consider this earlier phase of their life to be somewhat of a mystery. Still others find an explanation in the one-sex environment of a school or summer camp.

In order to stress the importance of age considerations, Ruth Tiffany Barnhouse speaks of a homosexual as one who has made "an adult adaptation characterized by preferential sexual behavior between members of the same sex."[7] Marc Oraison is satisfied with the qualification 'beyond puberty.'[8] A third theorist goes a step further in suggesting that the dividing line is whatever age a person can be said to be homosexual, not as a phase in the developmental process, but as a "constitutive element of the personality."[9]

Some homosexual activists are convinced that the definitive signs of homosexuality are clear from some period in pre-adolescence on, perhaps as early as five years old. But they provide no workable criteria to discern the difference between those who can trace back a confirmed homosexual identity into an early age and those who speak of homosexual episodes as a misstep in the growth process. As a result, a post-pubertal age criterion is deemed a minimum by most who have studied the issue. And some percentage of these favor a young adult standard as applicable in the majority of cases.

(c) A still further factor concerns the attitude toward the opposite sex. While some homosexuals deny that they experience any repugnance toward the opposite sex, some contributors to the discussion are not so sure. John Harvey, for instance, phrases it this way, "Basically, homosexuality is a neurosis of personality producing a sexual propensity for person's of one's own sex associated with fundamental repugnance for intimate relations with the opposite sex."[10] John Cavanaugh, who has collaborated with Harvey on occasion, gives a more restrained definition. "Homosexuality may be defined as a persistent, postadolescent state in which the sexual object is a person of the same sex and in which there is a concomitant aversion or abhorrence, in varying degrees, to sexual relations with members of the other sex."[11]

8

While the form of homosexual subculture in the United States has tended to isolate lesbians from male homosexuals, it is not clear how much stress should be placed on the negative affect that Harvey and Cavanaugh refer to. Does this preclude male-female friendships among homosexuals? Or is it rather that the thought of genital intimacy evokes a deep-seated psychic repugnance to the other sex. This problem is further complicated by the not insignificant percentage of homosexual men who have been heterosexually married and the high number of lesbians who have. Some want to claim that sexual orgasm is achieved in these instances by fantasizing a homosexual partner.

That there are some homosexuals who have a strong emotional hostility toward sexual expression with the opposite sex seems clear. But it is not generally accepted that this is always the case and the existence of warm friendships with both men and women in the lives of some self-described homosexuals seems to play down the significance of this factor.[12] It might be better to describe the prevailing attitude as one of indifference (as it probably is with heterosexuals who contemplate homosexual behavior).

(d) A fourth factor of definition has to do with whether the word 'homosexual' should be understood as an adjective or as a noun. For those who consider all patt erns of sexual identification as contingent and somewhat arbitrary, it is impossible to categorize a person according to a sexual type. In this way of thinking there are no homosexuals as such but only separate individuals who exhibit varying degrees of homosexual behavior. In this mode, Allen Young asserts that "the word homosexual was an adjective before it was a noun."[13]

However, this claim goes aginst the grain of those who stress that homosexual condition, when it really exists in a person's life, is firmly established and seemingly irrevocable. When an

9

individual in the adult stage of life continually experiences him or herself as homosexual, the noun form seems to be an accurate description at least of the individual's sexual propensity.

The evidence is indeed overwhelming that some percentage of human beings, after attaining an appropriate level of self-awareness and of maturity, experience themselves as 'homosexual' for the duration of their life. For these persons, the descriptive term 'homosexual' in the noun form seems justified. Still, since this captures only one dimension of their life and personality, it should be used with sufficient reserve. Just as we do a person a disservice to overplay the significance of their gender, racial, ethnic, religious, educational or economic backgrounds, so their sexual orientation captures only one dimension of their selves.

(e) A final factor to be considered in any adequate definition of the homosexual is whether or not he or she participates in a <u>unitary or pluralistic</u> phenomenon. Is it the case that each homosexual is so unique in kind that the common factors shared with other homosexuals are irrelevant to the descriptive task? One way of expressing the question is to claim that there is no 'homosexuality' (that is, a condition or state of being homosexual) but only 'homosexualities' (that is, separate and distinct patterns of causality and structures of sexual orientation).

Allen Bell makes the assertion, upon the basis of his research at the Kinsey Institute at Indiana University, that the category 'homosexuality' has been seriously misused.

> "By way of summary, our data appear to indicate that homosexuality involves large number of widely divergent experiences -- developmental, sexual, social, and psychological -- and that even after a person has been labeled

10

homosexual on the basis of his or
her preferred sexual object
choice, there is little that can
be predicted about the person on
the basis of that label."[14]

In fact, when Bell and Martin Weinberg came out
with the results of their extensive study of homosexuals in the San Francisco Bay Area, they titled
it Homosexualities: A Study of Diversity Among Men
and Women.[15] They say, "Ideally, 'homosexualities' (i.e., the numerous ways in which one can
be homosexual) should be exactly juxtaposed with
'heterosexualities'...there is no such thing as
the homosexual..."[16]

In a later chapter I will subject this important work to more extensive analysis, but suffice
it to say at this point that there is a strong
ideological claim built into such a switch in
language. The authors adopt a plural form of the
word because they wish to counteract the sickness
model of homosexuality. They wish to show that
homosexuals who are mentally ill are only a small
percentage of the whole group. And further they
wish to make the descriptive language as value-
neutral as possible. In the process, they imply
the normativity of a pluralistic tolerance of
sexual styles and orientation.

It is unlikely that social scientists and
others will cease to search for common factors in
the homosexual experience. In fact, Bell and
Weinberg offer a typology of their own. Thus the
continued use of the concepts 'homosexual' and
'homosexuality' in the singular can be expected.
But the introduction of plural forms does remind
us of the need for discrimination. The word
'homosexual' will necessarily refer to a particular person only at some highly generalized level
of their existence.

(f) Conclusion -- For the purposes of this book,
I will describe a homosexual as 'a person, male or
female, who experiences in adult life a steady and

11

nearly exclusive erotic attraction to members of the same sex, and who is indifferent to sexual relations with the opposite sex.

II. Homosexual Categories

In an attempt to broaden the range of our descriptive language, various writers on the subject have proposed a series of distinctions which are intended to more effectively capture the differences in the homosexual experience. These qualifying terms purport to distinguish a true from a false homosexual, to pinpoint homosexual roles, and to generally allow for a more accurate typology. To some extent, this is required by the recognition that homosexual behavior does not necessarily coincide with a homosexual identity nor with a desired homosexual future.

(a) Homosexuality as a phase or as a constitutive element of the personality -- Gregory Baum helped to popularize the distinction between phase and constitutive element.[17] For all of those persons who fall into the first category (for whatever reason), homosexual feelings and/or activity are temporary and non-determinative aspects of that individual's sexual self-expression. Presumably, these tendencies will be outgrown or a shift in circumstances will allow heterosexual feelings and relationships to take place more readily. On the other hand, for those who are constitutively homosexual, this element of their self will be a permanent attribute and an emotional focus for all social interaction.

This distinction highlights both the ambiguous meaning of some forms of homosexual expression and also the possibility of a settled disposition which will perdure across time. For Baum, the critical question is what is the moral status of the latter condition. However, at this point in our discussion, it seems sufficient to indicate that these two categories seem to be helpful in

12

speaking of two different meanings of homosexual feelings and behavior.

(b) Homosexuality as <u>inversion</u> or <u>perversion</u> -- In 1882 Drs. Charcot and Magnan wrote a paper title "Inversion of the Genital Sense."[18] This was the source of the term 'inversion' which began to be used to refer to the true homosexual disposition. An Invert is a person whose normal sexual feelings are reversed or turned inside out.

In a number of recent writings, however, inversion has been contrasted with 'perversion' where a normally heterosexual idividual has homosexual relations. Thus D. Sherwin Bailey restricts the applicability of certain Biblical passages because the homosexuality being referred to, in his opinion, is indicative of widespread social degradation and not a morality for inverts. He says, "the Bible knows noting of inversion as an inherited trait, or an inherent condition due to psychological or glandular causes, and consequently regards all homosexual practice as evidence of perversion."[19] John McNeill draws upon Bailey's categories to play down the moral significance of homosexual activity by genuine inverts. He claims that,

> "the genuine homosexual condition
> -- or inversion, as it is often
> termed -- is something for which
> the subject can in no way be held
> responsible. In itself it is
> morally neutral...The pervert is
> not a genuine homosexual; rather,
> he is a heterosexual who engages
> in homosexual practices, or a
> homosexual who engages in hetero-
> sexual practices."[20]

Once again this is not the place to examine the exegetical use that Bailey and McNeill make of this distinction, but it should be obvious that the term 'invert' refers to the same condition as

13

'constitutive element of te personality' in the first pair of categories. It is the second term 'pervert' which is being forced to fit too many contexts of sexual behavior. If there indeed is a phase in some peoples' lives when they have an uncertain or mixed sexual identity, the term pervert would seem excessively pejorative unless the activity itself were reprehensible whatever one's sexual disposition. In the traditional condemnation of homosexual behavior, it is the objective deficiency in the form of sexual expression which warrants the use of 'perversion,' and not the subjective feelings of the participant. While one may object to this form of argumentation, it seems that the distinction between 'inversion' and 'perversion' begs too many questions to make it very helpful in the kind of situations we are concerned about.

I will take the word 'invert' to be synonymous with confirmed adult homosexual. But I will not employ the term 'pervert' unless further specification is given of the value set that is being presupposed.

(c) <u>Homosexuality</u> and <u>Bisexuality</u> -- There is a wide divergence of opinion over whether the phenomenon of 'bisexuality' actually exists. Partly this is a result of disagreement about what is meant by the term. The concept of bisexuality seems to predate the scientific era and to have been one form of etiological explanation for the polarity of the created order.[21] However, it was Sigmund Freud who popularized the concept in psychoanalytic theory. Drawing upon the biological understandings of his day Freud presumed that the zygote was constitutionally bisexual. Through the course of development, one or the other gender inevitably began to become evident so that at birth the baby was denominated as male or female. In much the same way, he pictured the psychic constitution of the individual, at its earliest stages, as 'polymorphous perverse,' that is, capable of being attracted by a broad spectrum of sexual objects. In the vast majority of cases,

14

one or the other disposition predominated by the time of sexual maturation.

While Feud restricted his use of the term 'bisexual' to the potentiality for both hetero-sexual and homosexual attraction in the evolution of each individual's sexual identity, more recent commentators have tended to create a category of humans who are equally attracted to, and capable of pleasurable sexual activity with, members of both sexes. What would determine the choice of partner for such people would be the urging of the moment and/or the relative availability of men and women.

C.A. Tripp, for example, thinks that there are people who respond equally well to both sexes, but he suggests that two separate sets of criteria are brought to bear in rating and choosing part-ners of different sexes.[22] On the opposite side of the issue are Edmund Bergler and Irving Beiber who conclude that the heterosexual component of the behavior pattern of so-called bisexuals is always subordinate to the homosexual component which is more gratifying and fulfilling.[23]

It must be said that at the present time there is not sufficient proof that there is a third category of sexual orientation called 'bisexuality.' Rather there seem to be some pre-dominantly heterosexual or homosexual persons who, with varying degrees of frequency, have a strong erotic attraction to, and are capable of orgasm with, both sexes. There is some doubt about how to describe the psychological process which takes place. With some, fantasization of a homosexual experience seems to allow for erotic engagement in a heterosexual experience. This would be more critial with male homosexuals where physiological arousal is a sine quo non. With others, it is doubtful whether bisexual performance can be sus-tained over a significant portion of one's life.

Therefore, I would conclude that the term 'bisexual' is best understood as an adjective and

15

not a noun, that is, it qualifes the range of sexual experience of some persons who are basically either heterosexual or homosexual.

(d) The Contingent Homosexual -- H. Kimball jones has coined this term to describe those heterosexual persons who engage in some homosexual activity in one of three kinds of situation: (1) experimental (ii) variational (iii) situational.[24]

The experimental situation refers to those instances of adolescent sexual exploration which are precipitated by curioisty, ignorance, or the non-availability of opposite sex peers. In some cases, a whole group of adolescents may participate. But more often it seems to be a surreptitious experience between two juveniles who soon become disinterested or too fearful to continue. Experimental homosexuality is understood to be a relatively harmless part of growing up which has no long-range diagnostic value.

For Jones, the variational situation encompasses those heterosexual adults who have become bored with conventional forms of sexual release and wish to test their capability for homosexual orgasm. This would tend to be possible primarily in Bohemian settings where conventional taboos are systematically challenged. Or an individual could set out to have a fling in the homosexual subculture without fear of exposure or scandal. It is not clear that this category would refer to very many instances of homosexual behavior, especially after adolescence.

The third form of Homosexual activity is called situational and it seems to be the most prevalent. In prisons, military camps, boarding schools, seminaries and other one-sex environments, some individuals will tend to focus their erotic drives upon the available partners in the institution. Some of this may be very hesitant and concentrated at the level of masturbatory fantasy. But it can also take overt form in periodic engagements in clandestine settings. In response

16

to this possibility, such institutions frequently have rather rigid rules governing social interaction among the inhabitants. The United States military, for example, still considers the admission of homosexuality as grounds for dismissal, whether one has actually manifested this propensity or not.

In general, it can be said that those individuals who are heterosexual usually move away from homosexual behavior once they leave the confines of such restricted one-sex environments. And the younger the person, the less such a background seems to reveal about his or her sexual identity. But the importance of such experiences should not be totally dismissed since all of our human activity tends to live on, consciously or unconsciously, in our character as moral being.

At this point a brief word is in order about homosexuality in prisons.[25] Studies of the sexual behavior of men in prison have indicated that the majority do not engage in homosexual activity. However of those who do, most do not consider themselves homosexual and return to heterosexual patterns once they are released. In fact, the level of frequency of sexual activity in prison is much diminished, compared to the pre-internment habits of the same men, seemingly because of the deadening quality of the environment. It is the young and frail prisoner who most has to fear being homosexually raped by other prisoners. In these situations where choice is not involved, it is the trauma of brutalization that is the most important factor and not the gender identity of the other party. In prisons, such forced homosexual behavior is more often an expression of a power relationship than it is a manifestation of erotic preference. As Karlen asserts, "It seems that sexual deprivation is far from the chief motive for prison homosexuality. Rather, homosexuality becomes an instrument for establishing rank and status, validating masculinity, and creating protective-dependent relationships."[26]

17

By way of summary of the category of the contingent homosexual, what is being claimed is that some heterosexual persons have engaged in homosexual activity for some period of their lives without this affecting their ultimate sexual identity and preference. The experiemental and situational explanations of this contingency seem to be better borne out by the evidence than the variational one.

(e) <u>Transvestism</u> and <u>Homosexuality</u> -- Transvestism refers to the propensity in some individuals to dress in the apparel of the opposite sex as defined by a particular culture. Since at first sight this seems to be a manifestation of a desire to <u>be</u> of the other sex, it is easily confused with popular images of homosexuality. In fact, some transvestites are homosexual. But a higher proportion seem to be heterosexual. And the vast majority are males.

Most transvestites avoid the gay world and cross-dress normally in the privacy of their own bedrooms, usually as a prelude to heterosexual intercourse. The whole point of the pretense is to be a male passing. The small percentage of transvestites who are publicly visible are more likely to be effeminate homosexuals with transvestite tendencies. This is the case with the 'female impersonators' who entertain at gay gathering places.

The cross-dressing phenomenon is one of the major sources of confusion for those people who are unfamiliar with the homosexual world. For it contributes to a stereotype which pictures male homosexuals as basically swishy, effeminate types who fundamentally wish to be women. A recognition that the majority of transvestites are not homosexual may serve to balance the picture.

(f) <u>Transsexualism</u> and <u>Homosexuality</u> -- A very small percentage of the population come to a point in their life when they feel burdened with a body which gives them a gender definition different from their psychological sexual identity. Such people are called transsexuals because they wish to change their genital endowment accordingly. And in recent years medical technology has made some versions of sex-change surgery possible.[28]

Up to now most transsexuals who have sought surgery have been males. They look upon their bodies as a mistake of nature. These men do not see themselves as homosexuals since they are convinced that they are female. What they desire is a kind of psychic peace which they expect to come only through sex-change surgery. The difficulty is that such procedures are expensive, painful and often traumatic. and the end-result is not a normal or fertile person of the opposite sex.

Transsexualism is such a rare phenomenon, despite the preoccupation of late-night talk shows with the subject, that it is not a major consideration in this study. But it does force us to acknowledge that homosexuals tend to be persons who accept their bodily givenness as male or female and do not wish to change. What makes them unique is their objects of sexual preference and not their denial of biology.

III. The Language of the Homosexual World

(a) 'Gay' -- In Webster's dictionary there are three meanings given for the word 'gay':merry; bright in appearance; and licentious. But in recent American usage it has been more and more co-opted by the homosexual community as a term of proud self-proclamation. To describe someone today as gay is automatically to evoke in the listener a sexual frame of reference first of all, and only secondarily the traditional connotations. This change in meaning has been rather quick, prompted largely by the mass media and the homosexual rights movement of the last decade.

19

Jeanne Cordova gives a brief etymological history of the new usage in a short piece, subsequently reprinted for general consumption. She says,

> The word 'gay; comes from the French word 'gai,' which became popular in France in the Middle Frency burlesque theater as it was used to describe mock-feminine (swish?) roles. Because women were not allowed onstage, all the mocking and burlesque was done by gai men. Later the term came to be applied to any and all men who appeared feminine, on or off stage. The word was never meant or used to describe lesbian women.[29]

In more recent times, in the pre-liberation movement context of America, the word 'gay' seems to have functioned as a code word, the full meaning of which was available only to the initiated. Because of its other connotations, it could be safely employed in an ambiguous fashion.

Franklin Kameny, an early member of the Mattachine Society and a homosexual activist in Washington, D.C., is credited with coining the slogan 'Gay Power' which became a rallying cry for the movement of homosexual liberation. As a result, 'gay' became a way of expressing in a positive fashion the right to openly and confidently admit one's homosexual orientation. Peter Fisher calls it "an assertion of identity and legitimacy."[30] It reflects a change in the self-conception of homosexuals. Thus the word takes on an immense power to forge an unprecedented degree of public solidarity among homosexuals. And it is seen by some as a first step in the sexual liberation of all people.[31]

In its use by homosexual spokespersons, the term gay is far from being an objective

20

description of a person's sexual propensities. Rather it is intended as a means of liberation and world-creation for it attempts to shatter the stereotypes and repressions purportedly built into the psychological and moral histories of the more common term 'homosexual.' In much the same way that the shift from 'Negro' to 'black' or from 'chairman' to 'chairperson' reflects a new consciousness of minority rights and dignity, the shift from 'homosexual' to 'gay' is designed to have the same effect.

I think it is impossible to avoid using the term gay in a book about homosexuality. However, I have several problems with an unexamined canonization of the term. First, it is more popular among homosexual men than among homosexual women (who seem to prefer lesbian) and therefore it does not adequately reflect the full spectrum of the homosexual world. Second, it is not clear to me that the lingering connotation of 'happy' or 'merry' is true to the facts of homosexual experience. I am not sure that the Gay Way of Life is really gay, at least characteristically. And finally, unless one's ethical judgment of homosexuality as a way of life is affirmative, then to employ the term (as presently defined) is to falsify the situation by misdescribing the reality.

Thus I am left in the dilemma of wishing to avoid the use of a word which is generally accepted as a proper synonym for homosexual and which is casually employed by many of the authors I am dependent on. My compromise solution is to accept the term with the qualifications given above.

(b) <u>Homophile/Homophobe</u> -- At the most basic level, these two terms refer to a person who either loves or hates members of the same sex. This love can be taken in the non-erotic sense of acceptance or non-acceptance or it can portray a deep-seated emotional response. In homosexual literature these words have been used in a strongly polemical sense to refer to supporters or antagonists of the movement for homosexual liberation.

Accusations of 'homophobia' have become the most searing form of opprobrium in the homosexual vocabulary. George Weinberg has provided a theoretical base for this use of the term in his book Society and the Healthy Homosexual.[32] He sees homophobia as ultimately a form of 'acute conventionality,' that is, as an unanalyzed cultural taboo which is reinforced from childhood on by parental attitudes and educational reinforcement. This fear of intimacy with, and reluctance to express affection to, members of the same sex is especially acute among males. Weinberg discerns five main motives for the longevity of this pervasive prejudice. (i) The Judaeo-Christian ethic which proscribed homosexual behavior still exercises a strong influence in our culture. (ii) Many fear that they are homosexuals themselves and therefore overreact to its expression in the lives of others. (iii) The homosexual strikes a chord of repressed envy because he or she seems to belittle the very attributes (such as machismo) that heterosexuals work so hard to cultivate. (iv) Homosexuals are seen as a direct threat to one's values. (v) Homosexuals reawaken the fear of death because their lack of children remind the heterosexual of how inadequate this means of coping with death really is.

Among these possible explanations that Weinberg proposes the one which seems most compelling is the second, that is, unconscious fear of one's homosexual feelings and inclinations. Surely it is not uncommon for troubled individuals to conjure up imagined enemies and symbolic scapegoats. Demagogues throughout history have played on the fears of the masses (both conscious and unconscious fears) and homosexuals have often been coupled with Jews, blacks, labor organizers and other purportedly subversive groups. At times it was as if homosexuality were at the heart of every

22

suspected conspiracy. Whether the hostility takes a vitriolic public form or remains at the level of personal repugnance and social dis-ease, some percentage of people seem to have a disproportionate fear of homosexuals. The hypothesis that this is motivated by a non-acknowledged suspicion of their own sexuality is at least plausible.

The other motives listed by Weinberg may also come into play but the first and fourth are defensible within certain value configurations (that is, homosexuality may really be a serious threat to one's deeply held religious and ethical convictions). If this is the case, the real problem is whether the form of opposition is really consistent with the same value system. Represed envy and fear of death are so amorphous and conjectural that they are not very helpful.

I consider it fair to say that 'homophobia' does accurately describe some types of reaction to homosexuality in general as well as hostility shown to individual homosexuals. Incidents of random violence directed against homosexuals would be an example of this phenomenon. So would the inability of some individuals to be able to even discuss the subject in a rational manner. A more questionable situation would be the utter rejection of homosexual children by their parents since other psychological and social dynamics are probably also at work.

Thus there seem to be homophobic individuals in our society. What is not clear is whether all persons who make a negative judgment about the morality of homosexual behavior patterns can be lumped together under this pejorative category. I think not and I recommend to homosexual spokespersons that name-calling and imputations of subjective irrationality are no more effective on one side of an argument than they are on the other.

(c) 'The Act of Coming Out (of the Closet)' -- Throughout most of history the majority of homosexual persons seem to have been forced into a

23

pattern of schizophrenic existence. On the one hand, they sought sexual pleasure and companionship among others of a similar persuasion, most often in isolated oprotected locales. Some found this role-playing and necessity for pretense to be a source of excitement and stimulation. But the majority seemingly yearned for a more integrated and open manifestation of the fragmented parts of their lives.

This dilemma of the hidden homosexual has not, of course, disappeared. As far as we can tell, this is still the chosen route for the majority of homosexuals. However, in recent years the act of sexual self-revelation has become the focal point of the homosexual liberation movement. A 'closeted' gay is taken to be one who cloaks his or her sexual orientation from their family and work associates. In some instances, they may also refuse to admit it to themselves. The act of 'coming out' is the moment when a new freedom of self-accepatnce takes place. It is seen to be the culmination of a process of redefinition and affiliation with a movement of social reform. Whether or not it leads to explicit activism, it contributes to the creation of a new climate of sexual and social interaction. Peter Fisher describes the experience in these terms. "This is why the act of identifying and accepting oneself as a homosexual marks a turning point in so many lives. The inner conflict is over and one is suddenly free to be himself."[33]

I will have more to say about this strategic step in later chapters. However, at this point it must be acknowledged that this image is an apt and powerful way of expressing the act of acceptance of oneself as a homosexual. That some may do it prematurely or in a socially disruptive fashion is to be expected in such a time of transition. The act of coming out is an essential step in the entry process into the Homosexual Way of Life and thus merits a fuller discussion under that rubric.

24

(d) '<u>Cruising</u>' -- Cruising refers to the participation in a process of mutual search for sexual partners. It is almost exclusively a phenomenon of the male homosexual subculture (although it has its parallels in the heterosexual world). It occurs in various social locales and has its own code of manners and identification (which will be described in a later chapter). The sex that is desired can be had without obligation or commitment, although in some instances it must be purchased by one of the partners.

Cruising goes on continually in some components of the homosexual world. It is a style of sexual interaction which accentuates youth and physical beauty and therefore tends to be only a stage in the lives of many homosexual males.

IV. Conclusion

I have intended this brief introduction to the issues of definition, categorization and language as one part in this process of attempting to describe the Homosexual Way of Life. Some other related issues are better discussed under different topic headings. But what I hope is clear is that much is at stake in our task of definition and description. The very language we employ can clarify or falsify the human phenomena under consideration. If we can be alert to this dimension of our task, we may be able to avoid serious confusion in our ethical analysis.

Footnotes for Chapter 1

[1]Malcolm Boyd, Take Off the Masks (Garden City: Doubleday, 1978), p. 156.

[2]Arnie Kantrowitz, Under the Rainbow: Growing Up Gay (New York: Pocket, 1977), p. 155.

[3]Cf., Herbert McCabe, What Is Ethics All About? (Washington: Corpus, 1969), esp. pp. 68-103.

[4]Stanley Hauerwas, Vision & Virtue (Notre Dame: Fides, 1974), p. 102.

[5]Martin Hoffman, The Gay World (New York: Bantom, 1968), p. 28.

[6]C.A. Tripp, The Homosexual Matrix (New York: New American Library, 1975), p. 20.

[7]Ruth Tiffany Barnhouse, Homosexuality: A Symbolic Confusion (New York: Seabury, 1977), p. 22.

[8]Marc Oraison, The Homosexual Question (New York: Harper & Row, 1977), p. 13.

[9]Gregory Baum, "Catholic Homosexuals," Commonweal, 100, 1974, p. 481.

[10]John Harvey, "Morality and Pastoral Treatment of Homosexuality," Continuum, 5, 1967, p. 281.

[11]John Cavanaugh, Counseling the Homosexual (Huntington: Our Sunday Visitor, 1977), p. 38.

[12]Cf., Allen Young, After You're Out, edited by Karla Jay and Allen Young (New York: Pyramid, 1975).

[13]Allen Young, Out of the Closets: Voices of Gay Liberation, edited by Karla Jay and Allen

26

Young (New York: Harcourt Brace Jovanovich, 1972), p. 10.

[14]Allan Bell, "Homosexuality, an Overview," in Homosexuality and the Christian Faith: A Symposium, edited by Harold Twiss (Valley Forge: Judson, 1978), p. 21.

[15]New York: Simon and Schuster, 1978.

[16]Ibid., p. 23.

[17]Baum, loc. cit., pp. 479-482.

[18]Cf. Arno Karlen, Sexuality and Homosexuality (New York: Norton, 1971), p. 187f.

[19]D. Sherwin Bailey, Homosexuality and the Western Chrisitan Tradition (London: Longman, Green & Co., 1955), p. 38.

[20]John McNeill, The Church and the Homosexual (Kansas City: Sheed Andrews and McMeel, 1976), p. 42.

[21]Cf., Sandor Rado, "A Clinical Examination of Bisexuality," in Sexual Inversion, edited by Judd Marmor (New York: Basic, 1965), pp. 175-189.

[22]Tripp, loc. cit., p. 88.

[23]Cf., Edmund Bergler, Homosexuality: Disease or Way of Life? (New York: Macmillan, 1962) and Irving Bieber, "Clinical Aspects of Male Homosexuality," in Sexual Inversion, pp. 248-267.

[24]H. Kimball Jones, A Christian Understanding of the Homosexual (New York: Association, 1966), pp. 20-23.

[25]Cf., Karlen, loc. cit., pp. 552-556.

[26]Ibid., p. 554.

[27]Ibid., pp. 352-371.

[28]Ibid., pp. 372-384.

[29]Jeanne Cordova, in <u>After You're Out</u>, pp. 16-17.

[30]Peter Fisher, <u>The Gay Mystique</u> (New York: Stein and Day, 1972), p. 233.

[31]"Gay, in its most far-reaching sense, means not homosexual, but sexually free. This includes a long-ranged vision of sensuality as a basis for sexual relationships...It is sexual freedom premised upon the notion of pleasure through equality, no pleasure where there is inequality." Allen Young, <u>Out of the Closet</u>, p. 28.

[32]Garden City: Anchor, 1972, pp. 1-20.

[33]Fisher, <u>loc. cit.</u>, p. 24.

Chapter 2

Homosexuality in the Context of

History and Culture

Introduction

Much of the past history of the homosexual experience has been lost over the course of time. In some instances, it is because it was not considered a topic worthy of attention and remembrance. More probably, there were deliberate efforts to suppress what was known out of a fear that it might promote the life or prove culturally contagious. Thus, at our point in history, we can only work with the available resources: obscure references, implied behavior and snatches of literary discussion. But we have enough to at least make some estimate of how our historical and cultural experience of homosexuality compares with that of our predecessors.

In this chapter I will first give an overview of what we know about homosexuality in previous cultures. Then I will focus on one critical cultural factor of today, namely, the elaboration and structuring of sex roles and the corresponding concepts of masculinity and femininity.

I. Homosexuality in the Cultures of the Past

As far as we know, homosexuality has existed in all times and cultures of the past.[1] This would suggest that it is not a function of some uniquely Western causal nexus but it is rather rooted in more universal human dynamics. Despite all the attempts that have been made to suppress homosexual activity it has cropped up continually even in alien settings.

But to say that homosexuality has somehow perdured is not to indicate that it was ever wholeheartedly welcomed by any society. A few societies have permitted an unusual degree of openness about the subject. Yet even then there is no indication that the majority of inhabitants were very sympathetic. Marvin Opler has studied the matter and arrived at the conclusion that,

Actually, no society, save perhaps
ancient Greece, pre-Meiji Japan,
certain top echelons in Nazi
Germany, and the scattered
examples of such special status
groups as the berdaches, Nata
slaves, and one category of
Chukchee shamans, has let sanction
in any real sense to homosexuality.[2]

Heterosexual coitus has always been the dominant
form of sex activity for adults. As Karlen
expresses it,

Homosexual acts may be taken for
granted among the young; among
sexually isolated men or women;
between a man and a defined 'non-
man' such as a prepubescent boy or
transvestite. But there is no
known society that approves homosexual acts as a chief outlet or,
in most circumstances, among
adults in general.[3]

If homosexual behavior has never been exulted
by a whole culture, there do seem to have been a
few noteworthy times which are remembered for
their relative openness. I will now examine the
major ones.[4]

(a) The Greeks -- Of all the antecedent
influences on contemporary Western culture, the
one which has been most fondly recalled by homosexuals is Greece of the classic period. Some see
this epoch as a model of what might happen again
if the homosexual subculture is allowed sufficient
freedom to forge a social world in which love,
beauty and personal development are the ruling
values. The type of debate about homosexual love
that appears in Plato's Symposium is thought to be
representative of the level of discourse that
might be achieved. What some would suggest is
that, when the educated and sophisticated classes

31

of society can pursue homosexual relationships, the results will be a heightened quality of creative achievement in the human arts.

Greek homosexuality was practiced in a culture which had a strong patriarchal dominance mode of relating between the sexes. Women were downgraded and considered unworthy as intellectual and social companions. In most dimensions of everyday life, especially in the upper class, the sexes were strictly separated. Correspondingly, there was a strong cultivation of a male ethos which included military combat, athletic games and male nudity.

The most common form of homosexual engagement in this setting was 'pederasty' (literally, love of boys). Basically, this involved a relationship between an adult male and an adolescent boy after puberty. The favored type was a youth with smooth body, not overly muscular, and long hair. The chief jusitification for this erotic pairing was that the elder partner could teach the youth to be a brave person and a good citizen. However, it also included a preoccupation with the buttocks and a preference for anal intercourse. This dominance-submission pattern between adult and youth resembled the attitude exhibited toward women. Saul Fisher comments that

> It is striking that, in the Homeric period, the absence of pederasty coincided with the more elevated status of women, whereas, in the historic period, the prominence of pederasty coincided with the degraded status of women.[5]

Greek men considered exclusive homosexuals as odd and degraded. Most of those who engaged in pederasty were married and fulfilled the prevailing expectations of family life. Thus male homosexuality was a factor among the leisured class who debated the relative merits of boys and women as sexual partners.

It is among the literary apologists that the most vivid depiction of Greek homosexuality comes through. Sappho of Lesbos (7th Cent. B.C.) was the first voice for homosexual love in the Western world. In her poetry she celebrates love for girls and for men, although there is no explicit mention of homosexual lovemaking. Anacreon of Teos (6th Cent. B.C.) is the first male poet to rhapsodize about homosexual love. But he had a whole host of successors, the most famous of whom was Plato.

In general, the response among writers was not supportive of the value of homosexual love. Plutarch criticized the ancient philosophers as sexual seducers of young boys. And a number of authors mockingly belittled the fickleness and boasting of homosexual lovers. Aristophanes, for example, satirized pederasts and effeminate homosexuals. It is unlikely that the Greek experience of homosexuals was ever as pleasant and rewarding as subsequent generations have thought it to have been.

(b) The Romans -- As in Greece, most of what we know about Roman homosexuality is a function of the urban upper-class. Especially in the later stages of the Empire, a wide variety of sexual experimentation seems to have gone on. It was a culture which knew the extremes of the Colosseum and which accepted sadism as a source of emotional titillation. Even the rulers, especially after Julius Caesar, were prone to barbarity and dehumanizing performances as they sought sexual kicks. Some of this activity was homosexual in nature, but it can hardly be called admirable or anything akin to the homosexual expression that is being talked of so supportively today.

Two features of Roman homosexuality have relevance for our own discussion. First, it was usually connected with the baths, where male nudity in a leisurely setting seems to have allowed for some degree of solicitation. Second, the actors and mimes of Rome were expected to be homosexual by disposition. This is the beginning of a long association between the theater and homosexuality.

(c) <u>The Renaissance</u> -- 15th and 16th Century Europe are important primarily because this period of cultural renewal and creative ferment has been compared to ancient Greece by some homosexual apologists. The suggestion is made that homosexual literati were the leading edge of all that was great about the Renaissance. Thus Leonardo DaVinci and Michelangelo, among others, are seen as either 'homosexual' or 'bisexual.'

While it is difficult to know for sure, there is a great reason to be suspicious about the imputed homosexuality of just about every major figure in Italy, France and England. Oscar Wilde, for example, (himself a homosexual) first proposed the theory that Shakespeare was a homosexual in the latter part of the 19th Century. But all of his so-called proofs are internal and based on literary interpretation. There are no external records to substantiate the claim. That some of the leading figures of the day, like Francis Bacon, were homosexual seems clear. Yet it seems false to assert that it was a characteristic tendency (and thus the possible explanation for this sudden burst of artistic achievement).

(d)   <u>18th Century England and France</u> -- In regards to sexual mores this has been called the century for libertinage. Aristocratic delinquents pursued lives of unbridled lust and pleasure-seeking. In one form of club called 'Mollies', the men met to carouse dressed in women's clothes. Eventually, the word 'Molly' became synonymous with homosexual. Also in England the practice of flagellation or 'birching' was fashionable. In France, the Marquis de Sade published pornographic works which alternately depicted and

34

philosophically justified various practices of torture and sexual abuse.

But even in the age of libertinage, homosexual behavior was circumscribed by social disapproval. Some may have seen it as one more challenge to the traditional Western sexual ethic, yet the majority of the people could view the whole spectrum of sexual rebellion as correlated with the proverbial decadence of the upper class.

(e) <u>Homosexuality</u> <u>in</u> <u>the</u> <u>Arab</u> <u>World</u> -- Officially, the Muslim religion condemns homosexual behavior. This might be expected with its strong stress on marriage and family. However, reports of extensive homosexual activity, and even homosexual prostitution, are common in Arab countries. Some account for this discrepancy by pointing to the rigid separation of the sexes mandated in the Koran. Whatever the cause, the level of enforcement of anti-homosexual legislation seems to be weak in areas of the world where Muslim is the chief religion. Homosexuality seems to be tolerated in practice as little as it is condoned in theory.

(f) <u>Conclusion</u> -- We can conclude from this incomplete survey that even those cultures in history which allowed a greater degree of freedom in sexual expression still declined to accept homosexuality as a normal or desirable behavior pattern. Always homosexuals have been a minority (most often not a self-conscious group) who suffered social stigma and various degrees of persecution and suppression in the hands of the majority of the citizens. Furthermore, there is little evidence that homosexuality is a determining cause in the great creative ages of the past. Finally, there is no major religious tradition which gives its official approbation to homosexual conduct.

II. Sex Roles and Concepts of Masculinity and
Femininity in American Culture -- Among the many
cultural factors that could inform our discussion
of homosexuality, I will concentrate on the one
which seems most critical in Western society
today, namely, sex roles and sex stereotyping.
This topic is especially relevant because it is
the subject of extensive debate within the homosexual community itself. After some initial
considerations I will focus on two sex role manifestations: male effeminancy and male-female
relations among homosexuals.

(a) Biology and Role -- Biologically, there
are two sexes -- male and female. Although the
rare instances of hermaphroditism may cause some
difficulty of identification, the overwhelming
majority of human persons are born with external
genital organs which enable them to be readily
distinguished as male or female. Nevertheless, a
person's sexuality also includes other physiological elements as well: Chromosomes, the
endocrine glands, hormones, and internal sexual
organs.[6] It is possible for any of these components of our biological makeup to be deficient
and thus for our sexuality to be affected.

In addition to this biological rootedness,
there is also the psychological realities called:
'gender identity' and 'gender role.' Gender
identity is normally fixd very early in the
developmental process, usually by the end of the
first or second year. It refers to the consciousness that one gradually takes on that you are
either male or female and that this is a given
over which you have no control. This gender
identity usually determines a culturally-defined
path through which the child passes in the process
of learning a 'gender role.'

Gender role is a more amorphous concept than
gender identity since it varies from culture to
culture and from age to age. The prevailing
child-raising practices are capable of being
reformed by social reformers of various stripes

36

who wish to open up diversified role models among the sexes. Thus the contemporary struggle to accommodate households in which both spouses have a career yet wish to have children is tied in with notions of shared responsibility for nurturance and domestic education.

What remains to be sorted out is how flexible sex roles can really be. With the advent of biological technology and the birth of a test tube baby, even the maternal prerogative of childbearing (with all this seems to imply for infant identification) may soon be unnecessary. In futuristic scenarios the discussion has turned to the possibility of cloning a human, and the implementation of this intervention would potentially render the male irrelevant to the reproductive procedure. Whether or not our society goes to these extremes, the problem of sex roles would seem to be a critical one for the foreseeable future.

Sexual identity does not seem to be a source of tension among homosexuals. They know themselves to be male or female and, in most instances, do not wish to do anything about it. Even homosexual transvestites (a small percentage of the whole homosexual population) do not deny their masculinity since they derive a thrill out of passing as female. The real problem for homosexuals is one of sexual roles. For they claim to desire to break through the established stereotypes to achieve some higher level of sexual integration.

In the popular imagination what the homosexual protest against the rigidity of sexual roles leads to is the adoption of the culturally defined characteristics of the opposite sex. Therefore, male homosexuals are thought to be excessively effeminate and female homosexuals to be strongly masculine.[7]

(i) Stereotype of the Male Homosexual -- The stereotype pictures a man who is effeminate in

37

posture, appearance and speech patterns. Common descriptions would include items like: limp-wristed, swishy, lisping, high strung and fragile. It is supposed that such men are somehow physiologically different with a broad pelvis, fine skin (often beardless) and a high-pitched voice. They congregate in certain professions such as acting, hair styling, interior decoration, dressmaking and ballet.

(ii) Stereotype of the Female Homosexual -- The stereotype pictures a woman who is masculine in appearance with hair growth on the face, solid musculature, and a deep voice. She is athletically-inclined and relatively disinterested in aesthetic matters. Such women congregate in professions that require strength of character and aggressiveness, such as business, transportation, police work and manual labor.

Like all stereotypes, there are enough homosexuals who exhibit these characteristics that the classifications continue to have a certain plausibility. However, the majority of homosexuals seem to be relatively indistinguishable from the average citizen, especially outside the ghetto setting of some homosexual subcultures. Actually, what seems to have taken place in recent years is a strong overreaction by homosexuals to the prevailing stereotypes. Thus, in the homosexual worlds of San Francisco, Los Angeles and New York (which tend to set the styles for the whole subculture) gay men prize 'masculine' appearance in a partner, dress in casual, out-doorsman outfits and discourage effeminate homosexuals from the mainstream of the life. The same is true of lesbians who more and more have abandoned 'masculine' outfits and hard-nosed posturing.

(b) Effeminacy Among Male Homosexuals -- Effeminacy in a man (and masculinity in a woman), while fairly elastic concepts, cannot be used to ascertain a person's sexual preference.[8] Nevertheless, a small percentage of homosexual men do

38

cultivate effeminate characteristics (and cultivate is right word for it) and some other homosexual men do betray occasional lapse into mild
forms of effeminate mannerisms and bearing. With
some it may be simply a heightened fastidiousness
about appearance. With others, an emotional
sensitivity and concern about social dynamics and
gossip may be more common. There seem to be many
possible degrees of sex role reversal which would
conjure up claims about effeminacy. At one
extreme are drag queens and female impressionists
and at the other are men who self-consciously
strive to allow the feminine side of their personality to come to the surface in spontaneous ways,
like not being afraid to cry in public.

C.A. Tripp has offered a four part typology
to describe the various kinds of male effeminacy
in the homosexual world.[9] He calls them: Nelly,
Swish, Blase and Camp.

(i) <u>Nelly</u> -- This is an almost purely
feminine type of casual and authentic imitation.
Gestures are graceful and soft and lacking in the
quality of threat for heterosexuals. On the other
hand, homosexuals use 'nelly' as a term of opprobrium and are disconcerted by their presence. To
an observer a nelly appears as an almost perfect
copy of a self-confident woman.

(ii) <u>Swish</u> -- This type is characterized by a
high level of emotional energy which gets translated into rapid, rounded gestures and body movements. There is an element of hysteria and
perpetual confrontation which belies a practiced
skill at avoiding direct confrontation. The Swish
if often offensive to other homosexuals, probably
because he seems to derive sarcastic pleasure from
acting out the effeminate stereotype.

(iii) <u>Blase (the Queenly Gesture)</u> -- The
Blase is the counterfoil to the Nelly. Whereas
the latter is highly animated and frivolous, the
former is reserved and cool to an extreme. Like a
'Queen' living in regal indifference to the

misfortunes of the masses, the Blase attempts to avoid emotional involvements and confrontation. The tilt of the head, the control of movement, and affectation of an off-synch speech rhythm, all contribute to this studied role.

(iv) Camp -- Camp is a term that has passed into colloquial vocabulary from its roots in the homosexual subculture. It refers to a person who is skilled in acting out exaggerated roles for the purposes of satire or humor. A homosexual who goes to outlandish extremes to put gesture and language (and often costume) to use to shatter sex-role expectations is camping. No one really believes the role the person is playing and thus the appearance of duplicity magnifies the effect of the effeminacy.

Tripp claims that all four types of masculine homosexual effeminacy are a result of an over-supply of hysterical energy. In effect, they are coping devices which make one's life manageable. Whether or not this explanation is satisfactory, the typology does serve to highlight the different forms of behavior which are usually lumped together in discussions of homosexual effeminacy.

There are a number of issues which emerge from a consideration of these factors. First, why the frequent paranoia about effeminacy among male homosexuals? At first sight, it would seem to be a function of the often violent reaction that the stereotype induces in heterosexuals. The logical case in apologetic defense seems to run: Hetero-sexuals dislike effeminate males. They think all homosexuals are effeminate. If we can prove that most homosexuals are not noticeably effeminate, hetersexuals will discover that they can like most homosexuals. The difficulty with this form of reasoning is that it contradicts the professed desire to free the heterosexual world from the shackles of its sex-role oppression. Effeminate homosexuals are a living act of rebellion and should therefore by especially prized by other homosexuals. That this is not the case calls into question the seriousness or the extensiveness of the desire for radical reshaping of sexual roles.

Second, why the progressively greater stress on machismo among male homosexuals? In the Village in New York City, on Castro Street in San Francisco, in New Town in Chicago and in Griffith Park in Los Angeles, the young, militant gays tend to look more like the suave, sophisticated, virile cowboy of the Marlboro ads than the mincing, toady eccentric of the effeminate stereotype. Surely this macho group encompasses only a portion of the homosexual population, but in their publicity-conscious marches and speech-making they represent the gay world to others. Perhaps, it is all an overreaction which will moderate with time. But it may be that the problem of effeminacy is more critical to the homosexual resolution of the sex-role issue than most have admitted up to now.[10]

Third, is effeminate behavior simply one stage among many upon which the homosexual actor hones his skills of survival in a hostile environment? 'Coming out' seems to be so important in the life of a homosexual because it frees him or her from the contraints of a two-sided life. Along the way to this point many homosexuals become quite adept at pretense and simulation. It may be that this acting skill, in some instances, is transposed into a mocking caricature of the societal standards that have been experienced as oppressive. This would seem to be borne out by the evidence that most effeminate homosexuals can assume a new, less effeminate role if they want to.

I have devoted this much space to this relatively rare phenomena in the homosexual world because it raises, I think, some serious long-range issues. The limited data we have on 'masculine' lesbians could be interpreted in the same way, but much more hesitantly. The problem of sex roles (and the corresponding meaning of the concepts 'masculine' and 'feminine') will be with

41

us for a long time to come. The manner in which the homosexual subculture shapes itself in this regard will have many repercussions for the whole society.

(c) <u>Male-Female Relationships Among Homo-sexuals</u> -- The more immersed that liberated homosexuals (of either sex) become in their homosexual subculture, the less place there is for regular socializing with members of the opposite sex. This may be totally unreflective or it may be a result of conscious decision-making. It is not surprising that homosexuals would prefer to be in the company of others like themselves. Even heterosexual socializing patterns exhibit quite a bit of one sex membership in clubs, sporting groups, bars and recreational travel. Of course, the work context normally forces a certain amount of mixing, if only within the 9 to 5 parameters.

I have already defined a homosexual as one who is indifferent, but not necessarily hostile to, the opposite sex as a sexual partner. Still this minimalistic definition does not handle the question, whether homosexuals have friendships with and enjoy the relaxed company of the other sex.

In response to this question, the first bit of evidence can be sought in the level of cooperation in the gay liberation movement between homosexual men and lesbians. After the first flush of enthusiasm wore off, the two components of the movement seem to have gone their separate ways. Certain groups (the Daughters of Bilitis; Radicalesbians) have been exclusively female; and other groups (Mattachine; Gay Activists Alliance) have tended to be predominantly male. Part of the separation was motivated by a lack of women in the leadership roles outside of lesbian organizations. Another contributing factor was the feeling which developed among lesbians that it was more important to affiliate with the broader focus of the Feminist movement (because of their double oppression as both lesbians and women). But,

42

despite all of this, it is not yet clear that homosexual men and lesbians will be able to cooperatively and harmoniously work together in the immediate future.

Among homosexual men there do seem to be some women, called disparagingly 'fag hags' or 'fruit flies', who seem to enjoy the regular presence of gays.[11] They may just relish the non-competitive situation. Or perhaps some other dynamic is operative. A number of homosexuals work in professions such as hairdressing, interior decorating, and clothes design which put them into regular contact with women.[12] Some of thes customers can become friends. Still other women may get interested in homosexual men in order to seduce them out of their 'problem.' This is further complicated when the homosexual enjoys occasional sexual relations with women.

In the home setting, it seems to be the mother and/or the sisters who are the easiest to relate to once a male homosexual has come out (although it is not clear whether the parallel holds true for lesbians and their male relatives). It is not uncommon for a male homosexual to live with his mother in her old age. In a connected matter, some homosexual men seek out occupations which will give them regular contact with young children (not to abuse them as is sometimes erroneously suggested) but to experience the parental role vicariously. This can also place them in regular interaction with women who are mothers.

One of the more baffling phenomena in this series of social interactions "is the incredible attraction of the gay male community for certain female entertainment stars."[13] Judy Garland, Barbara Streisand, Liza Minelli, Bette Midler, Marlene Dietrich, Bette David, and Katherine Hepburn would head the list. Some have suggested that this is because of the struggles and hard lives that most of these women have had. Others think it is their 'campy' style which is full of

43

exaggeration and affectation. Or it may be a function of their psychic symbolization. But whatever the reason, a certain kind of woman seems to have an unusual appeal in the gay world.

On the basis of the available evidence, I would conclude that interaction between the sexes is somewhat minimal in the homosexual subculture. Part of this is explained by social and economic factors. There do seem to be some lasting and deep friendships, but it is possible to become so isolated that the chances of this type of friendship occurring are scant. It is primarily in the lesbian movement, at the present time, that the level of sexual hostility is the highest. The strident tone of much lesbian literature may be a passing phase, yet it is a cause for concern.

III. Conclusion

In this chapter I have presented a brief survey of pertinent cultural and historical factors which can help orient our discussion of contemporary homosexual life. Among the cultural factors I have concentrated on the issue of sex roles and sexual stereotyping, especially as this impinges on the homosexual subculture. One of the central claims that will be made by representatives of the Homosexual Way of Life is that it offers a viable alternative to the unfulfilling structures of sexual relating that presently prevail. As my discussion in this chapter has indicated, I think that many dimensions of the problem remain unresolved, even within the rhetoric of the gay liberation movement.

Footnotes for Chapter 2

[1]Cf., Marc Oraison, The Homosexual Question New York: Harper and Row, 1977), p. 67; Arno Karlen, Sexuality and Homosexuality: A New View (New York: W.W. Norton, 1971), p. 463; Gordon Rattray Taylor, "Historical and Mythological Roots of Homosexuality," in Sexual Inversion: The Multiple Roots of Homosexuality, edited by Judd Marmor (New York: Basic, 1965), p. 162.

[2]Marvin Opler, "Anthropological and Cross-Cultural Aspects of Homosexuality," in Sexual Inversion, p. 114.

[3]Karlen, Loc. cit., p. 476.

[4]For much of the following material I am primarily dependent on Karlen's book cited above, which is an outstanding contribution to the field.

[5]Saul Fisher, "A Note on Male Homosexuality and the Role of Women in Ancient Greece," in Sexual Inversion, p. 171.

[6]Cf., Richard Woods, Another Kind of Love: Homosexuality and Spirituality (Garden City: Doubleday, 1978), pp. 24-28.

[7]Cf., Joseph McCaffrey, "Homosexuality: The Stereotype, the Real," in The Homosexual Dialetic, edited by Joseph McCaffrey (Englewood Cliffs: Prentice-Hall, 1972), pp. 137-144.

[8]"Effeminacy is any style of male behavior that resembles the gestures, movements, or mannerisms usually associated with women. Although it is more frequent among homosexual than heterosexual males, effeminacy is relatively rare even in homosexuality and would not require as much attention as it does, if it were not that, in the minds of many people, it characterizes the whole group." C.A. Tripp, The Homosexual Matrix (New York: New American, 1975), p. 160.

[9]Ibid., pp. 180-189.

[10]The preoccupation with the size of the penis in male homosexual cruising may be related to this whole issue. Physiologically, genital size in heterosexual intercourse has little to do with either fertility or the inducement of pleasure in the woman. But among men it may be the quickest metaphor for easing deep-seated fears of insufficiency. One who is endowed with a large penis may see genital measurement as a kind of combat. One who is somehow deficient in his own eyes may seek a male lover who can provide a vicarious share of manliness.

[11]Cf., Allen Young, in After You're Out, edited by Karla Jay and Allen Young (New York: Pyramid, 1975), pp. 195-204.

[12]Cf., Peter Fisher, The Gay Mystique (New York: Stein and Day, 1975), pp. 63-67.

[13]Allen Young, loc. cit., p. 197.

Chapter 3

The Statistics of Homosexual Prevalence and

the Forms of Homosexual Activity

I. Introduction

To the majority of heterosexual persons, one of the mysteries about the world of the homosexual is how many individuals it includes. For every uncloseted gay who appears in the limelight there are rumors and allegations that a huge army may someday follow. Heterosexuals instinctively suspect that gays deliberately inflate the estimates of how many people are in fact homosexual in order to establish a claim about normalcy. If the cultural shackles were stripped away, suddenly homosexual men and women would appear almost everywhere and in sufficient numbers to disconcert the uninitiated. So runs the logic of some gay spokespersons. The first part of this chapter will attempt to make some sense out of the conflicting claims about the size of the homosexual population.

In the second part, I will examine another source of confusion -- the forms of homosexual genital activity. There is a common refrain in anti-gay polemics that what homosexuals do together is somehow degrading and unnatural. It is thought to be unnatural both because it diverges so far from the heterosexual norm and because it is esthetically deficient. I will look at the evidence available on gay sexual activity and the theoretical defense against the charges of unnaturalness.

II. The Statistics of Homosexuality

Alfred Kinsey, the Indiana University zoologist, was the first scientist to systematically survey the sexual preferences and practices of American males and females.[1] In 1948, he and his associates came out with the first volume of their results. In 1953 a companion volume on the American female was published. The combined effect of the two pieces was to seriously call into question many tradition-laden presuppositions about how the so'called 'normal' person experienced him or herself as a sexual being. Some saw the Kinsey statistics as part of a conspiracy to destroy the Judaeo-Christian sexual ethic. Others challenged the methodology employed which used sample populations of 6,300 male and 5,300 female volunteers. They wondered both about its representativeness and about the honesty of the respondents. But even Kinsey's worst critics had to acknowledge that his work was a watershed in the study of human sexual behavior.

One of the most influential contributions of the Kinsey studies was what he called the 'heterosexual-homosexual rating scale.' This scale used a 7 point system (0=exclusively heterosexual and 6=exclusively homosexual with 3=equally heterosexual and homosexual) to chart an individual's sexual history. The ratings strove to represent a balance between the homosexual and heterosexual elements in the history, rather than their intensity or the absolute amount of overt experience. By comparing the scales of the sample population, Kinsey could then give some indication of the relative percentages that fell into the different categories.

Among all of the findings in the two volume study, the following are the most important for our purposes.

(i) 4% of the males and 2-3% of the females are exclusively homosexual throughout their lives.

(ii) 37% of the males and 13% of the females have had at least one overt homosexual experience to the point of orgasm after puberty.

(iii) 13% of the males and 7% of the females react erotically to other males without overt experience after puberty.

(iv) 10% of all males are more or less exclusively homosexual for at least three years between the ages of 16 and 55.

51

(v) Persons with homosexual histories are to be found in every age group, in every social level, in every conceivable occupation, and in all geographical areas.

(vi) The average frequencies of orgasm are never high. the average frequencies are: 0.8 per week-early adolescence; 1.3-at 25 years; 1.7-at 35 years.

(vii) Long-time relationships between two males are notably few.

In general, it can be said that the Kinsey statistics have borne the test of time. In earlier and less extensive surveys, Havelock Ellis had estimated that 2-4% of English males were exclusively homosexual and Magnus Hirschfeld suggested that 2% of the males in Germany were exclusively homosexual and 4% were bisexual. In 1970 Morton Hunt attempt to follow up on the Kinsey findings to see if there had been any significant changes.[2] He concluded, "we find no reason to think that there has been an increase in adult male homosexual behavior in the past generation."[3] And the readings for the female population were about the same.

One critial problem in reading these statistics is, once again, the problem of definition. According to the definition of a homosexual that I proposed in Chapter 1, Kinsey would be estimating that 4% of the males and 2-3% of the females in America should be included.[4] This would mean relative to a rough figure of 220 million Americans that there would be almost 4.2 millin males and about 3.1 million female homosexuals. And according to Kinsey's statistics several times that number would have had some overt homosexual experience.

However, if one has a less rigorous definition of a homosexual than I have suggested, then the percentages go up accordingly.[5] In fact, there is no way of knowing for sure since no means

52

has been devised which can assure an accurate cross-section and truthful response to questionnaires or interviews. And there is the further compliation of standardizing a vocabulary which is precise enough yet understandable to the average person.

I would conclude that Kinsey's figures are helpful enough for the purposes of this book. First, they remind us that homosexuals constitute a small but noteworthy percentage of the population. Second, they can be comforting to those heterosexuals who thought they were the only ones who had had homosexual feelings and experiences. Third, they remind us that the process of arriving at a comfortable and confirmed sexual identity can be a traumatic experience for many people. Fourth, they open up the possibility of comparing exclusive adult homosexuals with other segments of the population in terms of various psychological and social traits.

But Kinsey's statistics cannot function as determiners of normalcy or appropriateness. Such descriptions of the human phenomena are not designed to settle questions of morality. They may challenge certain presumptions about how widespread so-called deviant sexual behavior really is. They may prepare the next generation for a greater openness to sexual experimentation. And they may provide a standard for comparing one's own sexual experience with that of other Americans. Nevertheless, they were ascertained in such a way that it is impossible to tell about how much guilt, regret and retrospective dissatisfaction was built into the various kinds of activity. They do not correlate the moral value schemes of particular individuals with their self-descriptions. Even the religious factor analysis is nothing more than a rough estimate of how influential a particular religious upbringing is in determining the prevalence of certain sexual behavior patterns.

The long-range question built into any analysis of statistical reasearch is: what difference does it make? Would more people become homosexual if they thought it was less aberrant? Would homosexual activists be able to proselytize more effectively if they seemed to be on the cutting edge of the sexual revolution? Would the legal prohibition against homosexual activity be repealed if it seemed to affect a larger percentage of the population? Would the churches suddenly look to ministry to homosexuals as a way of increasing the size of their flocks? These are possibilities. Yet my suspicion is that the use of statistics in the discussion of homosexuality serves two primary purposes. First, it penetrates through the aura of mystery which surrounds homosexuals life and makes the issue more manageable for public discussion. By knowing approximately how many homosexuals there might be (although in most cases not knowing who they are in particular), we feel more competent in discussing the ramifications of public policy decisions. Second, it allows gay spokespersons and their opponents to either maximize or minimize the significance of such decisions. If 20% of the population is actively homosexual at any given moment, the effect on established sexual mores is more dramatic than if only 4% is. At one time it may have been possible for heterosexual persons to go through a lifetime without much personal exposure to the gay world. Now that that is less likely, there is some comfort to the same people if the magnitude of the problem does not look overwhelming. On the other hand, homosexual activists would like to shock the public into remedial action and the bludgeoning use of statistics is one of their most effective tools.

III. Sexual Activity Among Homosexuals

        Contrary to popular opinion, homosexual men and women do not characteristically act out a vague imitation of the traditional heterosexual roles in marriage.[6] One partner does not always take the initiative while the other responds passively. Instead, the typical pattern seems to involve a great degree of variety in roles and in preferred forms of sexual expression. Sometimes one partner will control the rhythm of the engagement and sometimes the other. This is especially true after the individuals have had some experience of the possbilities in homosexual lovemaking. Because of the similarities of sexual makeup of the two participants, it is possible for them to have a more direct sense of what kind of effect a particular gesture or pace of expression might have on the other party.

Except for the most perfunctory kind of secretive orgasm among male homosexuals, the pleasure that can be experienced and sustained in homosexual coitus seems to equal anything that heterosexuals can achieve in their sexual bonding. At the level of sheer emotional release and sought-after senuality, there seems to be little to distinguish the two situations. In fact, homosexual pairs probably have a greater propensity for experimenting in sexual techniques, if only to compensate for the lessened sense of mystery in a same-sex partner.

At this point it will be helpful to say something specific about the male and female forms of homosexual activity.

(a) Male Homosexuals -- The most common form of sexual activity among gay men is solitary masturbation. The distinguishing characteristic is the prevalence of male fantasy objects. There is a flourishing trade in homosexually-oriented pornography directed primarily at men and this is as close as some men get to acting out. As with males in general, masturbation may be a coping technique which serves a variety of functions. It is probable that many homosexuals see masturbation as a relatively harmless release of sexual energy, and in some instances, as a protection against untoward and criminally-liable behavior.

55

Because men can be brought to arousal and orgasm rather quickly, it is possible for homosexual intercourse to be achieved in a variety of settings from public gathering places to a secluded bedroom. The extent of foreplay and dalliance as well as the length of the encounter are largely determined by the setting and by the nature of the relationship between the partners. And, as with hetersexual activity, more than two people can be involved simultaneously. There is homosexual lingo to describe various combinations of partners in situations of group sex.

The two most common means of achieving orgasm seem to be oral and anal intercourse.[7] Although some individuals may be exclusively insertors or receptors in these sexual acts (especially if there is a significant age or beauty differential between the partners), there is frequently a change of roles either on the same occasion or in subsequent moments of performance. Some homosexuals refuse anal intercourse, especially as a receptor, because of physiological discomfort or psychological distaste. In addition to these two common techniques, various forms of mutual masturbation and femoral (between the thighs) intercourse are also well known. Simultaneous mutual oral intercourse (69), whie often depicted as the ultimate sexual pleasure, seems to be unsatisfactory to a number of homosexuals. Some percentage of homosexual men also participate in anilingus and manual penetration of the anus.

With the increasing practice of oral and anal intercourse in heterosexual relationships (including marriage), the argument about homosexual acts as somehow being especially debased has been slowly defused. Peter Fisher argues, for example, "What homosexuals do in bed is precisely what heterosexuals do in bed; it is simply done with a partner of the same sex."[8] While such activity in both contexts violates the traditional norm for genital expression, on the basis of the shifting standars of Aemrican culture at large, it is hard to fault homosexual males as especially perverse.

The preferred ideal partner in much of the gay community seems to be a masculine, youthful, attractive person in his early twenties. With due allowance for individual taste, the main sexual attribute seems to be a larger than normal penis.[9] Although a small percentage of homosexuals are oriented toward pre-pubescent boys, these individuals are generally scorned in the gay world (if only because of the lurid publicity they generate). Older adolescents may appear as desirable partners to a percentage of other homosexuals, but the fear of mistake and arrest tends to inhibit this sort of pursuit. Obese, ugly, and aged homosexuals (as well a strongly effeminate ones) have a hard time competing for partners.

There seems to be the same variation in sex drive among male homosexuals that there is in the general male population. Some are intensely active, especially in the sexual marketplaces of the restroom, public park, and gay both. Others may go for years without any overt behavior. But the more open that a person is about his homosexuality, the more accessible other interested parties tend to be. As in heterosexual life, age is a decisive factor in shaping one's sexual needs and the energy directed at meeting them.

(b) Female Homosexuals -- Because of the different physiological and psychological response pattern of women, it is almost unheard of for lesbian activity to take place in public settings. There is also characteristically a much slower pace in the development of a sexual relationship. And it is not unusual for lesbian couples to play down the importance of sex in their own consciousness of the importance of the relationship.[10]

There is a frequent celebration of the joys of masburbation in lesbian literature. Nina Sabaroff, for example, declares,

Masturbation, really experimenting with masturbation, was the big transition for me between heterosexual and lesbian seuxality...I define masturbation in the broadest sense as a woman understanding and loving her own body, learning to give sensual and sexual pleasure to herself and exploring her changing rhythms, paces, and needs.[11]

To a large extent, this is pictured as an act of self-liberation and renunciation of the dependency on males for sexual pleasure. The Gay Revolution Party Women's Caucus asserted their position accordingly, "While the ability to relieve tension through auto-erotic stimulation is essential to woman's sexual autonomy, the emphasis in masturbation is heavily genital and orgasmic, rather than sensual."[12] What is happening is that a solitary, little-discussed form of sexual behavior among women has taken on a largely ideological function in lesbian circles.

The most common techniques of sexual expression between lesbian partners are: mutual masturbation, cunnilingus (or oral genital activity)) and tribadism (where one woman lies on top of the other and they simulate heterosexual intercourse).[13] Two other techniques that are less popular are: the use of penis substitues (like a dildo) and anilingus. The 'butch and femme pattern" which freezes the partners into roles, including expectations for sexual relatedness, seems to be declining. Therefore, it is likely that individual lesbians will participate as both initiator and receiver during the course of a particular relationship.

Most lesbian couples seem to be within the same relative age bracket. There is not the same premium on youth that exists among the male homosexuals. One of the most startling facts about lesbians is that a high percentage have had some degree of active hetersexual experience.[14] And quite a few have been married. One of the reasons for this, once again, is that there is greater social pressure on women to marry and it is possible for a homosexual woman to perform sexually in a heterosexual relationship in a way that is not feasible for most male homosexuals.

There seems to be much less instability in lesbian relationships than is true of male homosexuals. As a result, the number of sex partners that a particular woman may have had is often relatively small. This is also affected by the absence of a large lesbian subculture in most areas of the country.

(c) The Problem of Venereal Disease -- Because the level of promiscuity is high in some portions of the male homosexual subculture, the rate of venereal disease has reached epidemic proportions, especially in the large cities.[15] For those who have sex frequently, a blood test or culture every three months is advisable. The most common problems are syphilis and gonorrhea, both of which are curable if properly treated.[16] Gay women seldom contact either disease through homosexual coitus. Other venereal infections include: vaginitis, warts, herpes, crabs and scabies. There is no way that immunity can be gained from venereal disease. To have had it once does not prevent one from getting it again.

Venereal disease is best viewed as a social disease which can wreak permanent damange in those who suffer from it. Despite the moral punishment read into it by many, there is no justification for anything but the best efforts to treat it and stop its spread. But any sexually active person, heterosexual or homosexual, must realistically face the possibility of coming down with the disease. In the gay world, the habitues of the gay baths and other forms of anonymous, many-partnered sex are at special risk and should take extra precautions.

IV. Conclusion

In answer to the question, how many homosexuals are there in America?, I have adopted Kinsey's statistics as fairly accurate. In describing the sexual activity of homosexual men and women, I have given the spectrum of possibilities with some indication of the relative popularity of each technique. It is important to have some basic famliarity with each of these issues in order to understand how the homosexual world forms itself into ongoing social institutions.

Footnotes for Chapter 3

[1]Cf., Alfred Kinsey, et. a., <u>Sexual Behavior in the Human Male</u> (Philadelphia: Saunders, 1948); and Alfred Kinsey, <u>et. al</u>., <u>Sexual Behavior in the Human Female</u> (Philadelphia: Saunders, 1953).

[2]Morton Hunt, <u>Sexual Behavior in the 1970s</u> (New York: Dell, 1974).

[3]<u>Ibid</u>., p. 312.

[4]In an interview with William Simon of the Kinsey Institute, Arno Karlen got the following response. "Kinsey's and other studies would make me guess that 2 to 3 percent of the male population has a serious, long term homosexual pattern. Another 7 or 8 per cent have casual or episodic homosexual experience." In <u>Sexuality and Homosexuality</u> (New York: W.W. Norton, 1971), p. 456.

[5]Richard Woods betrays the problem of definition when he says, "Reliable estimates place the number of exclusive homosexuals at about four percent...It seems reasonable to accept about ten percent as a representative figure for those who are predominantly and exclusively homosexual in orientation and behavior." <u>Another Kind of Love: Homosexualty and Spirituality</u> (Garden City: Doubleday, 1978), p. 29. Those who work on a regular basis with homosexuals or who are a part of the homosexual subculture seem to naturally opt for the higher estimates (much as blacks who live in the inner cities of the North stress the black presence in America).

[6]Cf. Alan Bell/Martin Weinberg, <u>Homosexualities: A Study of Diversity Among Men and Women</u> (New York: Simon and Schuster, 1978), p. 111.

[7]Cf., C.A. Tripp, <u>The Homosexual Matrix</u> (New York: New American Library, 1975), pp. 94-98; and Peter Fisher, <u>The Gay Mystique</u> (New York: Stein and Day, 19172), pp. 96-100.

61

[8]Fisher, Ibid., p. 100.

[9]"The compulsive fellator is unwittingly re-enacting an ancient religious rite. By sucking the penis of what he believes to be an especially masculine male, he feels that he is incorporating some of this masculinity and vitality to his own person...This explanation fits in very well with the well-known emphasis on penis size among male homosexuals...This forms a recurrent topic of discussion among them." Martin Hoffman, The Gay World (New York: Bantom, 1968), p. 139.

[10]Bell/Weinberg, loc. cit., p. 115.

[11]Nina Sabaroff, in After You're Out, edited by Karla Jay and Allen Young (New York: Pyramid, 19175), p. 14.

[12]Gay Revolution Paty Women's Caucus, in Out of the Closets: Voices of Gay Liberation (New York: Harcourt Brace Jovanovich, 1972), p. 178.

[13]Del Martin and Phyllis Lyon, Lesbian/Women (New York: Bantom, 1972), p. 64f.

[14]Cf. Charlotte Wolff, Love Between Women (New York: Harper & Row, 1971), p. 12; and Jack Hedblom, "The Female Homosexual: Social and Attitudinal Dimensions," in The Homosexual Dialectic, edited by Joseph McCaffrey (Englewood Cliffs: Prentice-Hall, 1972), p. 52.

[15]"About two-thirds of the males in each race had at some time contracted a venereal disease as a result of homosexual sex, but of these, most had it only once or twice." Bell/Weinberg, loc. cit., p. 118.

[16]Cf., Julian Bamford, "Information on VD for Gay Women and Men," in After You're Out, pp. 256-266; and Edward Guthman, "Bottoms Up," Ibid., pp. 267-276.

Chapter 4

Theories of Causality

No one knows for sure why some percentage of the human race exhibit a homosexual orientation. A whole range of explanatory theories have been proposed, but no one of them has garnered sufficient support to be considered the prevailing wisdom on the matter. The most that can be said is that some theories have a greater plausibility than others.

In this chapter I will examine the major alternatives in the attempt at an etiology of homosexuality. This material is conveniently divided according to the two types of sciences that have given systematic treatment to the issue. First, I will review the Nature Hypothesis which springs from a natural sciences point of view. This includes various attempts to explain homosexuality on the basis of biological, hereditary and genetic factors. Second, I will explore the Nurture Hypothesis which is proposed by the social sciences of psychology, sociology and anthropology. These theories look for the origins of homosexuality in some concatenation of psychic, environmental, or cultural factors. Under the Nurture rubric, I will also take up the question of a 'cure' for the ingrained homosexual person.

I. The Nature Hypothesis

It is not uncommon to hear homosexuals explain their sexual preference in the phrase 'I was born that way.' What this seems to suggest is that something in the biological order, probably back in the fetal period, set off a course of development over which the individual had no control. If this is true, then to deny, or to seek to alter, this trend is to act unnaturally. While such explanations may appear a bit fatalistic, they do offer the comfort of identifying an unalterable structure of physical existence which sets the parameters of personal possibility.

The difficulty with the argument from biology is that very few scientists are convinced that it holds up to scrutiny. No one denies that there is a physical basis to human sexuality. It is just that this factor alone does not seem sufficient to account for the matter of sexual preference. William Perloff suggests the following division of function.

> Three elements are involved in the determination of human sexuality. The genetic factor sets the sexual pattern and defines the general limits within which the other factors may operate. The hormonal factor develops the organs needed for the sex act and increases their sensitivity to stimulation. The psychological factor essentially controls the choice of sex object and the intensity of sexual emotions.[1]

It is the first two of these elements, namely, genes and hormones, that are the subject of controversy. I will look at each in turn.

The evidence against the genes as the cause of homosexuality is strong.[2] The main reason is that it seems impossible to strictly correlate any particular character trait or behavior pattern with an individual gene or a group of genes. At one time it was thought that homosexuality might be a 'third sex' and that its genetic roots might be traced. Instead, what was discovered was that, although there is a kind of 'third sex,' namely, hermaphroditism, its members are not manifestly inclined toward homosexuality. Hermaphroditism is a result of abnormal sexual chromosomes, yet even here other factors seem to determine what the individual's sexual orientation will be.

If the explanation is not in the genes, some have that it might be in the hormones. According to this theory, homosexuality is the result either of an excessive presence of the opposite sex hormones or of the late appearance of the proper sex hormones. When experiments have been done with various types of hormonal injection, what is affected is not the nature of the desired sex object but rather the level of overt sexual drive. While hormones may account for the relative interest in sexual activity, they do not seem to determine whether or not one is heterosexual or homosexual.

While this brief treatment is not sufficient to reflect the extent of the available research, it does convey the general consensus that the reliance on physical factors alone to explain homosexuality is inadequate to the available evidence.[3] If homosexuality is not something one is born with, then it must be learned somewhere in the developmental process. But how this takes place, and what is the relative importance of various aspects in the familial, cultural and experiential contexts is the subject of the Nurture Hypothesis.

II. The Nurture Hypothesis

Simply stated, the Nuture Hypothesis suggests that at some point in the developmental process after birth an individual __learns__ to be a homosexual. This is not to imply that some conscious decision is made. It is more likely that a certain pattern of psychosexual relatedness is set off by other people and by the circumstances of one's life. But at some point in adulthood, some percentage of those who have had homosexual feelings and/or behavior patterns will find themselves unable to be attracted sexually by members of the opposite sex.

For purposes of convenience I will divide the different versions of the Nurture Hypothesis into two broad categories: psychological theories and other theories.

(a)   Psychological Theories of Causality   In 1973, after an extensive lobbying effort, the American Psychological Association finally declassified homosexuality as a form of mental illness. Some interpreted this change as a sign that the long-standing rift between psychologists and gay activists had finally been overcome. Others saw it as an irresponsible cop-out which reflected more the political realities among Association members than any detached scientific judgment. Since that time the debate has continued. I will set the stage for a discussion of the contemporary variance of opinion by first looking at the formulations of the great figures of the history of psychology.[4]

(a1)   The Classical Tradition

(i) Sigmund Freud -- Like most of his successors, Freud devoted his attention primarily to masculine homosexuality. However, since there is sufficient ambiguity to his whole system, and since he never wrote a sustained book on the topic, we must provide the organizing scheme ourselves. Basically, Freud pictures each person as 'polymorphous perverse', i.e., originally capable of being attracted to all sex objects and enjoying all sexual acts. What happens is that as each individual goes through the various stages of personal development, the majority of people achieve a predominantly heterosexual orientation.

Homosexuality is the result of an early fixation in the male child or a failure to work throuh the Oedipal stage at ages 6 to 8. From this perspective, homosexuality is a deficiency because not all of the steps toward emotional maturity are worked through in the proper sequence. In most instances this seems to be the result of a home environment where there is an absent father and an overpossessive mother.

But Freud did not rest on this explanation alone. He also saw homosexuality as a form of 'narcissism.' What happens in love-making is that the boy projects himself into another male and gives to this other person the mother-love he wants for himself. At a deeper level, homosexuality is also a defense against paranoia, a way of coping sexually in a potentially hostile world.

According to Freud, there are three forms of homosexuality:

(1) latent - a pansexual disposition which exists in everyone

(2) repressed - occurs in varying degrees in those who have failed to work through properly the stages of emotional growth

(3) overt - an obvious pattern in a person's life.

From his experience of dealing with patients in psychoanalysis, Freud doubted that most who came for treatment of homosexuality really wished to change.

(ii) Carl Jung -- Jung wrote even less about homosexuality than Freud did, but because his school of thought is quite popular in modern psychoanalytic theory, his views are worthy of mention. The key analytical category is the distinction between the 'animus' and 'anima' in each human person. Each male has an unconscious feminine self (an anima) and each female has a unconscious male self (an animus). True health comes from the balance and integration of these polar archetypes in one's unconscious life. Homosexuality in the male results from a Mother complex in which the boy identifies too closely with the feminine psychic framework. Behind every male homosexual is a failure in feminine parenting.

(iii) Other Early Figures -- While the theories of Freud and Jung have retained some currency even up to today, there has been no absence of alternate explanations. Alfred Adler saw homosexuality as one among many types of failure to cope with life, in this instance with a heterosexual world. It probably sprang from low self-esteem. Wilhelm Stekel focused on the role of narcissitic projection. Later theories took a new direction. "With Erich Fromm, Karen Horney, Clara Thompson, and Harry Stack Sullivan the emphasis began to shift from constitution, childhood and trauma to environment, family inter-action and social influences."[5]

(a2) The Contemporary Debate -- Sickness versus Sexual Variation

The question of causality has been tested out by psychoanalysts and psychologists of different persuasions. The results have been less than unanimous. A mainstream group continues to pro-pose some version of Freudian or Jungian theory. Others have attempted to recast the debate in new ways. And a third group have judged that the question of causality is misplaced since there is no conclusive evidence that homosexuality is necessarily a sickness, and therefore it is simply a primordial fact that may never be totally explained.

A. Proponents of the Sickness Theory

(A1) Edmund Bergler -- Bergler operates out of a Freudian framework and claims that homo-sexuality is a "neurotic distortion of the total personality...There are no healthy homosexuals."[6] He then list ten factors which characterize homo-sexuals.[7] They are: injustice collectors (psychic masochists); fugitives from women; prone to use other men as substitutes for the women they fear; constantly on the prowl; capable of only husband-wife camouflages in marriage; megalo-maniacs convinced of the homosexual's superiority; sufferers from inner depression and exorbitant malice; full of inner guilt; irrationally jealous; and unreliable.

Bergler traces the roots of both masculine and feminine homosexuality to an unsolved masochistic conflict with the mother of earliest infancy (the pre-Oedipal mother, the giantess of the nursery).[8] In his summary description he speaks of a homosexual as 'psychic masochist -- plus.' In his or her sex play, the active homosexual reenacts the role of the mother, and the passive homosexual assumes the role of the baby.

Contrary to the common presumption that male homesexuality is more frequent than lesbianism, Bergler considers the number of female homosexuals to be quite high. The main reason that they are not so evident to public scrutiny is that most of them are married.

> Male homosexuals habitually over-
> play, female homosexuals
> habitually underplay the per-
> version...The decisive
> difference -- it is easier for a
> wife to disguise here frigidity
> than for a husband to disguise his
> impotence -- leads to the fre-
> quency of 'alibi-marriages' in
> homosexual women and to the
> relative rarity of such marriage
> among homosexual men..."[9]

Bergler's opinons about homosexuality are a product of his experience as a psychoanalyst in private practice. He takes some basic Freudian theories and adjusts them to his shifting data base. His self-confident tone and penchant for hyperbole and sweeping generalization seem representative of an earlier era of unchallenged theorizing, especially in light of more recent studies.

(A2) Irving Bieber -- One of the best known and most influential studies of homosexuality was published in 1962 by Irving Bieber and other members of the Society of Medical Psycho-analystst.[10] It was based upon 9 years of

70

research. For purposes of comparison it involved 106 male homosexuals and 100 male heterosexuals who were patients in psychoanalytic treatment. Their doctors filled out questionnaires on each of the patients in the research group. Thus the information was based on the psychoanalysts' evaluations of the person in treatment rather than the patient's self-evaluations. After all the data from the questionaires was assembled, it was run through a computer program.

The sample had the following general characteristics. They were persons from the New York City area, of above average education and sufficient income to pay for treatment, disproportionately from the arts and other professions, and in most instances eager to conceal their homosexuality. Of the 77 psychoanalysts who participated in the medical analysis, 12 were female. Most of them (59) operated from a Freudian perspective, although a smaller number (18) described themselves as 'Culturalists.' However, all staff participants shared a common presupposition, namely, that

> the parents are the architects of family structure and fundamentally determine the ongoing interactive processes...The development of personality disorders in a child is almost always evidence of the pervasive effects of parental psychotherapy...In some families one child may bear the brunt; in others, most or all children may be seriously affected.[11]

The logic of the Bieber study goes something like this. The triangular system of the mother-father-child is the key locus of personality development. Since homosexuality in an individual is a personality maladaptation, it must have its roots in some distorted functioning of the triangular system. If we can find some common pattern in the family lives of homosexual

71

patients, then we will have isolated the most likely cause of homosexuality.

The central conclusion of Bieber and his associates is that "the triad characterized by maternal close-binding intimacy and paternal detachment hostility is the 'classic' pattern most conducive to promoting homosexuality or severe homosexual in the son."[12] According to the criteria laid down, about 70% of the mothers and about 90% of the fathers of homosexuals fit into these categories. Close Binding Intimate Mothers were characterized by four qualities.[13]

(1) They interfered with their sons heterosexual development -- acted seductively; were inhibiting; discourage masculinity; limited peer group participation.

(2) They interfered with the father-son relationship -- sought exclusive maternal possession; fostered father-son competitiveness; acted out a romance; included sons in inappropriate situations.

(3) They interfered with peer relations -- limited boyhood friendships and activities; fostered adult relationship; gave particular child preferential treatment.

(4) They interfered with development of independence -- preempted decision-making; encouraged timidity; infantilized; isolated son. While not all of the mothers did all of these things, they do describe the trends in their relationships.

The prime criterion in guaging the level of attachment between a father and son was the amount of time they spent together.[14] Most homosexual fathers were detached, hostile and rejecting. The response of the homosexuals to their male parent was hatred and fear.

One problem with this approach seems to be the presence of non-homosexual children in the same family as a homosexual. The authors of the study account for this by positing a series of separate triangles between the parents and each respective child. The assumption is that the parents form a special relationship with the homosexual son. For instance, the father might have warm feelings toward all the sons but one. Toward the end of the study, Bieber make the following suggestion, "a constructive, supportive, warmly related father precludes the possibility of a homosexual son; he acts as a neutralizing, protective agent should the mother make seductive or close-binding attempts."[15] Thus, although the CBI Mother is most often presented as the prime causal factor, the nature of the attachment between father and son may ultimately be the key.

Bieber presents homosexuality as a method of coping with the fear of heterosexuality. It is seen as acquired through the triangular dynamics of the nuclear family. Yet, every homosexual is potentially a heterosexual. All that is required is that this more basic, and fulfilling, sexual drive be reestablished.

(A3) Lionel Ovesey -- Ovesey's work is important primarily because he tries to distinguish homosexuality from pseudo-homosexuality.[16] He modifies the Freudian perspective to some extent and pictures three elements of behavior as causal factors in homosexual patterns of action: sexual, dependency and power.[17] Pseudohomosexuality occurs in those men who fail to meet successfully the standards for masculine performance laid down by society. It is not really a sexual problem at all. What happen is that individuals unconsciously make the following equation: I am a failure I am castrated I am not a man -- I am a woman -- I am a homosexual.

The true homosexual, according to Ovesey, is a neurotic who tries to overcome castration

73

anxiety by the phobic avoidance of the female genital. Correspondingly, success is equated with a large penis, and failure with a small one.

Ovesey's theory is not susceptible to proof. He has merely tried to explain why some men, who have had periods of homosexual behavior, may be led to a heterosexual adjustment. The key factor in his eyes is the desire to change.

(A4) Charlotte Wolff -- Wolff is the only one of the psychologists or psychoanalysts to be treated in this section who has concentrated on female homosexuality.[18] Her perspective is non-orthodox and is based on extensive counseling of lesbian clients. She describes emotionality as the central characteristic of lesbian love. And this has led her to coin the term 'homo-emotionality' to replace the standard categories of lesbianism and female homosexuality.

In order to evolve her theory, Wolff did in-depth interview with 108 lesbians. She found that the mother was the strongest force in the develop-ment of lesbianism. These female parents tended to be immature and unreliable. Out of this back-ground, lesbians tend to be searching for "nothing less than the wish fulfillment of an incestuous mother-daughter relationship."[19] Certain personality and experiential factors seemed to appear quite frequently among the lesbians studied. They were agressive, abusive, insecure, shy and had difficulties in adaptation. In addition, they were conscious of the disturbed relationship to their mothers referred to above. Unlike male homosexuals there was no particular fixation on the female sexual organs. In fact, most had had heterosexual experiences. The rate of masturbation was high and in some instances pets seemed to provide a surrogate for children.

While sympathetic to the problems of lesbians, Wolff basically considers their con-dition as undesirable and fraught with diffi-culties. The rates of alcoholism, neurosis and psychosis are higher than among heterosexual women. And the alternative of heterosexual marriage, which many had known first-hand, had soured them on any other sexual adaptation.

(A5) Marc Oraison -- Oraison is a French priest-psychologist of a strongly Freudian orientation.[20] He claims to have treated 6 or 7 homosexual clients a week for the past 20 years. On the basis of this experience, he has offered a balanced and sensitive theory which is one of the better versions of the sickness point of view.

For him, homosexuality is not an illness in the usual sense of the term. It is better seen as an 'anomaly' (which is a matter of statistics) than as an 'abnormality' (which presupposes some agreed upon standard of normalcy).[21] According to the laws of science, some thing has gone wrong in the developmental process, a psychic block of some kind which has prevented a person's full sexual potential from being actualized.

Oraison prefers to explain this inhibiting factor in Freudian terms. The myth of Narcissus, which suggests that we are attracted to our double, best describes the unconscious force at work. It is the phallus which is the focus of unconscious affective life and it is the fear of castration which sets off the problem of narcissism. The tragedy of the homosexual encounter is that it is "the doomed confrontation of two narcissistic personalities."[22] For this reason, the relationship between two partners is better viewed as a 'pair,' than as a 'couple,' since the chance of an enduring affective bond are minimal. The very drive to possess the other sets off the destructive forces which will prevent it from taking place.

Most homosexuals suffer from their homosexual tendencies, Oraison believes. By the age of 16 or 17 their sexual orientation is probably fixed so that there is no going back. The alternative of homosexual pairing may be the best of the

75

available alternatives, but it is no panacea. Ultimately the homosexual condition is indicative of the "basic, universal human tragedy."[23]

(A6) John Cavanaugh -- In a recently reissued manual which has had in the past a strong impact on Catholic attitudes and pastoral strategies, John Cavanaugh interprets homosexuality as a psychiatric problem.[24] The homosexual is an individual engaged in the frustrating pursuit of the impossible. The reason for this is that at an early age of development the libido became fixated.[25] While homosexual relationships contain many of the elements found in heterosexual attractions, there also tends to be more suspiciousness, less trust, and more selfishness. This leads to the prevalence of strife and to a high percentage of breakups.

Cavanaugh offers no new theories, but merely reechoes some of the established psychiatric perspectives. A person can be taken to be a confirmed homosexual when he or she is stimulated by thoughts about members of their own sex and sexually unmoved by thoughts about members of the other sex. Since this condition results from psychic dynamics over which the individual has no control, the real issue is what the genuine alternatives for sexual adjustment might be.

(A7) Ruth Tiffany Barnhouse -- Barnhouse is more inclined to a Jungian perspective than the other professionals considered in this section. In an interesting book, she tries to bring some order into the lingering confusion about the scientific data on homosexuality and then to relate this framework to the even more difficult consideration of the ethics of homosexual behavior.[26] She bases her analysis on her private practice as a psychiatrist.

It is the fundamental process of separation from the mother which is the key to the acquisition of sexual identity for both boys and girls.[27] Male children, however, seem to

76

experience more problems in this regard. Homosexuality, as we know it, is not a single entity. It is a symptom of any one of three main problems: unsatisfied dependency needs, unresolved issues of power or dominance, or fear of heterosexuality.[28] The person who experiences these difficulties may or may not participate in the homosexual sub-culture.

Barnhouse presupposes, under the influence of Jung, that there is a fundamental difference between men and women. The archetypal categories of animus-anima are one way of explaining that full sexual development takes place, not by a denial of one's gender identity, but by an integration of the contrasexual component in the unconscious. This task takes place over time, and in most instances, should not be considered completed before the age of 21.

B. Proponents of the Sexual Variation Theory

(B1) Martin Hoffman -- In 1968 Hoffman published a very useful study of the homosexual subculture of San Francisco called The Gay World.[29] Although himself a social psychiatrist, he deliberately set out to do a non-clinical research project using the tools of an ethnographer. The main motivation behind this shift in technique was the suspicion that the homosexuals who end up as clients of psychiatrists were not necessarily representative of the overall gay population. By widening the focus away from an exclusive concentration on mental illness, he hoped to show that there was a broad spectrum of life styles and degrees of personal contentedness in the gay world.

This attempt by Hoffman was one of the first examples of a high quality study on the subject of homosexuality which did not presuppose the sickness model. As Hoffman explains it,

77

> People don't like to think of
> homosexuality as sinful any
> longer, because the whole concept
> of sin has gone out of Western
> culture. To describe homo-
> sexuality as morally evil is now
> unfashionable. And yet the alter-
> native, considering it as a
> legitimate way of life for some
> people, is simply not palatable to
> very many. Hence, the popularity
> of the disease concept.[30]

But Hoffman does not wish to deny that homosexuality can be involved in various kinds of
psychotic breakdowns and other types of mental
distress and anxiety. Especially among males, the
achievement of masculinity, and therefore sexual
self-confidence, can be an arduous and painful
process. Thus Hoffman contends that, although
some percentage of the homosexual population
suffers from serious psychological problems, this
is not generally true.

A final contribution of Hoffman to this discussion is his wonderment about the therapeutic
claims of modern psychiatric treatment. Even pre-
suming that homosexuality is a form of mental
illness that can be cured, do we really think that
any method of one-on-one analysis can have much of
an impact on the problem. The factors of time,
available money, and personnel would seem to rule
this out except for the very wealthy or the
fortunate few.

Hoffman's rephrasing of the question about
homosexuality from: What kind of a sickness is it
and can it be cured? to: What kinds of adjust-
ments have homosexuals made to their condition and
how can these be improved has been supported by a
number of important theorists in the last decade
and a half.

(B2) Mark Freedman -- Freedman is an American psychologist who in 1967 undertook a study of 81 lesbian members of the Daughters of Bilitis (along with a volunteer group of heterosexual women).[31] A 12 scale test battery was used. As a result of this comparative analysis, he came to conclusion,

> there is not substantial evidence that there are more psychotic individuals among the population of homosexually oriented individuals than among the community of heterosexually oriented people...a slightly greater number of homosexually oriented than heterosexually oriented individuals manifest neurotic characteristics.[32]

The criteria by which such a judgment was made have to do with relative degrees of social adjustment and self-actualization. Freedman is optimistic about the ability of all of us (who are pansexual by nature) to handle the psychic shocks that may arise from assuming a non-socially approved sexual identity. For him, sex is only a means of satisfying a bodily need and therefore a source of temporary pleasure. As long as the individual does not become obsessed with the matter to the detriment of other personality factors, a healthy adjustment should be possible. Mastery of one's personal environment is the essential step in productive psychological functioning.

The move that Freedman has made is to shift the criteria by which sickness/health are determined. In his theoretical framework, adjustment to one's life circumstances is more important than conformity to some pre-determined pattern of appropriate sexual relatedness. Only those who fail to cope with a threatened homosexual identity should be considered mentally ill.

79

(B3) Paul Rosenfels -- Unlike the other studies in this section, Rosenfel's proposals have the quality of rhapsodic evocations of a dreamed of world of the future rather than a detached and clinical analysis of the existing condition of homosexual persons.[33] Rosenfels is a visionary who sees openness to homosexuality as the essential step in releasing human creative energy. He suggests a bipolar psychic structure in which love (feminine) and power (masculine) need to be fused. It is only by breaking out of the stereotypical masculine and feminine roles that this can take place. For men, this means that in polarized masculine friendships they may find an atmosphere in which love and power can be developed in their creative aspect.

Rosenfels recognizes that the break-up of established social patterns can lead to a higher incidence of promiscuity and irresponsible behavior. However, this the price that must be paid for the advance of our civilization. The psychological world of many has become more complex and less structured. Only a sustained defense of the potential for good that is stored up in this process can allow it to flourish.

Thus we see that Rosenfels is disinterested altogether in the question of causality. Without identifying at all with any of the psychological schools, he draws upon his medical training to evoke a cultural transition in which homosexuals must play a decisive role. They will be at the forefront of creative evolution as soon as they forge their capabilities for both love and power into an integrating style of living for all of culture. The prevalence of promiscuity and pettiness is but a regretful stage in the passage to wholeness.

(B4) Thomas Szasz -- Perhaps the best known figure in the revisionist attempt to discredit the theories about homosexuality propounded in orthodox psychiatry in Thomas Szasz.[34] He has unleashed an unrelenting critique of the theory of mental illness in general and of its diagnostic usefulness in the approach to homosexual clients. The medical practitioner has replaced the high priest as the new censor of modern mores.

> My contention that the psychiatric perspective on homosexuality is but a thinly disguised replica of the religious perspective which it displaced, as that efforts to 'treat' this kind of conduct medically are but thinly disguised methods for suppressing it, may be verified by examining any contemporary psychiatric account of homosexuality.[35]

The expected result of a healthy skepticism about the existence of a clinical entity called homosexuality would be to leave it to the individual to determine when his or her sexual orientation might be the source of conflict and pain. Illness brings stigma and social persecution. To be freed of such medical attribution is to assume a new identity full of the normal human possibilities.

Szasz is most effective as a gadfly in the psychiatric establishment. He challenges the facticity and objectivity of the very conceptual schemes that are most often employed by the professionals. Yet in his eagerness to rid us of the illness model, he goes overboard in minimizing the traumas and strains of homosexual life.

(B5) Franklin Kameny -- Kameny has no particular credentials as psychiatrist or psychoanalyst. His main role has been as a gay activist. He was one of the early members of the Mattachine Society and recently ran for political office in Washington, D.C. He does, however, succinctly state the main criticism of the psychiatric profession as rendered by the gay community.[26]

81

Kameny criticizes the studies done up to now on three grounds:[37]

(1) They employ inadequate definitions of such terms as pathology, sickness, neurosis, etc. The long-range effect of this misuse of language is the preservation of the societal status quo.

(2) They use poor scientific method, especially the sampling techniques. The patients chosen tend to be sick enough to seek psychiatric aid and are not typical of the broader homosexual population.

(3) They get away with poor logic and unclear thinking. The results are predetermined by the assumptions built into the data gathering and interpretive schemes.

According to Kameny, gay liberation is, in fact, primarily a freeing from the shackles of the sickness definition as generated by the psychiatric profession. Only in this way can the preoccupation with the insoluble questions of 'cause' and 'cure' be left behind.

(B6) George Weinberg -- Weinberg is a practicing psychotherapist who became disillusioned with the conventional wisdom of his profession. In a widely circulated book he called for a reversal of the categories of analysis which presupposed the biological and psychological superiority of the heterosexual option.[38] As he saw it, the central social problem was really the disease of 'homophobia.' A better standard of psychological health than the prevailing one of conformity to conventional patterns of sexual behavior is whether a person is harming him or herself or other people.[39]

For Weinberg, psychoanalytic theory misconstrues the real issue. Because it is committed to the position that one becomes homosexual because of some developmental failure, it sees a cure as the desired goal. What this leads to is

82

an attempt to suppress the individual's valid sexual feelings and desires and this amounts to a kind of forced punishment. Weinberg calls for a new 'gay' consciousness which will supplant this cycle of self-hatred and recrimination.

> A homosexual person is gay when he regards himself as happily gifted with whatever capacity he has to see people as romantically beautiful. It is to be free of shame, guilt, regret over the fact that one is homosexual...To be gay is to view one's sexuality as the healthy heterosexual views his...In essence, it means being convinced that any erotic orientation and preference may be housed in any human being.[40]

Weinberg says that he has discovered a number of homosexual people who have never been troubled by their sexual orientation. A clue may lie in the ready acceptance by some parents of their gay sons and daughters.. Contrary to the assertion of some psychoanalysts, no particular family configuation seems to predominate among homosexuals. Just as the sickness theory has been a self-fulfilling prophecy in the lives of many gays, so the discovery of healthy gays may set off a chain reaction that will shatter the old misconceptions and enable a higher percentage of homosexuals to realize their potentials.

Weinberg's book is designed as an antidote and a challenge. He turns the cards on the opponents of homosexuality by accusing them of homophobia. He belittles psychoanalytic theory for its methodological inadequacies. And he calls homosexuals everywhere to move in the direction of a gay identity which is the path to wholeness, health and peace.

(B7) C.A. Tripp -- Tripp is a sex researcher and psychologist who originally worked with Alfred

Kinsey at Indiana University. He undertook a research project on homosexually which took ten years to complete. On the basis of his findings, he has written a book which has generated much controversy.[41] I will merely summarize those of his conclusions which are relevant to questions of mental sickness and health among homosexuals.

In regards to the origins of homosexuality, Tripp thinks that the causes are multiple.

> No single element in homo-
> sexuality, no one original influ-
> ence, is by itself likely to be
> definitive. The final existence
> of any sexual orientation depends
> upon the extent to which its
> various parts have reinforced each
> other in producing a structure, a
> system of values, a pattern of
> responses.[42]

One key factor is probably a society's concept of maleness and the ways that it can be manifested. In most cultures, the stress on hetorosexuality is prevasive enough to gear most children in that direction. One curious fact is that homosexuals arrive at puberty earlier and start masturbating earlier.[43]

An essential component of Tripp's theory is his understanding of the place of mystery and dis-tance in the preservation of erotic attraction between the sexes. Men and women are usually segregated from puberty on in such a fashion that the unknown and the complementary elements that are hinted at in brief encounters are sufficient allure to heighten the desire for further explo-ration. In contrast, groups of all men or all women may find themselves in very intimate con-texts without setting off the same kind of sexual desire.

What happens, first of all, is bisexual indi-viduals is that a double value system is at

work. One set of criteria is used to judge
potential male partners and another to rate female
partners. But in the confirmed homosexual the
drive for union is focused exclusively on the same
sex.

> Homosexuality in all its varia-
> tions always means that same-sex
> attributes have become eroticized,
> have taken on erotic sig-
> nificance...In all their
> essentials, the sought-after
> rewards of homosexual and hetero-
> sexual complementations are
> identical: the symbolic pos-
> session of those attributes of a
> partner which, when added to one's
> own, fill out the illusion of com-
> pleteness.[44]

Tripp is among those commentators who see
nothing inherently promiscuous about homosexual
relationships. Stable partnerships are the hidden
side of the gay world. Yet he admits that,
expecially among male homosexuals, the problems
in sustaining a faithful commitment are numerous.
There is an intolerance of clashes. Arguments and
fights are so painful because each party knows
exactly where to sink the knife. "Homosexual
relationships are overclose, fatigue-prone, and
are often adjusted to such narrow, trigger-
sensitive tolerances that a mere whisper of disrapport can jolt the partners into making repairs,
or into conflict."[45]

Despite the difficulties to be found in the
life, it is critical that homosexuals admit to
themselves and to others their true sexual
identity. Too often they retreat into patterns of
denial. Tripp makes special mention of such
patterns of denial.

(1) In the 'Gender-Role Umbrella' the male
claims that since he always plays the male role

85

of the insertor, there can be no question about his heterosexuality.

(2) In the 'Personal Innocence Umbrella' seduction is presented as the cause of the behavior.

(3) In the 'Only-For-Now Umbrella' the homosexual pattern is seen as a temporary phenomenon.

(4) In the 'Special-Friendship Umbrella' homosexual feelings are only acknowledged toward one special individual. Otherwise, one is heterosexual.

All four of these devices are interpreted by Tripp as rationalizations and systematic denials of the real story of one's life.

Ultimately, Tripp favors a homosexual life style which is realistic about the difficulties to be faced, yet self-confident and proud. No one path will be proper for all. Each gay person will have to struggle to find a comfortable level of self-understanding and a viable support structure. But the chances are good that most will do all right.

C.   A Personal Assessment of the Psychological Theories of Causality

Is homosexuality a type of psychological maladjustment or one manifestation of sexual pluriformity? Are homosexuals sick people in need of therapy or normal people suffering from social stigmatization? As we have seen in the previous section, the answers to these questions vary across a whole spectrum of possibilities. If our experience tells us that a homosexual orientation is usually coupled with various symptoms of neurosis and psychosis (as most psychoanalysts claim), then we will search for some causal factor(s) which can provide a clue toward successful intervention in the client's life. If our experience tells us that, although some homosexuals are indeed mentally ill and in need of professional help, most are not, then we will want to reaffirm their homosexual identity and provide support structures which will facilitate the further development of their creative potential. It depends therefore both on our concrete experience and on the interpretive scheme we bring to bear on the issue.

In such a disputed context, how can we bring some balance into the discussion? My own perspective hinges on seeing the limits of the research that has been done up to now. For example, psychoanalysis began with the theoretical framework of Freud. Patients came to him because they had known some personal disease and wished to find a better way of coping. As Freud's reputation grew, more people came to him with their problems. Despite the proliferation of theoretical frameworks within the disciplines of psychoanalysis, psychiatry and counseling psychology, the basic situation has remained the same. The sick, or those who deem themselves sick, come for counsel, solace and therapy. The healthy, or those oblivious to their true state of affairs, stay away. And furthermore, for most forms of psychological therapy, only those of sufficient economic means and philosophical motivation even consider the possibility of therapy.

As a result of this situation, the access that psychiatrists have to the homosexual population is probably limited to those of a certain social strata. Therefore, the claim that many gay activists make that theories based on this restricted segment of the population many not be generalizable is surely plausible. Up to now, we have no way of knowing how representative the available sample really is.

The next question, having acknowledged the uncertainty about the data base, is whether the contrary claim should be accepted. Perhaps, instead of saying all homosexuals are sick until

proven healthy, we should say all homosexuals are
healthy until proven sick. But at this point we
run into some difficult problems of definition.
There is no consensus in the psychological disciplines about the dividing line between, or
relative degrees of, sickness and health. Irving
Bieber summarizes this divergence of opinion in
these terms.

> All psychoanalytic theories assume
> that adult homosexuality is
> psychopathologic and assign
> differing weights to consti-
> tutional and experiential deter-
> minants. All agree that the
> experiential determinants are in
> the main rooted in childhood and
> are primarily related to the
> family. Theories which do not
> assume psychopathology hold homo-
> sexuality to be one type of
> expression of a polymorphous
> sexuality which appears pathologic
> only in cultures holding it to be
> so.[47]

Although most of us may believe that we know a
sick person when we see one, that still leaves
open the problem of arriving at a common criteria
for judgment.

    In the midst of this morass of conflicting
opinion, I will venture the following proposition-
'A homosexual person should be considered mentally
ill only if he or she is unable to function as a
responsible member of society.' This phraseology
is deliberately elastic. The concepts 'function'
and 'responsible' are notoriously equivocal. Yet
this proposition does allow for testing out an
individual's ability to be self-supporting eco-
nomically, to engage in the normal duties of a
citizen, to make friends and to belong to social
organizations. From the evidence available, I
think that a significance percentage of homosexuals are capable in these areas of life.

Furthermore, such a social definition resists the attempt to make the matter of health dependent entirely on subjective consciousness. Since I believe that there are people who have a distorted view of reality, including some homosexuals, I think it undesirable to say that each individual should determine whether or not they have a problem.

When you look closer at the psychological literature, it seems possible to find greater support for this position than might appear at first sight. Oraison, for example, refers to homosexuality as a 'psychological birth defect.'[48] But he thinks that failure and human tragedy are inextricably linked to the quest for sexual fulfillment. In this relatively pessimistic view of reality, the homosexual struggle is not particularly unique. Or to take a second example, H. Kimball Jones, after reviewing various etiological theories, summarizes the points of agreement.

> While in each of these representative views homosexuality is seen as constituting a psychiatric abnormality, it is in no instance, with the possible exception of Bieber, seen as inherently constituting a serious and debilitating mental illness.[49]

In the instance of abnormality, the persons would not have their emotional life effectively integrated. But in this they would hardly differ from many heterosexuals. A third confirmation of this comparative placing of the homosexual condition comes from Arno Karlen. He says,

> Homosexuality probably does originate in emotional conflict or developmental distortion, but in a minority of homosexuals it seems to be minimally damaging... Meanwhile, anachronistic arguments

89

about health and sickness direct
attention from the many aspects of
homosexuality that need research
so that those who want treatment
and change will have a better
chance.[50]

Part of my motivation for minimizing the
claims of the sickness theorists is that only if
this is true will the ethical analysis be dealing
with individuals capable of making informed moral
choices about their sexuality. Otherwise, it is
the medical profession that will provide the
solutions, if any are to be found.

But this still leaves open the question why
some people are homosexuals and not others. The
most likely explanation is that many factors
contribute to this process. Especially in a
society where there are deeply ingrained social
influences to teach a heterosexual identity, something must interfere with this dynamic in a
percentage of lives. The family constellation is
surely one of the decisive factors. Whether a
Close-Binding-Intimate Mother and a Distant
Unaffectionate Father are the key familial context
is uncertain. I suspect that, at least in male
homosexuality, some combination like this is frequently present. But to look for some single
explanatory scheme is to go against the preponderance of the present data.

To say that homosexuality is not usually a
form of mental illness is different from accepting
its equivalency with heterosexual normalcy.
Certain psychological characteristics seem to be
quite common among homosexuals. Some of them
probably spring from unresolved tensions in the
family constellation. For example, the ability of
many homosexuals to relate comfortably to members
of the opposite sex seems to be curtailed. This
may reflect a tense relationship with the opposite
sex parent. Among male homosexuals, the prevalence of paranoia, bitchiness and authority
problems may have the same source.

Claims such as these always admit of degrees. We have no pure population samples to obtain our control data and no one knows how many undiscovered homosexuals there are who defy characterization. But on the basis of what we have discovered about publicly-acknowledged homosexuals, the road to self-acceptance is full of disappointments and a pattern of failures may exacerbate whatever inherent potential for psychological problems that is connected to the homosexual condition. This is especially true when homosexuality is linked with involvement in pedophilia, fetishism, voyeurism, exhibitionism, coprophilia, and sado-masochism.

By way of concluding this section, I want to repeat that I consider most homosexuals not to be mentally ill, even though many suffer from lesser forms of psychological disturbance. However, a heterosexual adjustment is desirable for those who are capable of making it. In the psychological literature, various claims have been made about the possibilities of such a cure. It is to this matter that I will now turn my attention.

(c) <u>The Question of a Cure</u>

It goes without saying that those who consider homosexuality a form of sexual variation fully the equal of heterosexuality will consider talk of a cure a barbaric intrusion into an individual's pre-given identity. In the previous section, I discussed a number of psychological theorists who fit into this category. But, even for those who deem homosexuality undesirable, there is a difference of opinion about the chances of effecting a cure. Much depends upon the underlying presuppositions of the particular therapist. Nearly every tool of personal transformation from external coercion and pain to self-disipline and heterosexual orgasm has been tried at one time or another.

The most common techniques outside of psychoanalytic therapy include the following.[51]

91

(1) Castration -- the removal of the male testicles can effect impotence but it cannot determine sexual orientation.

(2) Imprisonment -- Ironically, immersion in the prison environment may heighten problems of sexual identity and expose the individual to homosexual rape.

(3) Hypnosis -- while it may calm some sexual tensions, it cannot change one's desired sexual object.

(4) Shock Therapy -- a questionable intervention, whatever the problem.

(5) Brain Surgery -- in most instances it achieves nothing more than a deadening of some aspect of the personality.

(6) Association Therapy -- tries to make one's homosexual desires shift toward heterosexual ends.

(7) Moral Persuasion -- takes two different forms. In the first, drugs are used in conjunction with audio-visual materials to reverse one's homosexual drives and desires. In the second, emetics are used to induce nausea and dizziness when homosexual images appear on a screen.

There is general clinical consensus that none of these techniques have proven successful in the long haul. At best, they have achieved temporary modifications of behavior. Or in the instance of castration and brain surgery, they have done major damage to the individual concerned.

Almost all of the claims of success which have some credibility in the scientific literature have been made by psychiatrists and psychoanalysts who employ a one-on-one counseling technique over a long period of time. I will now examine some of

these declarations of success in curing homosexuality.

(C1) Edmund Bergler -- In 1956, Bergler made
the dramatic announcement,

> In nearly thirty years, I have
> successfully concluded analyses of
> one hundred homosexuals...Homo-
> sexuality has an excellent prog-
> nosis in psychiatric-
> psychoanalytic treatment of one to
> two years duration, with a minimum
> of three appointmens each week
> provided the patient really wishes
> to change.[52]

Later he set out three criteria which would determine whether a real change had taken place: (i)
complete lack of interest in the same sex (ii)
normal sexual enjoyment and (iii) character-
ological change.[53] As far as I know, there has
been no validation of his claims from outside
sources. We either take Bergler's word for it or
remain skeptical.

(C2) Irving Bieber -- In 1962, Bieber and his
associates reported some success in the treatment
of homosexual patients. They said, "29 patients
have become exclusively heterosexual during the
course of psychoanalytic treatment...These are the
most optimistic and promising results thus far
reported."[54] In order to increase the chances of
success they recommend at least 150 hours of
treatment. Most of those who had changed were
highly motivated to change. This sampling seems
more reliable because of the number of psychiatrists involved in the study and their ability to
check each other's results. But the methodology
they used is therapist-oriented and therefore susceptible to charges of professional status seeking
and excessively optimistic reading of the results.

(C3) Lionel Ovesey -- In 1969, Ovesey listed
the following factors as favorable signs in the

likelihood of a cure: strong motivation; strong ego strength; masculine sexual identification (for men); heterosexual social identification; low degree of homosexual consolidation (late onset; short duration; nonexclusivity; noncompulsive); and a high degree of heterosexual integrity.[55] The most important of these is the motivation to change. The ultimate test of whether successful therapy had taken place was in bed. "Sooner or later, the homosexual patient must make the necessary attempts to have intercourse, and he must make them again and again, until he is capable of a sustained erection, penetration, and pleasurable intravaginal orgasm".[56]

Two things strike one about this particular approach. In his list of criteria, Ovesey describes persons who have only a marginal homosexual identity. This type of patient is not a proper test of the possibilities of a cure. Second, the stress on heterosexual acting out seems to demean the other sexual partner into a non-cognizant experimental subject. This sort of pansexual problem-solving is morally questionable. A better test would be friendship, personal sharing and communication with the other sex which might later culminate in legitimate genital expression.

(C4) Ruth Tiffany Barnhouse -- In 1977 Ruth Barnhouse repeated the claim of these other practitioners of the counseling professions. She said, "many psychiatrists and psychologists with a more general type of practice (and I include myself in this group) have been successful in helping homosexual patients to make a complete and permanent transition to heterosexuality."[57] Once again she suggests that a desire to change is the sine qua non for successful therapy. And one of the inhibiting factors in the present context is the hostile reaction that many homosexuals in counseling receive from their former friends and associates.

By way of summary, each of these professional therapists have claimed that a cure was possible for those homosexuals who were committed to the counseling process. The chances of success were considered to be greater when the patient was younger, less immersed in the homosexual sub-culture, and ambivalent about heterosexual possibilities (thus not having ruled them out).

If any credence can be put in these clinical descriptions, and I think there can, what is being offered is the hope for a change in sexual orientation for some small percentage of adult homosexuals. The first inhibiting factor is the time, expense and trained personnel required for the counseling process. This effectively leaves out gays from the lower socio-economic groups and those who lack the stamina for long periods of one-to-one counseling. A second problem is that after a certain age or after a significant investment in the homosexual life style, it seems questionable that any dramatic change can be effected. Those who might best benefit from the type of intervention proposed would seem to be homosexuals in their 20's and 30's who became dissatisfied with their exposure to the gay world or those who consider themselves bisexual and want to free themselves from an ambiguous sexual identity.

Prior to the Gay Liberation Movement it was a commonplace in the gay world that those young people who had flirted with homosexual relationships but who were capable of heterosexual adjustment should pursue the latter alternative. The rationale behind this was that societal pressures made happiness more difficult for gays to achieve. This attitude no longer prevails. Now anyone who contemplates therapy in order to seek a sexual orientation change is considered a dupe of the psychiatric money-grubbers. This is decidely unfair. While I consider it next to impossible for such a change of orientation to occur with true adult homosexuals (according to my definition) there are many marginal types who have a greater prognosis of success. With these people it is desirable that they use the resources available to them.

One final question related to cure that needs to be addressed is heterosexual marriage. There is considerable evidence that marriage for a true homosexual will not solve the problem of sexual adjustment. As we have seen, a fairly high percentage of lesbians have married and had children. A lesser precentage of married men move into an exclusively homosexual pattern later on. The mere ability to complete sexual relations with a member of the opposite sex is no guarantee that the homosexual problem has disappeared. For many homosexuals acknowledge having fantasized a homosexual partner during heterosexual intercourse. Of course, the attraction of home and family, as well as the social cover it provides, is enough to sustain some marriages for considerable periods of time.

There is good reason for wondering whether a true homosexual can contract a valid marriage in the first place.[58] The central problem would seem to be psychological impotence. This is the grounds in the Roman Catholic tradition for considering homosexuality to be a diriment or invalidating impediment. Even the presence of children is not sufficient to belie this psychic block. But in the civil order such considerations are more likely to constitute grounds for divorce than they are to rule out marriage as a possibility.

(d) Other Etiological Theories

Most sociologists and anthropologists who have studied homosexuality have opted for a multicausal explanation. Evelyn Hooker, for example, says,

> homosexuality is a many-faceted phenomena not only in its manifestations in individual and social experience and behavior but

96

also, and correspondingly, in its
determination by psychodynamic,
biological, cultural, situational,
and structural variables.[59]

And Alan Bell speaks in the same vein when he concludes, "our data appear to indicate that homosexuality involves a large number of widely
divergent experiences-developmental, sexual,
social and psychological..."[60]

Since this conviction sets the context for
their work, and because the tools are not yet
available (if they ever will be) to precisely
determine the relative importance of the different
causal factors, most sociologists have concentrated on descriptions of the shape of the
homosexual subculture. They have effectively
forsaken the search for causes in order to explore
the hidden sides of the gay world. This is the
major reason that the methods of the ethnographer
(personal observation, note taking, sympathetic
reconstruction, and interviews) have led to the
most helpful results.

A good example of this approach is the study
by Martin Weinberg and Colin Williams called Male
Homosexuals: Their Problems and Adaptations.[61]
In their introductory chapter they sum up the presuppositions of recent sociological theory: (i)
Homosexuality is a variant of sexual expression.
(ii) There is no mandate to search for cures.
(iii) There is no need to posit heterosexuality as
a norm other than in a statistical sense.[62]
Taking these perspectives as a starting point,
they then identify their methodological position
as 'societal reaction theory.' This entails that
they will study three matters: how homosexuals
relate to the heterosexual world, how they relate
to the homosexual world, and what psychological
problems they might experience.

What we can expect from sociologists of this
type in the foreseeable future is an attempt to
describe the structure of gay life, one piece of

research building on another, and a defense of the
homosexual option as a manageable alternative for
the majority of gays.

III. Conclusion

I favor a multidimensional explanation of why
some percentage of the human race is homosexual
and not heterosexual. Biological, psychological,
sociological and experiential factors all have an
influence. We are fairly sure that homosexuality
is learned by some combination of influences at a
time after birth. It is unlikely that a homosexuality identity is firmly fixed until the age
of civic majority. But the more immersed an individual is in active homosexual experience,
especially in the context of the public gay subculture, the harder it is to change. According to
the strict definition of a homosexual proposed in
the first chapter, some homosexuals will remain so
their whole life and the prospects for sexual
reorientation are minimal.

The psychoanalytic tradition, which has provided the generally accepted theories of etiology,
has suffered from a limited data base. A higher
percentage of homosexuals, than was previously
speculated, seem to be able to function as
responsible members of society. But this
functional concept of health does not deny the
frequent experience of various levels of psychological problems in the homosexual population.

Footnotes to Chapter 4

[1]William Perloff, "Hormones and Homosexuality," in Sexual Inversion: The Multiple Roots of Homosexuality, edited by Judd Marmor (New York: Basic, 1965), p. 67.

[2]In a study that was just released, the sex researchers Drs. Masters and Johnson give new evidence that supports this claim. Cf. William Masters and Virginia Johnson, Homosexuality in Perspective (Boston: Little, Brown, 1979). Also see: Arno Karlen, Sexuality and Homosexuality: A New View (New York: W.W. Norton, 1971), p. 337ff.

[3]Cf., C.A. Tripp, The Homosexual Matrix (New York: New American Library, 1975), p. 11; C.M.B. Pare, "Etiology of Homosexuality: Genetic and Chromosomal Aspects," in Sexual Inversion, pp. 70-80; Marc Oraison, The Homosexual Question (New York: Harper & Row, 1977), p. 59; H. Kimball Jones, Toward a Christian Understanding of the Homosexual (New York: Association, 1966), p. 37.

[4]I will draw primarily on the handy summaries of Arno Karlen in Sexuality and Homosexuality, pp. 181-296. I have cross-checked his interpretation with a variety of sources and generally found it to be reliable.

[5]Karlen, Ibid., p. 296.

[6]Edmund Bergler, Homosexuality: Disease or way of Life? (New York: Collier, 1956), p. 9.

[7]Ibid., p. 13.

[8]Ibid., p. 245.

[9]Ibid., p. 244.

[10]Irving Bieber, et. al., Homosexuality: A Psychoanalytic Study (New York: Basic, 1962).

[11]Ibid., p. 42.

[12]Ibid., p. 144.

[13]Ibid., pp. 79-81.

[14]Ibid., p. 86.

[15]Ibid., p. 311.

[16]Lionel Ovesey, Homosexuality and Pseudohomosexuality (New York: Science House, 1969).

[17]Ibid., p. 28.

[18]Charlotte Wolff, Love Between Women (New York: Harper & Row, 1971).

[19]Ibid., p. 110.

[20]Mare Oraison, The Homosexual Question (New York: Harper & Row, 1977).

[21]Ibid., p. 40.

[22]Ibid., p. 53.

[23]Ibid., p. 131.

[24]John Cavanaugh, Counseling the Homosexual (Huntington: Our Sunday Visitor, 1977).

[25]Ibid., p. 49.

[26]Ruth Tiffany Barnhouse, Homosexuality: A Symbolic Confusion (New York: Seabury, 1977).

[27]Ibid., p. 77.

[28]Ibid., p. 51.

[29]Martin Hoffman, The Gay World (New York: Bantom, 1968).

[30]Ibid., p. 194.

[31]Mark Freedman, Homosexuality and Psychological Functioning (Belmont: Brooks/Cole, 1971).

[32]Ibid., p. 91.

[33]Paul Rosenfels, Homosexuality: The Psychology of the Creative Process (Roslyn Heights: Libera, 1971).

[34]An early version of his thesis appears in: "The Product Conversion -- From Heresy to Illness," in The Homosexual Dialectic, edited by Joseph McCaffrey (Englewood Cliffs: Prentice Hall, 1972), pp. 101-120. Since then he has published an endless stream of books debunking the psychiatric profession. For the purposes of this chapter, the most important are: The Myth of Mental Illness (New York: Haeber, 1964 and The Manufacture of Madness (New York: Harper & Row, 1970).

[35]Szasz, "The Product Conversion -- From Heresy to Illness," loc. cit., p. 112.

[36]Franklin Kameny, "Gay Liberation and Psychiatry," in The Homosexual Dialectic, pp. 182-194.

[37]Ibid., p. 185.

[38]George Weinberg, Society and the Healthy Homosexual (Garden City: Doubleday, 1972).

[39]Ibid., p. 21.

[40]Ibid., pp. 70-71.

[41]C.A. Tripp, The Homosexual Matrix (New York: New American Library, 1975).

[42]Ibid., pp. 85-86.

[43]Ibid., p. 77.

[44]Ibid., p. 93.

[45]Ibid., p. 157.

[46]Ibid., p. 125f.

[47]Irving Bieber, loc. cit., p. 18.

[48]Marc Oraison, loc. cit., p. 115.

[49]H. Kimball Jones, Toward a Christian Understanding of the Homosexual (New York: Association, 1966), p. 49.

[50]Arno Karlen, loc. cit., p. 596.

[51]Ibid., pp. 582-596.

[52]Edmund Bergler, loc. cit., p. 176.

[53]Ibid., p. 196.

[54]Irving Bieber, Homosexuality: A Psychoanalytic Study, p. 267.

[55]Lionel Ovesey, loc. cit., pp. 116-117.

[56]Ibid., pp. 106-107.

[57]Ruth Tiffany Barnhouse, loc. cit., p. 109.

[58]Cf., Walter Kenny, "Homosexuality and Nullity -- Developing Jurisprudence," Catholic Lawyer, 17, 1971, pp. 110-112.

[59]Evelyn Hooker, "Male Homosexuals and Their 'World,'" in Sexual Inversion, p. 86.

[60]Alan Bell, "Homosexuality, an Overview," in Homosexuality and the Christian Faith: A Symposium, edited by Harold Twiss (Valley Forge: Judson, 1978), p. 9.

[61]New York: Penguin, 1975.

[62]_Ibid._, pp. 20-21.

Chapter 5

Social Institutions of the Homosexual World

Introduction

Far more significant for the ethos of American culture than the isolated homosexual acts of individual men and women are the social structures which reinforce and promote such behavioral patterns. What has been happening during our period of history is that the greater tolerance of gay life, both in theory and in practice, has created conditions which are conducive to more explicit organization of the personal, social, economic and politcal lives of different types of homosexuals.

Most of this chapter will concentrate on the institutions of the world of male homosexuals. But I will begin with a brief look at the lesbian subculture, a picture which hopefully will be significantly enlarged when social scientists direct more of their energy to the study of this part of the homosexual world.

I. The World of the Lesbian

In the patriarchal society of the West, the thought of homosexual behavior among women has never generated the social disgrace and horror that male homosexuality has. As a result, legal scholars and historians have tended to neglect the lesbian phenomenon almost entirely. Because men dominated the intellectual disciplines, no one was available to speak first hand about feminine sexuality, including lesbianism. Therefore, in our research today we have had to rely on occasional bits of literary depiction, autobiographical anecdotes, and pornographic conjecture in order to appreciate the forms of lesbian life. What has happened in our time is that women homosexuals have finally begun to speak for themselves and with an openness heretofore unprecedented.

Our evidence is still sketchy, but the following general features can be gleaned from the studies that have been done up to now. First, homosexual women seem to be much less dependent on established public institutions which cater to their trade than homosexual men are.[1] For example, although there are lesbian bars (especially in the metropolitan areas), they are proportionately less numerous. In some of the smaller cities, lesbians attend mixed gay bars. The bars that do exist are meeting places and centers of conversation and gossip. Compared to the male bars, there is little partner shopping. However, these bars are a good place for lesbians from out of town to make contacts in the female gay community. There are no comparable institutions to the gay baths and the use of public parks and beaches as hustling spots.

Second, the most common support structure seems to be a loosely-defined series of friendship cliques. These groups may meet together regularly at each other's homes or go as a group to centers of public entertainment. For a new member of one of these groups the great advantage, in addition to the friends made, is the ability to recognize immediately other women of a similar sexual orientation. This foreshortens the sometimes excruciating process of signal giving and signal interpretation.

Third, the proportion of relatively stable lesbian couples seems to be higher than anything known in the world of the male homosexual.[2] This may spring from psychological factors peculiar to women or it may be a function of the lessened stress on the sexual side of the relationship. Whatever the cause, the more perduring the relationships are, the less dependent the individuals are on outside sources of support. It may be that as lesbian militant groups become more influential, the presumed standards of fidelity and loyalty will drastically change.

Another conclusion that can be drawn from the data is that lesbian organizations like the Daughters of Bilitis and Radicalesbians have

chosen to enter the feminist movement with much of
their energy and thus the homosexual focus has
been considerably blunted.[3] One reason for this
is that lesbians have a vested interest in salary
scales for women, preferential hiring and advance-
ment policies, and other matters where the broad-
based feminist coalition can be most effective.
Lesbians in the work force have often been afraid
to assert themselves lest their sexual life style
be brought to the attention of their employers.
Yet specifically lesbian organizations still serve
the purpose of bringing lesbians together to air
complaints and to derive encouragement from the
strength of numbers. Support for publications on,
and studies of, lesbianism in America has also
been forthcoming from these groups.

A fifth consideration is the existence of
lesbian mothers, who having abandoned a heterosexual marriage for a homosexual partner, now wish to
raise the children of the marriage.[4] In most
instances, this is done surreptitiously since the
courts will not normally allow a lesbian mother to
have custody of the children. However, this presents many complications for everyone involved,
including how to explain things to the children.
There are, also lesbian couples who wish to have
their own children, even though they have never
been married, either by adoption or by artificial
insemination donor. In each of these situations,
the dilemma of the one parent household is complicated further. While lesbian activists will continue to push for reform of law and social welfare
policies, it is doubtful that open lesbian mothers
will win widespread acceptance in the immediate
future.

On the negative side, a number of adjustment
problems seem to be common among lesbians. One is
the destructive impact of pervasive jealousy.[5]
Due to the absence of supportive legal structures,
once suspicion and mutual recrimination begin in a
relationship, the emotional toll can be quite
high. Another factor is the configuration of
depression and paranoia which seems to lead to

thoughts of suicide (in some cases) and to a
fairly high rate of alcohol addiction.[6] When
lesbians suffer from psychological and emotional
traumas, they may succumb to more severe reactions
than might be expected in the general run of
women.

But the negative factors are, obviously, not
the whole story. Many lesbians are reliable and
trusted employees and responsible citizens of
their communities. For some, their sexual identity has a minimum impact on their lives. For
others, their future will be full of hardship and
personal turmoil as they try to balance a twosided
existence. For still others, the comfortable companionship of dedicated women in the lesbian movement will offer an alternative to the sexual role
models of the prevailing culture. Whether the
euphoria of such a creative vision can sustain
itself amidst the ambiguity of real human lives is
the lingering problem of the future.

II. The World of the Male Homosexual

  A. Anonymous Sex-The Silent Stranger

In my discussion of the male homosexual world
I will begin with that proportion of homosexual
behavior which is characterized by its clandestine, furtive, anonymous quality. Here there are
no formal organizations or advocacy groups. It
many instances, the orgasmic encounter will
require but a few minutes. There is no desire for
continuity or expectation for gestures of affection. The pursuit is one-dimensional and
shockingly frank -- that in some semi-public
setting two or more partners will provide each
other with some degree of sexual satisfaction.

(a) Places -- In his excellent study of the
homosexual underworld, Edward William Delph
describes the distinctive features of 'erotic
oases.'[7] First, they must be physically contained
and obscured from direct observation by

passers-by. Second, there must be publically acceptable reasons for being present there. It is the combination of concealment and ambiguity of intention which allows such places to function for overt sexual purposes.

Each geographical locale contains some percentage of erotic oases, most of which are known explicitly only to those looking for anonymous sex and to the police who receive complaints about them. However, since enough mistakes are made by their denizens, a fairly high proportion of males will have been exposed to their existence at sometime in their lives. It can be presupposed that in any urban area such settings will be present in sufficient numbers to satisfy the demand although a particular place may vary in popularity, depending on the danger associated with it.

One of the most common types of oases are what are called 'tearooms' or public toilets. Usually located in the bus stations, office buildings and public parks, these facilities allow for a relatively innocuous presence for those who wish to linger there. Since any overt manifestation of sexual interest is fraught with some degree of danger or criminal liability, a whole ritual has evolved to provide maximum protection. In most instances, no word is ever spoken. The placement in the room, the display of one's genitals, eye contact, and the response to overtures are the means by which reciprocal signals are given. A whole scenario is acted out, sometimes involving multiple players, which provides a semblance of order in a stranger-filled environment.

Perhaps, the epitome of this sexual pantomime is the 'glory hole' or circular aperture gouged out of the wall between two toilet stalls. This hole permits sexual contact between two faceless participants who know each other only as genital objects. While the mystery and forbidden quality of such activity seem to heighten the pleasure for those who engage in it, it is the reduction of the

110

person to a sexual function which strikes everyone else.

A second type of setting for covert sexual activity is public land, particularly that reserved for recreational purposes, but visited in off-hours, usually at night. City parks, beaches, mountain overlooks and other scenes of casual interaction can be transformed once the sun goes down. In these situations, mere physical presence is normally a reliable sign of sexual availability. The one glaring exception is the criminal element which preys on the habitues without fear of prosecution. As a result, this world is both freer and more threatening.

A third locale is the city streets where hustlers congregate. Even relatively small towns often have a portion of a street or an intersection where homosexual prostitutes and their customers can be found. And in large cities there may be a whole series of such places with the men on the prowl making the rounds from hour to hour. While the social process is more open on the streets, and therefore less controllable, the actual sexual behavior is reserved for some other place (a car, a back alley, a room) where the chances of intrusion are slim.

(b) The Code -- Strange as it may seem, even this anonymous type of sexual pattern is controlled by certain expectations and rules of behavior among the participants. First, and most importantly, one's true identity must be preserved. If first names are used, no one considers it necessary or important. Most of the time, the silence cloaks any concern about uniqueness and personal history. The two parties are interested in each other almost exclusively for the sexual pleasure that is possible and after orgasm has been obtained, they wish to return to their other identity.

Second, the ritual of suggestion and response is designed to eliminate those who are

111

disinterested. This is not a world of rape or coercion. Even though occasionally a stranger or a youth may misinterpret the situation and thus seem available, the clear assertion of offense will send the pursuer scurrying away. It is because choosing among several potential partners is part of the game that such mistakes can easily occur.

Third, as in all instances of sexual interaction, physical attributes affect the status and role of the players. There is a premium on youth and genital endowment and masculinity. Some are the hunters and some are the hunted. In toilets and parks, money is seldom exchanged. But on the streets, the more desirable the hustler on the open market, the higher the expectation for remuneration.

(c) The Players -- To the non-participant, this whole world of covert sex in semi-public places may seem a fitting theater for the actualization of sexual libido. Much like houses of prostitution, there is no pretense of serving a higher purpose. Sexual release is the goal and the bursts of frenzied pleasure are divorced from whatever other pursuits take up a person's energy. Most of the characters move in and out of this setting with hardly a thought about what place it plays in their lives.

In a recent study of this phenomenon of silent, anonymous sex, Laud Humphrey found that there were basically three types of men who frequented this world.[8] The first grup are called 'trade.' They consider themselves heterosexual (a fairly high percentage are married) and will only take the insertor role. A second category includes 'closet queens' who admit to themselves that they are homosexual, but who fear involvment in the more public gay activities. Then there are the 'hustlers' who do it for the money and who may attempt to prolong a heterosexual self-image. In addition to these three groups, there are various others who have less in common and who are drawn

112

to the places out of curiosity, a desire for excitement, physical unattractiveness, or other reasons.

What emerges from this portrait is a strong sense that self-deception and fear of exposure are prime motives in sustaining such homosexual behavior. In his thinly-disguised novels, City of Night, Numbers, and The Sexual Outlaw,[9] John Rechy has given a searing and disturbing look at the self-identity and values of the homosexual hustler. In the process, he opens up the most hidden side of homosexual culture.

"The Promiscuous homosexual in a sexual revolutionary...To the sexhunt he brings a sense of choreography, ritual, and mystery...his is the only minority against whose existence there are laws."[10]

"Promiscuity, like the priesthood, requires total commitment and sacrifice."[11]

"I estimate I've been with over 7,000 people, but I know it's more...Thousands of sex encounters are not rare in the gay world."[12]

"I think of the hustling streets as a battlefield; two armies, the hustler and the client, yet needing each other."[13]

"Mutual exploitation -- the old corrupt, the young corrupt. That is the nature of the ugly, devouring, beautiful, lonely, exciting, devastating, dead-end, glorious, hustling streets."[14]

What can one say in response to this disarming honesty. Some might question how typical Rechy's attitude would be. Admittedly, he is a hustler and therefore only a representative of one portion of the homosexual underworld. Yet he does capture the simultaneous sense of lure and self-destruction which seems to haunt its regular participants.

113

It is rare for homosexual spokespersons to celebrate this dimension of homosexual life. It is a source of embarrassment because it so far violates the prevailing sexual ethic of Western society. One rejoinder is to claim that many of the people are really heterosexuals with homosexual urges or unliberated homosexuals. And this seems to be at least partially true. But the lingering question remains: on what grounds can we make judgments about such patterns of homosexual behavior? Because the promiscuity is unabashed and the language of love and commitment is irrelevant, is it possible to remain indifferent to such a subculture? Just as some critics have defended heterosexual prostitution as a necessary evil, perhaps the same judgment could be made here. Or we could posit the day of true sexual liberation (including homosexual self-determination) when such counterfeit sex would become unnecessary.

Whatever route our reponse takes, this 'silent community'[15] of clandestine homosexual behavior needs to be taken into account in any ethical theory on homosexuality. In the following sections of this chapter as I look at progressively more organized and self-consciously homosexual subcultures, this first subculture will seem either a correctable aberration in the process of liberation or else a true warning of the dangers of sexual permissiveness.

B. The Gay Bath

Insofar as the intentions of the members are concerned, there is little difference between the casual sex of the toilets and public parks and the activity available in the homosexual baths. However, because there exist certain physical facilities and membership requirements, such enterprises involve a higher level of organization and thus are a more firmly established component of the gay world.

114

Gay baths have existed in San Francisco for at least 30 years.[16] It is probable that the institution cropped up in the major cities around the same time. Today, there are baths in most areas with a large gay population. While there is some variety in their physical layout, three basic accommodations are provided: private rooms, a locker area and an orgy room.[17] The more luxurious baths also include snack bars, rest areas and a television room. And finally, a few have live entertainment.

In order to gain admittance to a bath, one must have a membership card or be recommended by a well-known member. There is a charge for each evening that one participates. Once inside, a towel is issued and your clothes are left locked in a locker. Ironically, it is not appropriate to go nude in the public places. If you have rented a private room, that will likely be the prime locus of activity. Normally, the door is kept ajar and you signal which type of sexual activity you are interested in by the posture you assume in the room. Since all of those present at the bath are explicitly seeking sexual partners, the only thing that remains is to find a proper partner for one's taste. Some remain in their room all night and others prowl from room to room.

Perhaps, the most distinctive area of the gay baths is the so'called 'orgy room.' This is a fairly large area, deliberately kept dark, where anonymity is carried to the extreme. Here silence prevails, except for the sounds of bodily activity. Depending on the size of the clientele, one may find innumerable partners and participate in the whole gamut of sexual possibilities. Arnie Kantrowitz has this to say of the baths.

> In our towels we could be sleeping
> with anyone, a garbageman or an
> astronaut, and never know the
> difference...with my stock of
> images I had sexual contact with a
> dozen men in a night...helped to

115

orgasm by a brotherhood of loyal
strangers...The dormitory was
popularly known as the 'orgy
room'...filled with anonymous
touches of men, surrounded by
total flesh, total humanity.[18]

What the gay baths do is facilitate the process of finding an endless succession of willing
sexual partners. Except for occasional police
raids, there is no fear ot entrapment. And the
subdued lighting and opportunity for groping sex
minimize the disadvantages of advancing age and
declining beauty. In a sense, there is a place
for every active homosexual at the baths as long
as the physical performance is the focus of attention.[19]

Unlike sex in semi-public places, it is not
uncommon for self-proclaimed and open homosexuals
to participate, at least occasionally, in the
world of the gay bath. It is the first of the
structured ways of being in an all gay environment
without penalty or social opprobrium. For some,
it seems to provide an outlet for a strong sexual
drive without the concomitant expectation for
investment in a relationship. This may be to the
detriment of the possibility of such a relationship or it may be a periodic escape from an
ongoing bond, especially in times of transition
between affiliated partners. For others, the gay
bath may be one step in the process of integration
into the wider homosexual world. Just as a
bachelor fling may be seen as a prelude to marital
stability in the heterosexual culture, a period of
bath attendance may later seem a function of
youthful impetuosity or sowing one's wild oats. A
final category of participants would include the
aging homosexuals who are frustrated in the street
and bar scene and yet who wish to satisfy their
sexual cravings.

The basic dilemma for the homosexual who
wishes to justify the institution of the gay bath
is whether he or she wants to give a general

approval to sexual promiscuity. As long as the language of caring, respectful tenderness, and personal communication is preserved in the homosexual subculture, it is hard to see how such a reduction of sex to entirely physical terms can be reconciled with these personality-involving values.

C. The Gay Bar

The central social institution of the homosexual world is the gay bar. Even those homosexuals who have never set foot in such an establishment are affected by the culture, attitudes and self-definition which is generated there. Gay bars serve a multiplicity of functions from sexual market place to refuge from a hostile society to communication center to recreational locus. Such bars come in all styles and sizes. The one common criterion is that they all cater to an exclusively homosexual clientele.

(1) The Place -- The number and location of gay bars is dependent on two factors: the size of the homosexual population in an area and the degree of repression exercised by the civil authorities. In recent times, especially in the large metropolitan centers, police interference has tended to decline, following the shift in public opinion. As a result, in certain areas a kind of clustering effect has taken place so that a series of gay bars may be found in the same area.[20] This has the added effect of sometimes transforming a whole neighborhood into a homosexual housing center as in the Village in New York City, New Town in Chicago and Castro Street in San Francisco.

It is estimated that there are 60 gay bars in Los Angeles, 70 in Manhattan and 50-60 in San Francisco.[21] The names of bars are typified to make for easy identification and to suggest the basic ambience to be found there. For example, some bars attract a young, fairly affluent, 'masculine' crowd where sexual availability and part-

117

ner seeking are part of the basic dynamic of the place. In many instances, these bars allow dancing and the jukebox or disco system is an all-pervasive feature. Furniture is sparse and most of the patrons stand, in tightly packed circumstances, for much of the evening. This allows for a stress on physical presence and sufficient mobility to facilitate social interaction. Because of the noise, conversation is difficult and appearance, posture and eye contact often constitute the main form of communication. These bars are one of the main meeting places of liberated, activist, attractive, young homosexuals. The dress is casual, but fashionable, and certain forms of effeminate mannerisms are totally out of place. Much like singles bars in the heterosexual world, it is a seller's market and the grounds for rejection are many. Age, physical deformity, social ineptitude, and unstylized appearance can disqualify one for consideration. The ultimate form of rejection is not being barred entry, but suffering a succession of evenings of total sexual rejection by other patrons.

One of the central phenomena of this type of 'hip' bar is the importance of dance. The current fad of disco music began in homosexual hangouts long before it penetrated the popular market. The repetitious, pounding beat, and the dancing that accompanies it seem to convey a kind of sexual liberation to its homosexual enthusiasts. It is not just dancing with other males that is important, but the freedom of self-expression that flows with the music. The rhythm and electric excitement of a packed gay dance floor seems to symbolize the quest for both personal autonomy and collective belonging that the homo-phile movement has brought to the center of attention.

In addition to the popular, youth-oriented gay bars, there are a variety of other types.[21] The western bars simulate the setting of Dodge City or dude ranches as portrayed in hundreds of movies. 'Piss-elegant' bars attract a more aristocratic crowd and have strict dress codes and

118

more subdued manners of interaction. Leather bars require a highly stylized costume which accentuates a tough, cynical and self-controlled posturing. Some leather bars are identified with motorcycle clubs and are reserved for the exclusive use of the membership. Others are connected with the weight-lifting and physical fitness subcultures. And a final group of leather bars are the prime gathering place of the sado-masochistic contingent of the homosexual world.

(ii) Sado-Masochism -- It is not clear what percentage of homosexuals have participated in this form of sexual behavior. Surely it is a minority and probably a fairly small one. Yet there are some indications in the advocacy literature of the homophile movment that S & M experimentation is increasing. Carl Wittman, for example, has this to say, "sado/masochism, when consensual, can be described as a highly artistic endeavor, a ballet the constraints of which are the thresholds of pain and pleasure."[22] And Peter Fisher continues in the same positive vein, "Generally viewed as cruel and brutal, S & M sex is often based on a greater degree of trust and tenderness than more conventional sex."[23]

This attitude may horrify more conventional observers. Yet it reveals the difficulty that exists of ruling out any form of consensual sexual behavior once the inherited ethical traditions have broken down. S & M seems to be in direct contradiction to the desire for pleasure that is identified with the experience of orgasm. But, for some, pleasure can only be gained by yoking it with its opposite and acting out perverse fantasies with similarly intentioned partners.

There seem to be three main arguments in favor of S & M, or perhaps better put, in allowance of its appropriateness for those so inclined: (1) it merely imitates nature (2) it involves a new dimension of love and (3) the fantasy absorbs the potentially destructive reality.[24] It is not clear what would count as rational rejoinders to

119

these types of arguments for those who offer them. But they do reveal how attractive the borderline of the forbidden can be. Perhaps, one bit of evidence is the increasing toll of death and crippling that has resulted from the practice of manual penetration of the anus.[25]

While not necessarily representative of the gay world, nor even defended by many homosexuals, S & M behavior is a critical test case for the evolution of a coherent sexual ethic in the homosexual movement. Even on purely experiential grounds, most humans look with repugnance on such tendencies. Perhaps, John Rechy is overstating the case, but his words should be heeded by all who have a stake in homosexual liberation.

> The proliferation of sadomasochim is the major internal threat to gay freedom, comparable only in destructiveness to the impact of repressive laws and persecution by cops. The basis of both is the same: self-hatred. The hard-core of S & M is relatively small -- perhaps tiny -- in proportion to the vast gay worldly -- and much of S & M is soft-core fantasy. Nevertheless, its grip on the gay world -- by reverberation, and perhaps more psychically than physically -- is fiercely strong.[26]

(iii) The Ritual -- Each type of gay bar has its own pattern and standards of behavior. Yet if we leave out the extreme manifestations of the leather and S & M crowds, certain features seem to predominate. First, the initial entry into the gay bar scence is frequently a rite of passage for a person.

> Walking into a gay bar is a momentous act in the life history of a homosexual, because in many cases it is the first time he publicly

120

identifies himself as a homosexual. Of equal importance is the fact that it brings home to him the realization that there are many other young men like himself and, thus, that he is a member of a community and not the isolate he had previously felt himself to be.[27]

Such a person may be totally unfamiliar with the customs and ways of relating in such places, but he will soon have plenty of guides to aid him. Because there are always new males undergoing this process of initiation, the bar scene retains a certain liveliness despite the relative rigidity of its modes of relating.

Second, the attention of those present is focused on each other, and particularly on new faces and recent arrivals. Since the bar is a kind of sexual marketplace, appearance and poise are all important. The ground rules of a particular type of bar determine the parameters of the dress code and the degree of overtness of behavior. However, within these limits each person is attempting to stand out and to seem attractive to others. Whatever fantasy a particular person might have of an ideal lover is searched for among the denizens of a bar or a series of bars on a specific evening. This quest for sex and love can be an occasional interlude in an otherwise humdrum existence or it can be the conscious center of all one's activities. Martin Hoffman has described this bar setting as "a stage on which is played out a fantasy in which the hero never arrives."[28] To be both cool and exciting, disinterested and interesting, at home and accidentally present, require a skill of participation which is only learned by experience.

Third, the stress on masculinity and youth in most gay bars force the role definitions in a certain direction. Because fear of rejection is high, the first overture is a delicate process.

121

Once two men are interested in each other, the eye contact and physical proximity are keys of setting the stage for one of the two to make a proposal. As in all human social situations, the communication may be more or less direct depending on the self-confidence of the initiator. In every bar as the night wears on some percentage of those present begin to suspect that no one will approach them and thus they must make some moves of their own. If someone is too bashful or too proud, the impact of the closing hour can be devastating. One compromise it to accept an invitation to a private party where the hunt can be continued. A successful evening is one in which a particular person can leave the bar with another attractive person in order to pursue the possibility of an active sexual relationship, at least for the remainder of the waking hours.

(iv) Problems -- Drinking places in many parts of the worlds have functioned as one of the central social institutions, particularly among men. So the preeminent role of the gay bar in the homosexual male world is not unprecedented. Neighborhood taverns, cocktail lounges in hotels and convention facilities, and singles bars have had a long life in this country as well. However, the gay bar has its critics, even among homosexuals.

Some object to the environment created in the bars.[29] In some areas, especially in the cities of the East, the Mafia seems to be in control. As a result, a conspiratorial, corruption-ridden management seems disinterested in the complaints of their customers. But even when bars are owned by gays themselves, the profit motive and preservation of the status quo seem to reign supreme. Prices tend to be high and severe overcrowding is commonplace. It is difficult to cultivate a friendly, warm atmosphere.

Because the basic service provided by the bars is the serving of alcohol, many homosexual spokespersons recent the promotion of addictive

122

tendencies in such places. Our information is incomplete on the percentage of gay alcoholics, but it seems to include a significant number.[30] Richard Wood, who has done considerable counseling with homosexuals in Chicago, has this to say. "The main function of the gay bar is to provide an open environment for drinking, mixing, cruising, and often dancing and other forms of entertainment...alcoholism becomes a serious problem for many gays as a result."[31] Not only is alcohol generally available in the bar setting, it is also a handy escape for the rejected and a courage-maker for the shy.

The final problem with the bar scene is that it promotes a model of promiscuous relating in the gay world, which seems designed for the youthful and the beautiful. The 'one-night stand' may allow for a degree of immediate pleasure, but it does not bode well for significant human relatedness. If the ideal lover never appears, then the ultimate story is one of repeated failure and frustration. Perhaps, this is why some homosexuals so quickly search for some other alternative. The toll of surviving in the gay bar scene for very long may not be worth the price.

D. Social Cliques and Couples

Until recently, almost all of the studies of the homosexual world were composed of either descriptions of patients in psychotherapy or analyses of the promiscuous social scene of the gay bath and the gay bar. By implication, the options available to homosexual men were seen to be some sort of attempt at cure or else reconcilement to a truncated, ephemeral context of relatedness. Occasionally, gay spokespersons would assert that they knew some couple who had sustained a bonded relationship for a long period of time, but even among homosexuals this was treated with some degree of skepticism.

What has changed at the descriptive level is that we now have available a number of large scale

123

studies of the full spectrum of homosexual possibilities. In addition to the formal institutions of the gay subculture, various types of friendship groups, communes and individual couples have also been discovered by social scientists. While the data is far from complete, there is enough material available to, at least, discern some trends and to characterize these more informal arrangements.

(i) Social Cliques -- One of the advantages of the gay bar as a social institution is that the mere physical presence of a person in such a setting is tantamount to formal acknowledgement of one's homosexual orientation. The same can be said about the gay bath and even, to some extent, the gathering areas of the furtive world of sexual outlaws. For those who have become disenchanted with these alternatives, or who have never participated in any of them, the main problem is finding a context in which homosexual partners may be safely discovered and cultivated. Criminal liability, cultural stigma, and personal hesitance can all contribute to a foreshortening of one's social space.

One route taken by an increasing number of homosexuals is to settle for a network of gay friends and acquaintances who gather at one another's houses, spend recreational time together, and sometimes pair off for various lengths of time. This is much easier to bring off in large metropolitan areas where relative anonymity provides some protection, where gay housing patterns are concentrated, and where a degree of affluence makes travel and vacation interludes fairly convenient. These friendship groups tend to form around men of similar backgrounds and interests, unlike the bars where sexual identity and availability are more important than educational and economic factors.

In one of the first studies of these social patterns, the ethnographer Evelyn Hooker has stressed their multi-faceted nature.

124

In this world are to be found men
who have established long-term
living relationships with other
homosexuals and who rarely, if
ever, go to bars and other public
establishments because of their
sexually predatory and competitive
character...In the cliques,
groups, and networks of friends,
social occasions like evening,
dinner, and cocktail parties are
frequent, ranging from the sim-
plest to the most elaborate and
from the most intimate to the
large spur-of-the-moment affairs
...In the main, members feel
uncomfortable in the social presence of heterosexuals, and prefer
social occasions in which the
guest list is made up of homosexuals.[32]

Sexual belonging seems to far outweigh sexual
availability as a stimulus for these groups and in
many ways they enable their members to cope with
the pervasive disenchantment which accrues to
living in a predominantly heterosexual society.

Another alternative which has been pursued by
some homosexuals, especially among young
activists, is some version of an urban or rural
commune. A group of several gay men will buy or
rent a home of sufficient size to accommodate
them and share the household expenses and chores.
The kinds of relatedness among the participants
may vary from active sexual partnerships to casual
friendships to minimal tolerance.[33] Like many
such experiments in communal living under other
auspices, gay communes have tended to be short-
lived up to now.

At this moment of homosexual history it is
likely that variety will continue to be the order
of the day. And this complicates the attempt to
characterize the male homosexual phenomenon.

125

However, a recent effort to bring some order into the discussion can serve as a fitting transition into an analysis of homosexual couples.

(ii) Homosexualities -- In 1978 the most extensive study yet completed of homosexuality in America was published by Alan Bell and Martin Weinberg.[34] It is called <u>Homosexualities: A Study of Diversity Among Men and Women</u>. It was sponsored by the National Institute of Mental Health and the Kinsey Center at Indiana University. Approximately 5,000 men and women in the San Francisco Bay Area were recruited to participate. While acknowledging that the Bay Area is not representative of American society in general, it was thought that the sexual permissiveness that obtains there might well foreshadow future developments in other sections of the country. In order to perfect the testing procedures a pilot project of 450 white homosexual males was completed in Chicago in 1967.

The basic format was a face-to-face interview which involved 528 questions and took between two to five hours to complete. A control group of heterosexual men and women, chosen at random, was used to provide some comparative data. The interviewers were usually graduate students from the local universities, but the field staff followed up with about half of the interviewees. The truthfulness of the oral responses was accepted, but certain cross-check questions were used as a source of confirmation.

The goal of the study was twofold: first, to exemplify the existence of 'homosexualities' (the numerous ways in which one can be homosexual) and second, to correlate various homosexual lifestyles with levels of social and psychological adjustment. The implicit presumption was that some types of homosexual patterns are better than others.

While this study can be criticized on a number of grounds, it does provide some extemely

126

helpful data.[35]   For our present purposes, the main contribution is a five-fold typology of homosexual life.[36]

(1) Close-Coupled -- a quasi marriage between two men (67 out of 485)

(2) Open-Coupled -- involved in a 'marital' relationship but not exclusively (120).

(3) Functional -- 'single,' sexually active, many partners, low level of regret (102).

(4) Dysfunctional -- sexually active, promiscuous, numerous problems and regrets (86).

(5) Asexual -- low level of sexual interest and activity, many problems and regrets, less exclusively homosexual, more covert (110).

The first two categories include those homosexuals who participate in homosexual cliques and bonded relationships.   By way of percentages the authors of the study come to this conclusion.

> There were many more Open-Coupleds
> than Close-Coupleds among the male
> respondents. This suggests that a
> monogamous quasi marriage between
> homosexual men is probably diffi-
> cult to achieve, and that most
> such relationships   involve the
> pursuit of sexual contacts with
> persons other than one's part-
> ner.[37]

While the Close Coupled pairs are   the best adjusted, they do not occur with the same frequency as the Open-Coupled ones.

One major insight to be gained from this distinction is that a homosexual couple is a multifarious phenomenon.   Even in the eyes of the partners there are different levels of expectation

127

about what constitutes infidelity and the shattering of the bond.

(iii) Homosexual Couples -- In its pure form, such a relationship seems to refer to an explicit commitment to another homosexual which is intended to be both exclusive and permanent, much as the institution of heterosexual marriage has been constituted. It includes sexual sharing, a domestic arrangement, and some kind of public recognition, if only among other homosexual friends.

The first problem in getting a handle on homosexual couples is that there exists no socially recognized procedure by which such a relationship is formally begun., And furthermore its termination is simply a matter of mutual agreement, even after many years together. Because there are no children (at least as a result of the male relationship), the main tangible signs of the existence of the bond are property and household goods which may be jointly purchased. Thus a homosexual couple is a legal non-entity and the attitudes of the partners is all important.

The Bell/Weinberg study suggested that a noteworthy number of homosexuals have lived with one other sexual partner in what could be described as a 'couple' for some period of their lives. We do not know for sure what the relative percentages would be. And what is critically lacking is some rough estimate of how many homosexual partnerships have lasted for 5, 10, 20, or 40 years. That there are some long-term, relatively exclusive relationships seems sure. But how to account for them is an open question.

In the homosexual community there is a divergence of opinion over whether the Close-Coupled or the Open-Coupled arrangement is preferable. The first alternative has the advantage of imitating an existing societal institution. Thus Tom Hurley aruges that "at this stage in gay history,

128

many gay people believe that a marriage relationship is the best way for two people in love to
build a life together."[38] This accounts for the
development of a liturgical ritual for the
exchange of public promises in some components of
the gay church. On the other hand, the Close-
Coupled bond seems too restrictive and oppressive
for those who look with disfavor on the institution of the nuclear family.[39] For example, Peter
Fisher projects a more radical understanding of
the superiority of the Open-Coupled pair.

> Gay couples call themselves lovers
> because the word expresses the
> nature of their relationships. It
> is love that holds a gay couple
> together: they receive no
> approval or support from the
> state, the church or even from
> their families in most cases...
> There is no reason lovers cannot
> have sex with whomever they please
> if both are comfortable with such
> an arrangement and their relation-
> ship is basically strong.[40]

It is this confusion about what constitutes a
gay couple which has compounded the difficulty of
ethical analysis. In some of the homosexual advocacy literature in the Christian context, homosexual couples are spoken of with all of the reverence accorded to newlyweds. It is then claimed
that as long as the same values are employed to
make judgments about appropriateness of sexual
activity (e.g., mutuality, fidelity, love,
patience), a heterosexual couple and a homosexual
couple should have the same status in the church.
But this is the very point at issue. If many
homosexuals consider Close-Coupled pairs that we
are talking about. Consider, for example, this
statement by Harold Brown.

> Among the established couples I
> know, about a third are completely
> monogamous, a third allow each

129

other total sexual freedom, and a third (behaving a good deal like the proverbial errant spouse) have occasional affairs, which they try to conceal from their partners.[41]

It is not the success rate that is important (since heterosexual marriages are having the same problems) but rather the self-definition of homosexual coupling provided by the partners. What is in doubt is whether exclusivity for a life-time is ever considered desirable and/or possible by homosexuals who enter such relationships.

We are thus left with a situation in which there is no common agreement about whether homosexual couples should forge a whole new understanding of what sexual bonding might look like or whether coupling (of an Open or Closed sort) is simply the best alternative available in the homosexual subculture. Are we seeing the shattering for once and all of a too narrow definition of sexual intimacy and fulfillment or rather discovering a sustained threat to the sexual differentiation and dimension of fertility which have sustained the heterosexual monogamous marriage through all these milennia?

I suspect that the answers to these questions will emerge in a lower rhetorical key. Homosexual couples will be found with a wide variety of self-descriptions. Some will see the pairing as an inevitable step in the process of self-discovery and reciprocity. Others will be seeking an illusive ideal lover who will never appear. Still others will adjust to a less than best sharing of bed and table, with few demands placed on the other party. The percentage of couples which survive past 5 or 10 years will continue to be small, both because numerous social forces are against them and because many homosexuals do not consider it desirable in the first place.[42] The central problems will continue to be:

(1) the absence of sexual differentiation with a corresponding loss of mystery and allure.

(2) the relative impossibility of children providing a serving dimension to the relationship.

(3) the legal and economic sanctions which prevent a genuine sharing of goods.

(4) a high level of experience with promiscuous patterns of interaction prior to entering the relationship.

(5) the onset of old age with the desire for security and passing on a tradition to another generation.

It seems self-evident that homosexual couples can more easily embody some of the more important values of the Western sexual ethic than is possible in the impersonal context of other gay social institutons. A degree of pleasure, tender concern, love and sacrifice are all possible in such situations. But the continuity and exclusivity of these relationships will remain in doubt for the foreseeable future.

E. Homophile Organizations

The most public form of participation in the homosexual subculture comes with active membership in various homophile organizations. Once an individual abandons the cloak of anonymity, the resulting shift in consciousness can have a profound impact on his or her perception of reality and/or discernment of the viable courses of homosexual life. Some gays then spend a highly active period of time when the movement for gay liberation becomes the central focus of their lives. Others jump from one group to another searching for a comfortable format to express a new-found sense of affiliation. And still others quickly become disenchanted with the limits of the

131

political process and opt for more private methods of societal transformation.

Whether or not a particular homosexual person has ever joined a group or not, his or her life is inevitably affected by the forceful, and sometimes conflictive, presence of homosexual organizations. The themes of 'gay power' and 'gay liberation' have become part of the common phraseology of the day primarily because of the media coverage of homophile rallies and protests. And efforts at changing civil legislation have been spearheaded by such groups.

(i) Early Movements -- It was not until the 1950s that homosexual activism began to emerge in a formalized way in this country. As might be expected, the initial attempts at organizing homosexuals met with much resistance and fear. Individuals hesitated to join lest their their names appears on membershp roles and be used against them. The tenor of these groups was restrained and relatively conservative.[43] Much effort was expended at getting at the root causes of homosexuality. In addition, counseling help was available to homosexuals. Representatives of these organizations concentrated on projecting a balanced, respectable image in order to belie the unflattering stereo-types which predominated in the culture.

The first significant male organization was the Mattachine Foundation which had its start in Los Angeles in 1950. The name was chosen as a deliberate obfuscation of the purposes of the group. Only the members tended to know that 'mattachines' were medieval court jesters who told the truth to kings while hiding behind masks.[44] While the Mattachine Society (a more recent name) was the NAACP of the gay movement, it has through the course of time ceased to have a major role. Presently its two major tasks are: homosexual civil rights and personal counseling. It has ceased to hold formal meetings.

132

One, Inc. was founded in 1952 as an offshoot of the Mattachine Foundation. It served an important functional role in the early days of the movement. On the female side, the Daughters of Bilitis began in San Francisco in 1955. Once again its name was chosen for its vagueness, a reference to an obscure poem on lesbian love. Its journal The Ladder was one of the first publications to give exclusive attention to homosexual concerns. In 1954 an umbrella organization called NACHO (North American Conference on Homophile Organizations) began in San Francisco. It was the closest thing to a unifying agency prior to its breakup in 1970.

In the 1960s gay organizations took on an increasingly activist tone. There were attempts to systematize the work of smaller groups by banding together on a geographical basis. Thus ECHO ©East Coast Homophile Organizations) in 1963, SIR (Society for Individual Rights). Council on Religion and the Homosexual in 1964, and NACHO in 1968 all emerged as possible routes toward a national homosexual presence. During this same period of time, the churches also gave evidence of some stirrings toward including homosexual ministry in their overall agenda.[4]

(ii) After Christopher Street -- On June 27, 1969, the New York police raided a gay bar called the Stonewall Inn on Christopher Street in the Village. The situation seemed nothing out of the ordinary. Police raids were a common experience in the gay bar scene and the Stonewall Inn was just another place. However, to the surprise of everyone involved, the gay men present began to hurl bottles and accumulated debris and soon the police had to lock themselves inside and await reinforcements. For the first time in memory, gays had fought back against the establishment. In the days after, the minor riot that ensued on the raid began to take on epic proportions in the homosexual community. It functioned as a symbol that the days of passive acquiescence to oppressive and prejudicial laws were over. On the first

133

anniversary of the Christopher Street protest, a
large march and rally were held in New York City,
culminating in speeches in Central Park. Now the
American public began to perceive a new spirit of
militancy in the gay community.

The late '60s and early '70s was a time of
general social upheaval and protest in America so
it is not surprising that the survival rate of gay
organizations has been somewhat low. One compli-
cation was the mixing of causes, with some wanting
to focus almost entirely on homosexual issues and
others seeing gay liberation as one element in a
general need for social and radical reform.
Another factor was the lack of structure of the
organizations themselves. Leaders came and went,
the meetings often degenerated into shouting
matches, and financial support was spotty at
best.[46]

In 1970, the Gay Activists Alliance was
formed in New York City. It was a one-issue
organization which sought to harness the energy
generated by the radical spirit of the time.
Another group was the Gay Liberation Front (GLF)
which provided a forum for confrontation,
demagoguery, appeals to solidarity,and the generation of new strategies of protest, all at the
same time.[47] And Radicalesbians became the
leading organization to create a common front
between the radical feminist movement and lesbian
liberation.

In the midst of this proliferation of gay
organizations, there seem to be three major types
of structures.[48] The conservative groups are
mainly social, providing dances, parties and other
recreational activities in a protected and stimu-
lating environment. The reform groups combine
educational functions, social service and legal
defense. The radical groups involve themselves in
political action and confrontation. It is likely
that there will continue to be a need for each of
these kinds of services, even though the radical
organization may get the most publicity. The

long-term pattern of affiliation is still unclear. The strident tone and threat to personal security that some of the more militant groups generate would seem to limit their attraction to the youngest and most alienated segment of the homosexual population. Much would seem to hinge on the quality of gay leadership. Up to now no particular individual, with the possible exception of the Rev. Troy Perry (founder of the Metropolitan Community Church), has emerged as a recognizable and credible gay spokesperson on the national level.[49]

The general response to homophile organizations by the American population at large will, most likely, vary considerably from one part of the country to another. In the major metropolitan areas, which tend to have a more liberal social orientation and a more extensive homosexual subculture, the efforts at legal reform and a greater overall tolerance will win support. In the smaller cities and towns, in rural areas, and in highly ethnic or religious enclaves, the prospects are not as promising. The potential surely exists for a reactionary response, especially if some sensational incident precipitates public discussion.[50] Because the issue of homosexuality evokes such deep-seated responses, the homosexual movement will continue to chart a perilous course between legitimate appeals for civil and social rights and controversial attacks on the nuclear family (as well as challenges to the restrictive configuration of sexual alternatives that has won public approbation up to now).

III. Conclusion

In this chapter I have given a summary description of some of the major social institutions of the homosexual world. Unfortunately, most of the available material is focused on the masculine component. This is partly explained by the absence in the lesbian subculture of certain public facilities like the gay bath and, to a

135

lesser extent, the gay bar. In order to familiarize us with the lesbian patterns of social interaction, it is necessary for social scientists to immerse themselves in the informal context of friendship groups and couples. And, so far, it has been lesbians themselves who have provided the basic clues. This has the advantage of immediacy and first-hand experience but it lacks the distance and attempt at objectivity of analysis that might better be provided by others.

On the other hand, the male homosexual subculture has been the object of increasing attention by analysts from a wide variety of disciplines. Because of this it is possible to balance off apologetic and critical literature and arrive at a working descriptive consensus. At best, we have some sense of the framework of institutions which present themselves to any homosexual male as he chooses whether, and how far, to self-consciusly participate in the more public and militant forms of gay life.

It has been the governing presupposition of this chapter that the progressive passage from the secretive and anonymous setting of tearoom and public park sex to participation in long-term bonded relationships with one other partner is full of meaning not only for the persons involved but also for the broader society of which they are a part. The problems of promiscuity, depersonalized sex, sadomasochistic behavior, venereal disease, and various personal forms of instability may or may not be endemic in the homosexual situation. Apologists have continually argued that if societal strictures were only relaxed, the structure and context of homosexual life would vary little from that of heterosexual life. No one is clear on how such a case could be proven, except by plunging in and doing it. But that is just the point at issue. Many observers of the gay scene remain unconvinced that the intimacy, commitment, and perseverance of the idealized gay couple is possible for the majority of homosexuals. In the meantime, the other alternatives (the gay bath, the gay bar, social cliques and movement membership) would seem to be the range of options for the uncloseted, self-conscious gay. The debate will continue on whether these institutions are basically a form of flourishing or a form of coping. At the descriptive level alone, there is no way that this controversy can be adequately resolved.

Footnotes to Chapter 5

[1]Jack Hedblom, "The Female Homosexual: Social and Attitudinal Dimensions," in The Homosexual Dialectic, edited by Joseph McCaffrey (Englewood Cliffs: Prentice-Hall, 1972), pp. 31-64.

[2]"By and large, most Lesbians opt for a one-to-one, long-term relationship as an ideal." Del Martin and Phyllis Lyon, Lesbian/Woman (New York: Bantom, 1972), p. 103. Also Arno Karlen, Sexuality and Homosexuality: A New View (New York: W.W. Norton, 1971), p. 548.

[3]"A lesbian is the rage of all women condensed tothe point of explosion...lesbianism, like male homosexuality, is a category of behavior possible only in a sexist society characterized by rigid sex roles and dominated by male supremacy," Radicalesbians, in Out of the Closets: Voices of Gay Liberation, edited by Karla Jay and Allen Young (New York: Harcourt Brace Jovanovich, 1972), p. 172.

[4]Martin and Lyon, loc. cit., pp. 140-168.

[5]Karla Jay, In After You're Out, edited by Karla Jay and Allen Young (New York: Pyramid, 1975), p. 42. Also May Roman, "Sexuality and Homosexuality in Women," in Sexual Inversion: The Multiple Roots of Homosexuality, edited by Judd Marmor (New York: Basic, 1965), p. 297.

[6]Charlotte Wolff, Love Between Women (New York: Harper and Row, 1971), p. 161.

[7]Edward William Delph, The Silent Community: Public Homosexual Encounters (Beverly Hills: Sage, 1978), p. 60. I am indebted to him for much of what follows.

[8]Laud Humphrey, Tearoom Trade: Impersonal Sex in Public Places (Chicago: Aldine, 1970).

[9]John Rechy, City of Night (New York: Grove, 19163); Numbers (New York: Grove, 1967); The Sexual Outlaw: A Documentary (New York: Dell, 1977).

[10]Rechy, The Sexual Outlaw, p. 28.

[11]Ibid., p. 32.

[12]Ibid., p. 46.

[13]Ibid., p. 154.

[14]Ibid., p. 161.

[15]This is Delph's term, although I doubt whether the word 'community' is appropriate in this context.

[16]Alan Bell/Martin Weiniberg, Homosexualities: A Study of Diversity Among Men and Women (New York: Simon & Schuster, 1978), p. 233f.

[17]Delph, loc. cit., p. 135.

[18]Arnie Kantrowitz, Under the Rainbow: Growing Up Gay (New York: Pocket, 1977), p. 169.

[19]One man claimed 48 anal receptions in one night at a gay bath. Martin Hoffman, The Gay World (New York: Bantom, 1963), p. 48.

[20]Cf., Evelyn Hooker, "The Homosexual Community," in The Same Sex, edited by Ralph Weltge (Philadelphia: United Church Press, 1969), p. 29g; Martin Weinberg and Colin Williams, Male Homosexuals: Their Problems and Adaptations (New York: Penguin, 1975), p. 45f.; and Evelyn Hooker, "Male Homosexuals and Their 'Worlds,'" in Sexual Inversion, p. 94f.

[21]Cf., Delph, loc. cit., p. 111f.

[22]Carl Wittman, in Out of the Closets, pp. 338-339.

[23]Peter Fisher, The Gay Mystique (New York: Stein & Day, 1972), p. 94.

[24]John Rechy, The Sexual Outlaw, pp. 259-259.

[25]Ibid., p. 256.

[26]Ibid., p. 253.

[27]Hoffman, loc. cit., p. 14.

[28]Ibid., p. 55.

[29]Cf., John Murphy, Homosexual Liberation: A Personal View (New York: Praeger, 1971), p. 108f.

[30]Kevin McGirr quotes a figure of 25%. In After You're Out, p. 287.

[31]Richard Woods, Another Kind of Love: Homosexuality and Spirituality (Garden City: Doubleday, 1978), p. 67. It is worth noting in passing that some homosexuals sniff amyl nitrate in order to heighten sexual pleasure. In addition, the use of marijuana and other drugs can create an expectation that sexual activity will always take place in a state of alcohol or drug-induced euphoria. Cf. Rechy, The Sexual Outlaw, p. 75.

[32]Evelyn Hooker, "Male Homosexuals and Their 'Worlds'," in Sexual Inversion, edited by Judd Marmor, p. 101.

[33]Arnie Kantrowitz describes the creation and demise of such a commune in New York City in the 1970s. Under the Rainbow, p. 183f.

[34]Alan Bell/Martin Weinberg, Homosexualities: A Study of Diversity Among Men and Women (New York: Simon and Schuster, 1978).

[35]It seems to me that the following criticisms can be validly raised: (1) By choosing the San

140

Francisco Bay Area for its sample it skews the data base in a permissive direction for both the homosexual and the heterosexual population. This city has symbolized a tolerant and obliging social environment throughout its chaotic history. It is not clear that there is some kind of evolutionary progression from acceptance in avant-garde San Francisco to general permission in America at large. (2) It can be suspected that homosexual respondents in such a major study would be motivated to answer questions about adjustment in a positive vein since the results were likely to influence American opinion for years to come. Whether or not one felt good about being a homosexual, it would serve a political purpose to say 'yes' in the hope that it might come true. The absence of corroborating evidence from sources other than the respondents themselves leaves the question about the reliability of the answers unresolved. (3) While the researchers seem to have adopted a value-neutral perspective, the operative standard is a certain understanding of psychological and social adjustment. All sexual activity is taken to be of equal value or disvalue dependent only on the degree of integration and self-acceptance of the individual. This is surely one possible point of view, but it is not self-validating and it is never argued for in the course of the study.

The book, however, makes two great contributions. First, it provides a look at the most liberated components of the gay world. And the tendencies that appear there, may tell us more about the homosexual configuration than we have heretofore known. Second, a convincing case is made that homosexuality is not necessarily pathological, i.e., not a mental illness. Therefore, the ethical analysis can be freed from the strictures of the disease model and reestablished in the value realm where it belongs.

[36]Ibid., p. 132f and 219f.

[37]Ibid., p. 138.

141

[38]Tom Hurley, in _After You're Out_, p. 149.

[39]Cf., Karla Jay, _Ibid._, p. 36.

[40]Fisher, _loc. cit._, p. 210.

[41]Harold Brown, _Familiar Faces/Hidden Lives_ (New York: Harcourt Brace Jovanovich, 1976), p. 132.

[42]C.A. Tripp accounts for the tendency for breakdown in homosexual pairings in these terms. "Homosexual relationships are overclose, fatigue-prone, and are often adjusted to such narrow, trigger sensitive tolerances that a mere whisper of disrapport can jolt the partners into making repairs, or into conflict." _The Homosexual Matrix_ (New York: New American Library, 1975), p. 157.

[43]Cf., Foster Gunninson, "The Homophile Movement in America," in _The Same Sex_, pp.113-128.

[44]Cf., Laud Humphreys, _Out of the Closets: The Sociology of Homosexual Liberation_ (Englewood Cliffs: Prentice-Hall, 1972), p. 51f.

[45]This will be covered in detail in a later chapter.

[46]"Gay liberation has shown little tolerance of parliamentary procedures or the straight world's standards of fairness and good manners." Humphreys, _Out of the Closets_, p. 112. "The radical left gay organizations were largely unstructured and sought to combine the more attractive features of participatory democracy and rational anarchism." Fisher, _loc. cit._, p. 188.

[47]Cf., Murphy, _loc. cit._, p. 75f.

[48]Laud Humphreys, _Out of the Closets_, p. 130f.

[49]"One of the most striking features among homosexualities active in the movement is the

prevalence of persons who have had a ministerial or religious vocation...Although it is possible to speculate that a vocation in the church is particularly attractive to homosexuals -- or that the single-sex environment of Roman Catholic seminaries encourages homosexual tendencies -- there are no empirical data to support either hypothesis. More likely is that special verbal skills (along with a'pastoral sensitivity' for afflicted persons) developed and transmitted within the gay community tend to equip homosexuals for such work." Ibid., p. 143.

[50]Cf., John Gerassi, The Boys of Boise (New York: Macmillan, 1966).

Chapter 6

Homosexuals and the Civil Law

Introduction

I do not intend the question of civil law regulating homosexual conduct to be a major focus of this book. However, it is impossible to appreciate the full dilemma of the self-proclaimed homosexual without acknowledging the impact of formal social sanctions. Even if the average gay person is never arrested or brought to trial, the potential for scandal and/or economic hardship is always present. To be dishonorably discharged from the military, to be denied job promotion, to have one's family subjected to embarrassing questions, to be blackmailed by petty criminals, or to be mistreated by the police are all more likely as long as restrictive legislation remains on the books.

It is sheer maliciousness or hardheartedness that leads many citizens to favor retention of such laws. These people value the educational function of the criminal law and they fear that decriminalizaton will be tantamount to approbation. Whether it is possible to liberalize the law without surrendering the traditional Western sexual ethic will be the concern of this chapter. I will begin with a brief historical review and then proceed to a discussion of the arguments for and against decriminalization.

I. A Short History of Anglo-American Civil Law on Homosexuality

The task of formulating a coherent and integrated legal code is much easier in periods where common values are held in an identifiable and public way. Without doubt, the Judaeo-Christian religious tradition has been the source of many laws in the evolved Anglo-American criminal codes. Nevertheless, as this religious grounding has broken down, to a large extent under the pressures of modern life, it has become questionable whether there is a 'public ethic.'[1] The consequence has been a severe challenge to any laws which cannot be shown to directly harm the common good of the body politic. Since many of the laws regulating sexual conduct are said to be peculiarly religious in origin, it is this area of life which has generated the most controversy.

It is true that Jewish law and custom proscribed homosexual conduct.[1] However, it is not clear to what extent this was ever a major problem. In the book of Leviticus (18:22; 20:13) the penalty of death by stoning was laid down. As with so many other areas of Jewish life, the religious, cultic and social laws were intermixed in Leviticus so that commentators have given various explanations of why references to homosexual acts appear.

The Christian community inherited this abhorrence for homosexual activity and equated it with the immoral customs of the pagans. Even the Roman civil law of the early period of Church history rendered a negative judgment on homosexual practices, especially when minors were concerned. But it was not until the time of Emperor Justinian in the 6th Century that the Christian rationale and the civil statutes were brought into line. In 538 and 544 laws were enacted which made homosexuality a major offense to be punished by torture, mutilation, parading in public and execution. The prime concern of the legislation was to control male homosexual prostitution and the corruption of boys. As D.S. Bailey points out, however, the patristic period generated a mere hundred items of legislation on the matter in the course of some one thousand years, so that it cannot be said that it was considered a major social problem.

If the Code of Justinian solidified the Christian opinion on the matter, it was the teaching of St. Thomas Aquinas which gave it a theoretical basis. By the end of the 13th Century, the common teaching of the Christian Church on homosexuality as a form of sexual expression was overwhelmingly negative. In both

147

canon (Church) law and civil law, harsh penalties were exacted. And the tendency began to appear which equated homosexuality and heresy, as if there were some causal relationship. The word 'bugger' for example, which refers to anal intercourse, has its origin in the attribution of heresy to the Bulgarians. By the time of the Inquisition, where public burning was the common punishment, the word 'faggot' (as in the pile of sticks used for the burnings) began to refer to homosexuals. The moral fault and the civil crime (as well as the religious rebellion) were seen as one.

What happened in England under the auspices of the Church-State relationship of the Middle Ages was that the ecclesiastical courts were held responsible for the trial of those accused of sodomy. The first major statement of English law on homosexuality was the statute of 1533 enacted by King Henry VIII who complained about the non-enforcement of prior legislation. What was forbidden was 'buggery' (i.e., anal intercourse) and bestiality. The penalty for these offenses was death. In 1548 a new statute renewed the prior one, with some minor revisions. After some uncertainty under Mary, Queen Elizabeth returned to the 1533 version in her statute of 1563. For the next 275 years, this was to be the operative law of England.

In 1861, under the influence of a wave of humanitarianism the death penalty for homosexual offenses was finally abolished. A further reduction came with the Criminal Law Amendment Act of 1885 where homosexual acts (even when performed in private) were made a misdemeanor and punishable by up to two years in prison. This law included all forms of homosexual acts, in addition to buggery which was already prohibited.

In the United STates, the state laws followed the British example, although there was considerable variance in both the acts covered by the statutes and the penalties exacted. In neither

148

Britain nor the United States was there much of a movement for legal reform on this issue until the 1950s. What happened was that, at about the same time, two study groups were formed which subsequently issued recommendations which called for sweeping reforms. The Model Penal Code in the United States (1955) and the Wolfenden Report in England (1957) both suggested that homosexual acts taking place in private between consenting adults should no longer be subject to the criminal law. This precipitated a wide-spread discussion of the merits of such a move, a controversy which continues up to the present day.

The Wolfenden Report explicitly preserved three types of situations as valid concerns of the law: (1) offenses against minors (2) offenses against public decency and (3) exploitation of vice for the purpose of gain. Thus the key feature of the reform was decriminalizing 'consensual acts done in private by adult males.' In 1967, after considerable parliamentary debate, the main features of the Wolfenden Report were made into law in the Sex Offenses Act.

The story in the United States has been much different. Only Illinois (in 1961) of all the states has adopted the recommendations of the Model Penal Code Committee. It is true that some local municipalities have done so, but even the legal victories which are won are subject to reconsideration at later dates. The efforts of some conservative Christians in the Bible Belt to stand adamantly opposed to legislative reform has garnered extensive publicity. It is fair to say that American public opinion (and therefore the sense of urgency the issue has for public officials) lags behind that of England.

II. The Forms of Discrimination in America

There have been three basic forms of discrimination against homosexuals in America. The first, and most obvious, is the civil law ban

149

against homosexual acts as found in the legal codes of the various states. Among the nations of the West, the United States has the most severe antihomosexual laws.[4] Penalties range in severity from a maximum of one year to possible life imprisonment.[5] What is illegal is usually oral or anal intercourse, but these acts were also prohibited in the heterosexual context. Nevertheless, in the vast majority of instances, homosexuals are not prosecuted under these explicit statutes. Instead, a number of vaguely worded misdemeanor statutes are involved which apply to behavior in public places.[6] Most arrests are made in regard to solicitation in rest rooms, parks, or street corners or during the course of raids on homosexual establishments. The proof employed in court is the testimony of the police officer. In most cases, there is no complainant.

While the law allows for a significant penalty to be conferred for those convicted of homosexual offenses, this seldom occurs. Instead, everyone involved wants to proceed with dispatch.

> The participants in the courtroom drama, both the judge and the defendent, and in very many cases the prosecutor also, are all somewhat embarrassed by the whole affair and wish to get it over as quickly as possible. . .knowledge in the community that one is homosexual is much more damaging to a man's life than any sentence which is likely to be imposed by the court.[7]

Thus the public indignation which precipitated the formulation of strong laws with harsh penalties is considerably transformed in the day to day workings of the criminal justice system.

A second form of discrimination is the federal government policy which generally has excluded homosexuals from government employment and from access to security clearances. In recent years, there have been some changes made in this regard so that the long-range prospect is for some significant loosening of these restrictions. The prime rationale behind this historic policy has been the fear that homosexuals would be subject to extortion and blackmail and thus targets of enemy agents. It is ironic, therefore, to hear claims (which seem to have some basis in fact) that a high percentage of American foreign agents have been homosexuals.[8] The freedom from family responsibilities and the ingrained habits of living in discrepant worlds simultaneously may in fact make homosexuals better qualified for some types of government work than heterosexuals.

An allied concern about homosexual presence in government, in addition to the blackmail possibility, is the suspicion that homosexuals might congregate in particular areas of government employ and make the social situation unpleasant for others. Accusations of favoritism and of dark conspiracies might develop much as other minority groups have been resented when they succeeded in certain businesses. Of course, this possibility cannot be ruled out in advance, but the present indications are that homosexuals have gone over-board to avoid such entanglements. And at the level of civil rights, it seems an unreliable basis for discriminatory treatment.

The third form of formal discrimination against homosexuals is the complete rejection from induction or enlistment in the armed forces.[9] If a person is discovered to be homosexual while on active duty, he or she is discharged from the service. (It should be pointed out that, although legal sanctions against lesbians tend to be seldom invoked in other areas of American life, in the military this is not the case). The higher courts have recently refused to review this military policy.

III. The Arguments for a Change in the Law

In a well-known series of essays, Sir Patrick Devlin has argued that the civil society has a vested interest in regulating the moral conduct of its members, even at times that which is done in private, as long as it can be shown that the common good is being served.[10] Devlin employs the standard of 'the reasonable man' (i.e., the ordinary citizen in the jury box) as his guide to what kinds of conduct should fall under a ban. His operative principle is that "there must be toleration of the maximum individual freedom that is consistent with the integrity of society."[11] However, he interprets what promotes 'the integrity of society' with a strong concern to defend the religious foundation of the social order. Thus he argues, in the British context, that

> it seems to me therefore that the free-thinker and the non-Christian can accept, without offense to his convictions, the fact that Christian morals are the basis of the criminal law and that he can recognize, also without taking offense, that without the support of the churches the moral order, which has its origin in and takes its strength from Christian beliefs, would collapse.[12]

Despite Devlin's suspicion that the historical intermeshing of religious principles and civil law have made it impossible to abandon the first without sacrificing the integrity of the second, a whole host of critics have challenged his assumptions and offered a contrary perspective on the legal control of adult moral conduct.[13] One popular way of phrasing the issue has been to talk about the difference between 'crimes with victims' and 'crimes without victims.' Edwin Schur has defined 'crimes without victims' as "the willing exchange, among adults, of strongly demanded but

legally proscribed goods or services."[14]   He sees
the problem as emerging out of an attempt to
legislate morality for its own sake.   What is
characteristic of these situations is that any
harm which accrues to the activity is inflicted on
the participating individuals themselves.
Normally, there is no complainant to bring the
matter to police attention so that only surreptitious observation or entrapment can lead to
arrest.

It is primarily on utilitarian grounds that
the opposition to laws regulating homosexual
conduct among adults has won a measure of support.
It is asserted that, whatever one's personal
attitude or moral judgment about homosexuality in
general, the social harms that derive from trying
to make this a matter of prohibitory legislation
far outweigh the social goods.   The case for this
claim is based on a series of empirical factors of
which the following are the most important.[15]

(a) The laws are ineffective -- The vast
majority of homosexuals are not directly affected
by the existing legal situation.   They have never
been arrested, no less convicted, for a homosexual
offense.   At best, they experience a vague threat
or a demeaning social taboo through their knowledge of such efforts at control.   But even those
gay men who are active in the underworld of public
sex do not sense a sufficient threat to deter them
from their pursuit of partners.   Thus the present
laws seem not to be an effective deterrent.

(b) The laws are capricious -- As I have
already indicated, the range of penalties attached
to sodomy laws in various states indicates a wide
variance of opinion about the relative importance
of this matter.   In addition, most homosexual
arrests are made on the basis of misdemeanor laws
that have nothing specifically to do with sexual
activity.   But even in the felony arrest situations, the judiciary is reluctant to impose even
minimally unpleasant penalties.   For example, in
one year in Los Angeles of the 457 homosexuals who

were convicted at the felony level, only 3 went to prison.[16] And of the felony convictions, 95% were later changed to misdemeanors.

(c) The Laws can only be enforced when police use illegal tactics -- Since there is usually no complaint, individual police officers (normally from the vice squad) are assigned the responsibility of ferreting out homosexuals and making a convincing case that can hold up in court. It is a unpleasant duty and the temptation to take shortcuts is ever present. The difference between 'enticement,' which presumably means that the cop posed as a potential partner but did not take the initiative, and 'entrapment,' in which he lured the other party to a level of interest that would have been non-existent otherwise, is difficult to specify in practice. This one-to-one situation of propositioning is tedious and effective only against a small percentage of the unsuspecting. The professional gay prostitutes are too streetwise and too alert for the presence of police in an area to be caught, except by accident. The other major police tactic of mass arrests during periods of crackdown, for example, in a public park tend to abridge the normal civil protections and function primarily as a form of harassment.

(d) The laws create a condition where wealthy, powerful or influential homosexuals can be extorted and blackmailed -- In the Bell/Weinberg study, one-quarter of the white male homosexuals and approximately the same perspective of females claimed that attempts had been made to blackmail them.[17] Primarily, it would seem, it is those who are best off, and who have not acknowledged their homosexuality publicly, who are most susceptible to this type of criminal threat. Whether financial gain or jealousy or revenge is the motive, such a condition penalizes some gays by, in their minds, summarily removing them from the protection of the legal system.

154

For each of these reasons, the supporters of anti-discrimination laws have called for legal reform. The side effects of laws prohibiting homosexual acts between consenting adults in private seem to be harmful enough to outweigh the social good achieved by having them on the books.

IV. A Personal Conclusion

I consider the effort to win basic civil rights for homosexual persons a step in the right direction. But it is important that the proper distinctions be made so that the principles that underly this judgment be properly understood.

Let me begin by suggesting the kinds of conduct that should not be protected. First, offenses against minors are a proper area of legal concern. While pedophilia is probably less common among homosexuals than among heterosexuals, it does occur and a few individuals with this emotional problem can act out with a surprisingly high number of underage partners. It is not just a question of seduction and innocence. For in some situations the child or youth may, unconsciously at least, make explicit overtures. What society says is that adults in their relationships with non-adults must recognize a heightened level of responsibility. What might be tolerated among adults becomes unconscionable when there is a significant age (and corresponding emotional and experiential) discrepancy between the parties. This does not, of course, determine what an appropriate penalty for the adult offender should be. In some cases, a program of long-range therapy may be the best alternative. In others, imprisonment may better protect the common good.

One critical factor in the discussion is deciding what age should be the boundary line between youth and adulthood. The prepubescent child is surely deserving of special protection. But it could be possible to argue the relative merits of the ages of 16, 18 and 21 for the

155

purposes of legal enforcement. I would favor the age of 18 since it seems to be the normal time when an individual in our society moves away from home, becomes eligible for military service, and assumes a new level of personal responsibility. It will be up to the judge and jury in a particular case to determine the significance of the age factor.

A second form of prohibited conduct (again following the Wolfenden Report) should be offenses against public decency. In this situation no distinction between heterosexual and homosexual orientation is implied. The boundaries of public common space should not replace the bedroom as the focal point of sexual expression. In most instances, cultural mores provide sufficient protection. But on occasion, the right to protection against lewd displays will be infringed. Then it is up to the civil authority to reestablish the desired status quo. Obviously, there must be sufficient flexibility in this regard since levels of sensitivity vary tremendously from one region and cultural group to another. What is needed is a set of laws which will only be invoked when children, the elderly, passers-by, home owners, vacationers, and other are needlessly forced to witness someone else's exercise of sexual freedom.

A third form of offense, homosexual prostitution, is not as clearcut an issue. A long tradition in Christian ethics, going back to Thomas Aquinas, allows for a civil tolerance of the evil of public prostitution. According to this point of view, those forms of vice which cannot be suppressed should, while tolerated, be regulated so that their harm can be minimized. In some parts of this country this is already done with heterosexual prostitution. The challenge to the public authorities is how to regulate without becoming embroiled in the same kind of payoffs and uneven enforcement which has prevailed under the present legal ban.

A policy of benign neglect is subject to the complaint that it does not give sufficient attention to the educative power of the law. Might not a more open environment lead the young and innocent to experiment more readily than they would otherwise? It is hard to know what the long-range consequences of such social changes might turn out to be. All societies in history have seen fit to limit the kinds of allowable sexual conduct. If we just look at the short-range effects according to some utilitarian calculus, we could be missing the deeper dimensions of the issue.

I think that, at a minimum, all forms of prostitution should be regulated by the civil authority. This should include: periodic health checks, prevention of participation by juveniles, guarantee of free passage for those who wish to leave th life, and geographical confinement to set areas of a city or county. All of this would apply to both heterosexual and homosexual types of prostitution. However, I am in sympathy with the desire to eradicate this demeaning social institution from our midst. It is just that such an effort has never worked. It has led to the corruption of the criminal justice system and to the virtual enslavement of prostitutes kept controllable through the creation and maintenance of alcohol and drug addiction. A policy of tolerance, with regulation, seems to me to be the better alternative.

A fourth type of prohibitable offense is homosexual rape. The heinousness of any type of rape derives from the violent and debasing treatment of another human being as a sexual object. No society can allow such conduct to go unpunished. Male homosexual rape often takes place in the context of struggles for power and dominance, and therefore is not motivated by lust but by anger or revenge. Such is the situation in many American prisons where the young, inexperienced or unaffiliated inmate is soon subjected to such physical insults. It is a sad fact that these acts have often gone unreported or unpunished because of the indifference of the authorities. Laws against homosexual rape (which is often engaged in by predominantly heterosexual inmates) should be rigorously enforced.

What I have done up to this point is to discuss the kinds of homosexual conduct that I do not think should be protected by the law. Now I will turn to the more difficult issues that have been the central focus of the call for reform.

I agree with the main recommendation of the Wolfenden Report and the Model Penal Code proposal. There should be no interference with consensual acts done in private by adult homosexuals. This position in no way authorizes or recommends homosexual conduct. It merely reflects a realistic appraisal of the present situation in which the sodomy laws do not deter homosexuals from following their sexual preferences, do lead to various social problems such as corruption of public officials and haphazard enforcement policies, and do cause more harm than the good they produce.

This policy of non-interference should not be extended to the question of empowerment in other areas. I do not favor the creation of a category of homosexual 'marriage' (by whatever name). Nor do I support the right of adoption of children by homosexual couples. In both of these instances, the societal values at stake are too basic to be overridden by adherence to libertarian criteria. When it comes to economic matters such as joint income tax returns, inheritance, and property sharing it seems feasible to allow for a slow evolution of policy here. If religious communities, and various collectivities are granted special status in the financial realm, I see no reason why some such protection could not be extended to homosexual parties.

Among the basic civil liberties presently being sought by gay men and women are protections

158

against discrimination in housing and employment. Generally, I support such efforts. But the question of homosexuals in certain occupations where they deal regularly with young children and adolescents (such as teaching, counseling, etc.) is a complex issue. On the one hand there is no evidence that the rate of sexual solicitation or abuse by homosexual teachers is any higher than it is for heterosexual teachers. On the other hand, the public proclamation of a counter-cultural identity by a significant-other such as a teacher can have a profound effect on the interpretation of the world that is available to impressionable youngsters. All of us need role models at critical stages in the development process. What is in doubt is what kind of impact gay teachers as role models may have on their students.

Since teaching has been one of the occupations most attractive to gays, it is obvious that homosexual teachers have often given devoted and loving service to their charges. What has changed is that now, uncloseted gay teachers, have become publicly identified according to their sexual orientation. I doubt if there is an easy solution to this dilemma. While it is desirable to attract to the teaching profession the very best people we have, in a pluralistic culture it is hard to preclude individuals from the profession simply on the basis of sexual preference. While I oppose the granting of a wholesale protection, I favor the just and humane acceptance of publicly homosexual teachers, except in those instances where there is genuine cause for alarm that they will either be seductive with students or inculcate a promiscuous pattern of behavior. I fear, however, that soon this level of protection will only be available outside of the public school system.

In regards to the issue of government employment, especially at the higher or more sensitive levels of government, I can see no reason for the retention of the traditional discriminatory laws.

Judgments about reliability, stability and dedication should be made on a person-to-person basis.

When it comes to the military the issue is less clear. Because the living and work situation are usually the same, sources of antagonism and mutual suspicion, like sexual preference, can easily lead to a diminishment of overall effectiveness. This might especially be the case in isolated or constricting environments. However, the degree of paranoia generated by the present legal structure is far our of proportion to the reality of the difficulty.

I favor the elimination of the dishonorable discharge for homosexuals dismissed from the service, except in situations comparable to those for which heterosexual offenses would be similarly punished. The prime function of the dishonorable discharge is to give an individual a criminal record and thus, often, to blackball him or her from gainful employment in the future. I think it would be advisable for the separate services to accept a sample group of avowed homosexuals in order to test their work record and general compatibility. If the results proved positive, then the present ban on recruitment and admission could be lifted. It would still be possible to take sexual preference into account in making assignments.

What I have argued for in this last section of the chapter is a reexamination of the present laws regulating homosexual conduct. While I favor the general thrust of the Wolfenden Report, I am more wary of some other proposals which move closer to a general approbation and social ratification of the homosexual way to life. I think it is possible to embrace a moderate policy of legal reform without abandoning the values of the Judaeo-Christian sexual ethic.

Footnotes for Chapter 6

¹For an insightful discussion of the notion of a 'public ethic,' see: John Courtney Murray, We Hold These Truths: Catholic Reflections on the American Proposition (New York: Sheed and Ward, 1960).

²For much of this historical review, I am relying on two sources: Norman St. John-Stevas, Life, Death and the Law (London: Eyre & Spottiswoode, 1961), pp. 198-231; and Derrick Sherwin Bailey, Homosexuality and the Western Christian Tradition (London: Longmans, Green & Co., 1955), pp. 64-152.

³Bailey, loc. cit., p. 99.

⁴Cf., Arno Karlen, Sexuality and Homosexuality: A New View (New York: W.W. Norton, 1971), p. 608; H. Kimball Jones, Toward a Christian Understanding of the Homosexual (New York: Association, 1966), p. 79.

⁵Cf., Gilbert Cantor, "The Need for Homosexual Law Reform," in The Same Sex, edited by Ralph Weltge (Philadelphia: United Church Press, 1969), pp. 83-94.

⁶Martin Hoffman, "Homosexuals and the Law," in The Homosexual Dialectic, edited by Joseph McCaffrey (Englewood Cliffs: Prentice-Hall, 1972), pp. 121-136.

⁷Ibid., p. 129.

⁸"For most of this century, in Britain as well as in the United States, the very highest levels of governmental confidentiality (particularly diplomatic and espionage services) have been in the hands and often under the leadership, of homosexuals." C.A. Tripp, The Homosexual Matrix (New York: Signet, 1976), p. 201.

[9]Cf., Colin Williams and Martin Weinberg, Homosexuals and the Military: A Study of Less Than Honorable Discharge (New York: Harper & Row, 1971).

[10]Patrick Devlin, The Enforcement of Morals (New York: Oxford U. Press, 1965).

[11]Ibid., p. 16.

[12]Ibid., p. 23.

[13]H.L.A. Hart, the British legal scholar, has been the prime opponent of Devlin's position. Cf., Punishment and Responsibility: Essays in the Philosophy of Law (New York: Oxford U. Press, 1968) and Law, Liberty and Morality (Stanford U. Press, 1963).

[14]Edwin Schur, Crimes Without Victims (Englewood Cliffs: Prentice Hall, 1965), p. 169.

[15]Cantor, loc. cit., pp. 90-91.

[16]Hoffman, loc. cit., p. 129.

[17]Alan Bell and Martin Weinberg, Homosexuality: A Study of Diversity Among Men and Women (New York: Simon and Schuster, 1978), pp. 192-193.

Chapter 7

The Homosexual Way of Life

The   homosexual way   of life   is   the social
fabric created by the interweaving of   the diverse
personalities who have come to identify themselves
as homosexual.   It is   made up   of both male   and
female members.   Only quite recently has it been a
self-conscious   product   of   specifically   focused
energies.   Prior to   that, it was much more   sub-
terranean and   discreet; the result   of inevitable
processes of nurturance and support. In its female
component   it still inclines in this   direction of
inconspicuous affiliation.

Like the   social organization   of   many other
minority   groups,   the   homosexual   way   of   life
remains a   mystery to many who do   not participate
in   it.   It is   always at   a distance and   safely
ensconced beyond some ghetto boundaries.   And yet,
it is very much a part of the observable   world of
contemporary society.

By lingering   over some   of   its constitutive
elements,   it   may   be   possible   to   construct   a
portrait of the homosexual way of life   which will
make analysis of its ethical status a   bit easier.
Let us begin with the <u>via negativa</u>.

(1)   <u>Participation in homosexual   activity is
not   sufficient   grounds   for   inclusion   in   the
Homosexual Way of Life</u>.

As we have   seen, a   fairly large minority   of the
male and   female population admit   to   having
experienced orgasm some time after puberty   with a
member of   the same   sex.   The   context   of such
activity,   the age   of the   participants   and   its
connection with later sexual development   must all
be taken into account in assessing the   meaning of
any particular sexual encounter.   Even periods of
homosexual behavior stretching over   several years
may   not   have a   decisive impact   on   one's later
sexual identity.

Adolescent crushes, the lustful seeking of an
outlet in   one-sex environments, the   seduction of
the   young,   homosexual   rape,   fumbling   sexual

164

experimentation and misguided therapeutic counseling can all lead to homosexual activity without
necessarily fostering a confirmed and comfortable
identification with a homosexual object choice.

(2) Absence of homosexual activity is not
sufficient grounds for exclusion from the
Homosexual Way of Life.

While usually the evolution of an acknowledged
homosexual orientation is the product of a pattern
of homosexual behavior, this is not necessarily
the case. One could be a celibate gay or have
some physical or psychological handicap which
prevented the actualization of one's sexual preferences. In these cases, it is still possible to
participate in the gay sub-culture, to consider
gay liberation also self-liberation, and to make
significant contributions to the lives and well-
being of other homosexuals.

(3) A preference for any particular mode of
physical sexual expression is not determinative of
the Homosexual Way of Life.

In the western cultural tradition heterosexual
vaginal intercourse has functioned as the pardigm
form of sexual activity. However, since at least
the Courtly Love movement of the Renaissance,
other interpretations of the meaning and appropriateness of foreplay, orgasm and other stimuli
of sexual pleasure have had their defenders. More
recently, especially in the 20th Century, the full
variety of manual, oral and anal techniques, as
well as the use of mechanical substitutes, has
become a part of the theoretical and practical
sexual knowledge of many adult people.

As the former taboos have broken down, so has
the radical difference between the preferred techniques of heterosexual and homosexual love-making.
The preponderance of emphasis on oral and anal
intercourse among homosexuals no longer distinguishes them as easily as it once did.
Admittedly, the parallelism breaks down at the

point of gender identity of the partner, but the broad descriptive categories of vaginal, oral and anal do not separate one sexual group from the other.

(4) Style of dress and physical posture are not reliable criteria for the Homosexual Way of Life.

Operative cultural stereotypes about homosexual men and women are discredited by the available evidence. Only a minority of gay men and lesbians are inclined to dress in a style normally attributed to the opposite sex. In fact, the youngest age groups of liberated homosexuals seem to go to the opposite extreme, especially among the men where the 'macho' look, with all of the paraphernalia this requires, is the fashion of the day. On the other hand, it seems that the majority of transvestities are basically heterosexual in orientation.

What has been said of style of dress also applies to the manner of physical self-presentation. Patterns of 'effeminate' posturing among male homosexuals and of 'masculine' posturing among lesbians are a cultivated manner of bodily presence which is a periphery phenomena in the gay world. It is unlikely to disappear, but there is no indication that it is prized as a desirable sexual style by other gays. There is probably as much hostility toward such dramatic creations of an alter ego in the homosexual world as is evidenced in the wider society. And furthermore, a number of people who unconsciously exhibit such mannerisms are very much heterosexual.

(5) High levels of creativity, of refined esthetic sensibility, and of flamboyant dynamism are not typical manifestations of the Homosexual Way of Life.

Homosexual people come in all shapes and sizes and they have no corner on the market in cultural

166

productivity. In an understandable reaction to the pariah status accorded them by their critics, gay apologists have succumbed at times to the temptation to make grad niose claims about homosexual giftedness. Long lists of famous personages have been brought forth to prove the case. Yet, even accepting the validity of some of these claims, this kind of characterization no more admits of generalization than do similar claims about other disadvantaged groups. The prevalence of gays in certain of the artistic professions is just as easily explained in terms of lack of work-related discrimination as it is by any special charism.

(6) Adult interest in sexual relations with children or young adolescents is not common in the Homosexual Way of Life.

It seems that the preferred sexual partner for the majority of adult gays is either of the same age or in the 20s or early 30s. There is no evidence that pedophilia or pederasty are any more prevalent among homosexuals than among heterosexuals. In fact, there is a genuine scorn expressed for gay child-molesters by other gays. Occupations in which gays have access to children on a regular basis (such as school teacher and camp counselor) are only dangerous physically to the children when they encounter the small percentage of homosexuals who are especially attracted to them. But this same qualification applies among heterosexual teachers and counselors as well.

Thus far we have seen that the homosexual way of life cannot be discerned simply by invoking certain cultural expectations. Overt homosexual activity is at best an ambiguous clue. Style of dress and contrasexual posturing are not determinative of sexual identity. There is no special homosexual giftedness which promises unlimited cultural creativity. And the same percentage, or less, of homosexuals as of heterosexuals are interested in children as sexual partners.

167

Having given a brief account of what is not characterstic of the homosexual way of life, I will now turn to the more difficult task of describing what I take it to be.

(1) The Homosexual way of Life is a matter of a self-conscious sexual identity.

I think that the Gay Liberation Movement is perfectly correct when it says that 'coming out of the closet' is everything. Numerous homosexual escapades are not the equivalent for the individual of one act of self-acknowledgement of a confirmed homosexual orientation. Not that we are disembodied slaves who can cavalierly make ourselves something just by declaring it. This is not what I take 'uncloseting' to involve. Rather it is to look back at one's life and reinterpret it by a whole different value scheme. In this regard, the phenomenon of a change of name (which is popular in certain ethnic circles at the point of reidentification and which of course has deep roots in Judaism and Christianity) might best capture the reality involved.

Presumably one is capable of this degree of introspection only after passing into adulthood, althought the passage does not take place in a moment. A whole period of profound confusion, increased anxiety, inarticulateness, and attempts at avoidance will normally precede such turning points. Premature ventures into gay activism may seem to resolve the conflicts, but they are different from the intense looks into the solitary vistas of one's inner world. Only the individual can accurately say to her or himself that 'I am a Homosexual' and know that it is an honest appraisal of one's sexual possibilities.

The first and most critical step into the homosexual wayof life involves a kind of personal monologue in which the only passage taken is one of self-interpretation. This person who was once indifferent or hostile or confused about his or her sexual identityis now confident that honesty

168

is better than self-deception. To say the words
to oneself (or a trusted other) is to forge a new
identity. However hesitant or afraid the person
might be, from now on the world will be seen from
a different point of view.

(2) The Homosexual Way of Life involves a
public manifestation of one's self-conscious
sexual identity.

Most human beings have an innate sense of privacy
about their innermost thoughts and feelings.
Normally, the pre-established roles of society
provide sufficient protection to allow this inner
reserve to go unthreatened. With a trusted friend
or a close circle of relatively intimate companions, a higher degree of self-revelation may
take place. But a few bad experiences in this
regard may be enough to shut off any but the most
perfunctoryforms of personal sharing. This seems
to be why communication is so difficult even in
the marital context.

For a person who has come to the conclusion
that he or she is a homosexual, the majority of
human instincts caution against public disclosure
of that fact. There is a great degree of risk
involved, even being cut off socially from one's
family and peers. This accounts for the long
tradition in American culture for gays to lead a
two-sided existence full of role-playing and pretense. Within this mentality, one has two sets of
relationships -- one set includes family and work
associates, the other homosexual acquaintances.
Neither world interacts with the other, except by
mistake. To perpetuate this dual existence
requires a definite set of social skills and an
ability to tolerate a certain amount of tension.

Nevertheless, another kind of dynamic is also
present in each of us. We wish to be accepted for
who we are, to be respected and loved for that
combination of qualities which make us unique.
From this perspective, to live a lie, to seek to

169

win recognition and acceptance on the basis of some concocted self, is the ultimate hypocrisy. It is this basic human desire that is being appealed to when gay liberation calls for homosexuals to come out of the closest, to assume adult responsibility for the shape of their lives.

The decision to say to another person 'I am a homosexual', especially to a significant other, is another pivotal point in the process of entry into the homosexual way of life. It may be the intention of the individual so revealed to restrict this knowledge to one other person, at least for the time. In such a case, promises of secrecy and confidentiality will be imperative. But having been done once, there is always the possibility that the circumstances will be right again. Or one may find oneself caught up in a social circle where the level of threat seems minimal and so the secret is shared again. This slow and carefully programmed scenario seems to be more common than the brash and often vitriolic public confessions of the instant revolutionaries in the gay movement.

However a person goes about publicly admitting his or her sexual orientation, the same temptation exists. This is the impulse to allow the sexual dimensions of one's personality to become the focus of one's identity. When this occurs, the most significant thing that can be said about youis that you are gay. Even those who resist the temptation do so with great difficulty. For the more one becomes immersed in a predominantly, if not exclusively, gay subculture, the less possible it is to leave the sexual question blind. Therefore, it seems that the very environment which allows for the freest expression of personality (i.e., the homosexual world) is also the most restrictive when it comes to minimizing the significance of one's sexual identity.

(3) <u>The</u> <u>Homosexual</u> <u>Way</u> <u>of</u> <u>Life</u> is sustained
by an <u>interlocking</u> <u>network</u> <u>of</u> <u>social</u> <u>institutions</u>.

In the chapter on the social institutions of the
homosexual world, I described six basic types of
affiliation among gays and lesbians. The under-
ground world of anonymous sex is an almost exclusively male phenomenon. It has its own places,
rituals and code of behavior. Some who participate in it would not identify themselves as
primarily homosexual, but in most instances this
does not affect the nature of the sexual exchange.
Because of the potential danger and scandal
attached to this hidden arena, some gays have
never been attracted to it. Others know it as an
occasional marketplace in times of sexual frustration or thrill seeking. But there is a third
group, personified by the male hustlers and sexual
outlaws of the urban scene, who express their
gayness entirely within this ambit.

The gay bath, another male institution, is
one step up in structuring of interaction.
Because membership is a prerequisite for admittance, a certain security from arrest and
undesired intrusion is a postive feature. In
addition, sheer physical presence is tantamount to
admission of an interest in sexual activity. The
desire for anonymity is preserved, and the potential for sexual pleasure-seeking is unlimited.
The gay bathis a place where lust reigns supreme
and the need for involvement in communication of
personality is kept to a minimum.

The third institution, the gay bar, although
predominantly masculine, has its lesbian counter-
parts. It is the best established of the contexts
of homosexual affiliation. It is first of all a
sexual marketplace where a series of individuals
look for partners for the night or more unrealis-
tically, for a lifetime. But beyond its immediate
function of match-making, the gay bar also serves
as a communication center, a locale for initiation
into the gay world, and a rallying point for the
grievances of the moment. Gay bars are

171

multifarious and each type of bar has its own
clientele and its own style of dress, of music, of
communication and of behavior.

The stress on youth and appearance, coupled
with the sustained consumption of alochol, lead
many gays to abandon the bar scene after a certain
point in their lives. Yet the concentratin of gay
bars in certain neighborhoods often leads to a
special housing market for prospective gay buyers.
Thus, whether individual gays involve themselves
in bar life or not, they are still affected by the
secondary repercussions of this institution.

Social cliques or friendship groups are a
fourth form of institutionalization. Here the
focus is not upon a place, but upon the relationships among the members. Gathering together for
meals, recreation and discussions, they tend to
exclude non-homosexuals from the mainstream of
their lives. In the intimate setting of a home,
apartment or summer cottage, they derive support,
encouragement and affection from others like themselves. There maybe an active sexual relationship
between different combinations of participants but
thisis not a prerequisite for belonging. In such
circles, a distinction is made between 'friends
and 'lovers.'

Such patterns of interaction seem to be the
most common form of homosexual social life among
lesbians. The unobtrusive and contained quality
of these arrangements have an appeal to those who
wish to leave the hostile world behind. They
provide sufficient diversity to make getting
together interesting yet are manageable financially and otherwise.

The fifth type of institution is the homosexual couple. Here there may be a variety of
understandings between the partners about the
nature of their relationship and about the type of
commitment each expects from the other. Some
attempt to imitate the model of faithful, monogamous heterosexual marriage. Others consider

172

this particular relationship the primary one among a series of affective and sexual unions. Still others see their time together as transitory and bound only by their mutual satisfaction in the relationship. Since there is no formal, publicly-recognized way of celebrating such couplings, the individuals are forced to determine for themselves what they mean.

The available evidence would suggest that lesbian couples are more stable and longer lasting than male couples. There may be many reasons for this. But the absence of children in both situations (except for recent efforts to adopt) is surely one of the causes. Whether civic approbation of such bonded relationships (with the concomitant change in tax and inheritance status) would increase their chances for survival is not clear. I suspect it would to some extent.

The final form of homosexual institution is the most recent, namely, homophile organizations. With the Gay Liberation Movement has come the proliferation of cause-oriented groups that vary from the staid and conservative to the most revolutionary. Some sponsor social events like dances and parties and rest content with this improvement in the leisure life of gays. Other groups offer educational and counseling services as well. But the most significant change in the social climate has been the creation of activist groups who work for legal, economic and cultural transformation.

Homophile organizations are diverse enough to provide a conducive environment for the positive utilization of gay talent and energy. They provide a sense of belonging and the potential for satisfying involvement in the process of society change. But their chaotic lack of structure and inability to mobilize behind a common efforts have been sources of disenchantment for some gays.

It is unlikely that a very high percentage of homosexuals will ever be actively involved in homophile organizations. But even those who are not can sympathize at a distance and draw encouragement from whatever successes they are able to achieve.

These six types of organization -- the underworld, the bath, the bar, the social clique, the couple, and the homophile organization-structure the range of possibilities for those who would desire to live out a publicly gay life. The further along in this sequence that one goes the less possible it is to pull back and seek some other pattern of life. The ultimate form of participation in the homosexual way of life is to not only be homosexual, but to represent all other homosexuals. This is what comes with active involvement in the gay movement.

(4) The Homosexual Way of Life severely limits one's ability to render negative judgments, on the basis of consistent criteria, about any kind of sexual behavior.

The most common accusation made by heterosexuals against homosexuality is that it is inherently promiscuous. The two main types of rejoinder are either 'so what' or 'that is not an accurate description of the homosexual possibility.' I take it that 'promiscuity' in this case refers to 'indiscriminate sexual union.' Now at this point it makes no difference whether some homosexuals live active sexual lives with one partner exclusively. What is critical is whether that is an acknowledged moral requirement for membership in the homosexual way of life. I think it is not.

The homosexual world is so described by its defenders that it necessarily must remain open to a wide spectrum of life styles and forms of sexual expression. While some gays may regret, or castigate, or abhor what a certain percentage of other gays do, there are no grounds in the gay subculture bywhich they can dissociate themselves

174

from these patterns of behavior. One-night stands, tearoom sex, sado-masochistic relations, dominance and bondage, and similar manifestations cannot be ruled out without threatening the very freedom of sexual self-determination that has been so ardently advocated.

What I am suggesting is that the homosexual way of life includes more modes of sexual behavior than any particular gay might wish to include. Any argument about the immorality or inappropriateness of a specific expression seems to spring more from personal preference and personal values than from any perspective identifiable in the movement. If I am correct, there is a dynamic built into the call for sexual liberation which if carried to its logical conclusion would rule out only those behaviors which involve excessive violence or corruption of the innocent.

(5) The Homosexual Way of Life is sustained by the continual addition of new participants who emerge from a great variety of backgrounds.

There is no one path by which homosexually-oriented individuals attain that degree of self-consciousness and of public courage that is required for full participation in gay life. For those who grow up in rural or small town settings it is likely that passage to a major urban center will facilitate the process. The percentage of gays in the major cities, especially in certain neighborhoods, is much higher than in the population at large. If societal attitudes keep changing, this may cease to be so common, but for the present moving away from home to the city is, for many gays, the first step toward freedom of sexual identity.

For others, military service may provide a comparable opportunity for getting a feel for a new range of possibilities. Here the risks are greater. Yet the strict official policy of anti-homosexual discrimination has been tempered by the realism of military officials who can tolerate some divergence as long as public scandal is avoided.

More and more college campuses have become protected enclaves were divergence of opinion and practice are accepted modes of living. As a result, young homosexuals may find active gay organizations where support and encouragement is received and survival clues are offered bythose who know their way around. In these environments, a quick radicalization is not uncommon and the potential trauma of familial rejection is easly overlooked.

There are, obviously, many other paths by which individuals can solidify a homosexual identity. But whatever the route, the fear that heterosexual observers often have is whether intense recruitment to the homosexual way of life creates more homosexuals than there would be otherwise. It seems to me that the best answer to that question is: it all depends.

On the one hand, itmust be acknowledged that a certain percentage of young people of late high school and college age have confused or uncertain sexual identities. For them, active and self-conscious involvement in the gay subculture may trigger, especially over a protracted period of time, a stronger inclination in that direction than would have been the case. Since I believe that we are creatures of habit, and that habits can be reinforced or diminished by their exercise or disuse, any significant level of experience affects the kind of person we are. However, this is only true if there is a real homosexual potential in the individual. Otherwise a few attempts at acting out would reinforce feelings of repugnance and disgust.

For young persons of this sort, the homo-sexual movement may create a context in which the word 'recruitment' (in the sense of leading in a direction that might not have been taken otherwise) is appropriate. A more difficult question is what exposure to the gay option does to the post-pubertal adolescent who never becomes actively engaged in homosexual relations but who has fears aroused that might have lain dormant. I suspect that this is a price that any society pays which allows for pluralistic expressions of sexual orientation. In the same way that neighborhoods dominated by 'adult' entertainment establishments may have varying effects on the young who regularly are exposed to their existence, so, depending on the family context and the maturity level of the individual, young teens may react to discovery of the gay world with curiosity, suspicion, humor or a premature insouciance.

A second category, on the other hand, cannot be said to be 'created' in any sense of the term. These would include the vast majority of adult age persons who have made a personal transition from one state of sexual consciousness to another. For them, the institutions of the homosexual way of life are simply pictured as natural outlets for a new freedom of self-expression. It is not so much a matter of activation from without (i.e., by the persuasion or propaganda of others) but of seeking a means of properly manifesting a new sense of self.

(6) The Homosexual Way of Life is plagued by three key social problems: aging, alcohol/drug addiction and suicide.

Gerontology is one of the growth industries in American society. As we live longer, with better quality of health, we inevitably run into unprecedented problems in distribution of social services. The proliferation of homes for the elderly, of planned retirement communities, and of outreach programs are signs that aging is a problem not confined to the gay world. Yet it is a commonplace in homosexual literature that gay life, with its stress on youth and appearance (especially in the male arena) is ill-adapted to those beyond 40 and even more so those in their

177

60s and 70s. The absence of a family and children makes support, both financially and emotionally, a difficult achievement. While all Americans are troubled by old age to some extent, gays seem to have a greater struggle with the aging process. Perhaps an organized effort to provide support structures would help, but the problems of loneliness, unrootedness and one-generational living are real nonetheless.

The same can be said of alcohol/drug addiction and suicide. Both of these are dilemmas which face all of the industrialized societies. What is troubling about homosexual variants of these social problems is the relatively high incidence that seems to prevail. On the basis of various theories about human forms of coping, it is clear that social stigmatization and personal unhappiness can accentuate the tendency toward alcohol/drug addiction or suicide when these exist. What is not so obvious is whether a freer social climate would bring the gay rates into conformity with comparable heterosexual samplings.

(7) The Homosexual Way of Life exhibits certain negative characteristics which can be said to shape, in many instances, the form of homosexual interaction.

(a) Gossip - Perhaps all disenfranchised groups have resorted to words as the most available weapon to seek revenge against their oppressors. To know, in fact or in imagination, details about an enemy's private life is to have a control over that person's reputation. The more the person depends ont he appearances of integrity and uprightness, the more critical knowledge of a fatal flaw can be. As individuals forced so often to play a role and to pretend to be like everyone else, gays seem to develop a pervasive suspicion of public images. The import of this instinctive reaction is that there is always more to be known, a fuller story to be revealed.

178

It goes without saying that such realism contains many elements of truth. The private sinner/public saint is the stuff of our experience. The heroic dimension of lives runs afoul of the potential for malevolence and deceit. Yet the task of accurately describing another's character presupposes our ability to take an accurate reading, to balance off with what we see what a person pretends to be.

The problem with gossip as a form of social discourse is that it allows conjecture and imagination to have priority over concrete experience and a common history. As a result, truth and falsehood become inextricalbly mixed to the detriment of any rooting in a real situation or person. Gossip among gays can be directed outward, against the hypocritical heterosexual world, or inward toward the latest patternings of fellow gays. It seems to take up a high percentage of gay social conversational time. Because of the considerable turnover of homosexual partnerships and the tendency to be perpetually on the prowl when unaffiliated, interest and curiosity are high when it comes to the affairs of others. But, as is usually the case, one can be on both ends of the rumor mill and those on the receiving end can be deeply crushed by the suspicion and willingness to believe the worst when manifested against themselves by others.

(b) Jealousy - In reflecting on the affinities between sex and violence, a number of commentators have pointed out that the degree of passion that is shown in the most pleasurable experences of orgasm, when side-tracked by the emotion of hate, can often lead to the cruelest instances of violence. Murder, for example, is frequently committed by spurned lovers and jilted spouses. Jealousy has the same potential for deadening relationships which once flourished.

In the gay world, jealousy seems to be a function of the precarious grounding of many partnerships. Since society provides no protective institutions, legal or otherwise, and since the gay institutions that are available do not implicitly respect particular pairings, the potential for collapse is always present. This is especially acute when there is an age, beauty, economic or educational discrepancy between the partners. Even when exclusivity is not a part of the defined nature of the relationship, strong instincts of possessiveness may rise to the surface.

Although the gay subculture is not particularly known for its overt violence, there are some instances of this effect of jealousy. What is more likely is a barrage of character assassination and recrimination. And the closer two people have become, the more intimate their sharing, the better able they are to destroy each other in ways that cut to the quick.

(c) Authority Problems - In suggesting that the family nexus is the key to understanding sexual developments and aberration, psychologists have isolated one central dimension in human experence. While I have argued that the child's relationship with his or her mother or father is not sufficient causal explanation for the homosexual orientation (though an important one), I do think that an inability to relate comfortably with one or both of them is a common pattern among homosexuals. If this is indeed the case, then it is understandable that other authority figures, later in life, might also pose a problem.

This difficulty may be further exacerbated if the confession of a homosexual identity to one's parents has led to rejection and hostility. In a sense, every person who wields determinative power in one's life, whether at work or in the civic sphere or in the Church, becomes a surrogate parent with all of the historical stresses that accrue to this role. The preference in homophile organizations for an anarchistic style of leadership may betray this same tendency to fear centers of power outside of oneself.

As with any other generationalization about a diverse group, each of these three characteristics of the Homosexual way of Life must be qualified in their applicability. They do not apply to all homosexuals and they are surely evident in the heterosexual world as well. What I am suggesting is that in terms of degree they are more prevalent in the gay subculture than elsewhere.

Conclusion

In this last chapter of the first section of the book, I have brought together some descriptive comments about the Homosexual Way of Life. I have drawn upon a diverse set of materials to arrive at these conclusions, but in their present form they reflect my own sense of the gay world rather than any consensus in the social scientific literature. Since in the second section I want to construct a picture of the Christian Way of Life, against which the Homosexual Way of Life will be juxtaposed, it has been necessary to create an impressionistic image of the first alternative.

The central claim of this first section of the book can be phrased in the following manner. The Homosexual Way of Life is a pattern of social organization that takes certain characteristic forms which find a common focus in the ultimate commitment to unrestrited personal sexual freedom. Whatever other values individual homosexuals may hold and pursue, this liberation conviction is at the heart of their common identity with other homosexuals. To accept homosexuality as a way of life is to call into question any attempt to enforce sexual standards of a more restrictive sort, whether based on political, social or religious grounds.

Part Two

Christian Ethical Reflection on the

Homosexual Way of Life

Chapter 8

The Scriptural Evidence

This chapter will be divided into two main
parts. In the first section, I will summarize the
current state of discussion on various texts from
the Bible which have been taken, at one time or
another, to refer to homosexuality. In the second
section, I will draw some theological conclusions
about the proper way that such materials should be
used in arguing an ethical position on homosexual
behavior.

I. References to Homosexuality in the Bible-

There are six key passages, three in the Old
Testament and three in the New Testament, which
seem to be especially pertinent to an analysis of
homosexuality as an ethical issue. Each of them
has been used as part of the traditional prohibition against homosexual acts as it has been formu-
lated in the Christian community. Until quite
recently, it was thought tht the matter was
closed. Slowly but surely, however, as modern
biblical criticism has become a central tool of
the scholarly world, even these passages have been
subjected to a new and more intense scrutiny. Out
of this reexamination has come a variety of of
exegetical opinions. No longer can the theological interpreters be said to be speaking with
one voice.

In addition to these classical texts, a number of other stories and references have assumed a
new importance. Some of these are more signficant
for what they leave open to the imagination than
for what they actually assert, but these texts too
must be put in a suitable context. The second
half of this section will take on this task of
interpretation.

A. The Classical Texts:

(1) Sodom and Gomorrah (Genesis 19:4-11)-[1]

They had not gone to bed when the
house was surrounded by the men of
the town, the men of Sodom both

young and old, all the people
without exception. Calling to Lot
they said, 'Where are the men who
came to you tonight? Send them
out to us that we may abuse them.'

Lot came out to them at the
door, and having closed the door
behind him said, 'I beg you, my
brothers, do no such wicked thing.
Listen, I have two daughters who
are virgins. I am ready to send
them out to you, to treat as it
pleases you. But as for the men,
do nothing to them, for they have
come under the shadow of my roof.'
But they replied, 'Out of the way!
Here is one who came as a foreign-
er, and would set himself up as a
judge. Now we will treat you
worse then them.' Then they
forced Lot back and moved forward
to break down the door. But the
men reached out, pulled Lot back
into the house, and shut the door.
and they struck the men who were
at the door of the house with
blindness, from youngest to
oldest, and they never found the
doorway.

The story line in this part of Genesis is
easily reconstructed. Lot, Abraham's nephew,
settles in the town of Sodom, which, it turns out,
has a reputation as a center of evil behavior.
God hears of these charges and sends two
messengers (angels) to check on the matter for
themselves. Before they arrive, Abraham inter-
venes with God to restrain his wrath provided ten
good men can be found. Eventually, Lot greets the
two visitors and offers them hospitality for the
night. Then the incident takes place. Later the
visitors warn Lot and his family to flee the city.
After they do so (except for Lot's wife who is
turned into a pillar of salt when she looks

187

back), God destroys Sodom and its neighbor Gomorrah with fire and brimstone from heaven.

It seems that the moral of the story is that sin will receive its appropriate reward. Through much of Christian history the sin of Sodom was understood to be the desire to commit homosexual acts upon Lot's guest. In such a patriarchal society, Lot's offer of his two daughters, as gruesome and unfeeling as it might seem today, was a secondary element which reinforced the presumption that sexual lust was the central issue. As a result of this reading of the story, the Sodom episode was considered to be a major proof-text that homosexual acts were contrary to God's law.

The first major challenge to this interpretation in the modern period came with the publication of D.S. Bailey's book, Homosexuality and the Western Tradition.[2] Bailey argues that the destruction of Sodom and Gomorrah was an historical event, probably due to natural causes, and that there is no reason to think that the reason was sexual, still less that it was for homosexual sin.

But why has the homosexual interpretation of the story become so well established? Bailey thinks that this is a rather late accretion which began with th late books of the New Testament, 2Peter and Jude. According to him, the Old Testament writings depict Sodom as a symbol of utter destruction, but nowhere specify that the great sin committed was homosexuality. Even the New Testament condemnations of homosexuality made no mention of Sodom in this regard. By the end of the first century A.D., the homosexual emphasis began to carry the day and with the Fathers of the Early Church it became the accepted opinion.

Bailey's own interpretation hinges on his exegesis of the Hebrew verb 'yadha'. Traditionally this has been taken to mean 'engage in coitus.' But he claims that this usage is exceptional in the Old Testament.[3] He conjectures that 'get acquainted with' may be closer to the truth. If this is so, a different reading of the story would be in order.

> Is it not possible that Lot, either in ignorance or in defiance of the laws of Sodom, had exceeded the rights of a ger (Sojourner) in that city by receiving and entertaining two 'foreigners' whose intentions might be hostile, and whose credentials, it seems, had not been examined?[4]

This would give a non-sexual focus to the story. Lot's offer of his daughters would then be seen as a spontaneous attempt to appease the crowd with the only barter he had available.

The sin of Sodom in Bailey's interpretation would basically consist in a failure to render hospitality to the stranger. Whether the form of the failure was sexual or not, this deliberate refusal would be considered a major fault among nomadic peoples whose very survival while traveling was often in the hands of others.

Before looking at some criticisms of Bailey, I want to indicate how influential his opinion has been. In 1966 H. Kimball Jones provided a review of the biblical material, with a special stress on the Sodom story. His overview was taken almost entirely from Bailey.[5] In 1974, Robert Treese also relied on Bailey.[6] But most importantly, John McNeill in his long suppressed book The Church and the Homosexual (1976) follows Bailey step for step.[7] These are only three examples in a vast literature, both theological and secular, which has granted Bailey's interpretation a sacrosanct status.

Those who wish to counter Bailey's interpretation argue that he goes overboard in playing down the threat to commit homosexual acts.

189

It is not necessary to eliminate the horror of
this form of attack on privileged guests in order
to balance off the traditional interpretation.
Tom Horner, for example, contends that the act in
question was homosexual rape. There are no mitigating details to see it differently. "They were
ugly, callous, dirty-minded and unfeeling rapists.
There is no point in trying to depict them as anything else. Their intent was homosexual rape..."[8]
Horner remains unconvinced that the verb 'yadha'
can mean anything but 'to have intercourse with.'

From a different theological position Don
Williams would preserve the same homosexual interpretation of the threatened acts, but once again
as a matter of rape and not as a sensual pleasure
seeking.

> What then is the sin of Sodom?
> The clear answer from the text is
> homosexual rape...There are three
> aspects to Sodom's sin. The law
> of hospitality is broken, the dis-
> tinction between angels and men is
> threatened, and the prohibition of
> sex between males is violated.[9]

Another conservative exegete follows much the
same line of reasoning. "It seems to me to be
beyond reaonable question, therefore, that the
incident in genesis 19:1-11 is an incident of
attempted homosexual rape. However, to say that
the sin of Sodom was homosexuality alone is much
to oversimplify the story."[10]

It seems to me that a credible case can be
made for the position advocated by the critics of
Bailey. The act in question was homosexual rape
and the context in which the threat was made constituted a violation of hospitality. Whether
Sodom was a society which tolerated widespread
homosexual practices, we have no way of knowing.
The elements of fact and legend are so interwoven
that a true depiction of the characteristic

sin(s) of the Sodomites, as interpreted after the events of the destruction of the town, have been lost to us. In the form in which the story appears, it is probably the violence of the rape, as much as the sex of the participants, which made the deed so offensive.

So it appears that Bailey's central point, that the passage in question originally was not (up until the 1st Century) and should not today be seen as a condemnation of the homosexual condition in general or homosexual behavior by consenting homosexual adults, can be upheld. The Sodom story is not validly used as a proof-text against every form of homosexuality. But Bailey's effort to defuse the story of all homosexual implications remains unconvincing. Sexual rape was bad enough, but homosexual rape implied a more degrading form of abuse of the strangers who came to the town. At this point in history it is probably impossible to separate the meaning of the story from the relevant details which make it memorable. The very word 'sodomy' captures the staying power of the biblical reference.

(2) The Holiness Code:

> You must not lie with a man as with a woman. This is a hateful thing. (Leviticus 18:22)

> The man who lies with a man in the same way as with a woman: They have done a hateful thing together; they must die, their blood shall be on their own heads. (Leviticus 20:13)

None of the major commentators on these passages disputes the interpretation that sees them as a legal prohibition against homosexual acts between men. The main areas of disagreements are: (i) how significant were they for the everyday life of the Jews? and (ii) what relevance should they have in the Christian era?

191

We have no evidence in Scripture to suggest that homosexuality was ever common among the Old Testament Hebrews. There does seem to be some indication, however, that ritual acts of homosexuality were sometimes a part of pagan religions in the Middle East. What is not clear is whether the laws in <u>Leviticus</u> were designed to preserve cultic purity against idolatrous influences or whether they simply repeated standard social judgments to be found in the operative legal codes of their neighbors.

On one side of the issue we find D. S. Bailey. He says,

> There is no reason to suppose that unnatural practices were so markedly characteristic of the nations which surrounded Israel that they specifically endangered Hebrew morals. . .The Hebrew attitude to homosexual practices differed but little from that of the Egyptians and Assyrian. . .we may cautiously hazard the opinion that homosexual practices were ordinarily of infrequent occurrence in Israel.[11]

His view is supported by Don Williams who says, "There is no reason to suppose that homosexual behavior endangered Hebrew morals and that the law against homosexual acts was designed to combat idolatry."[12]

But the protection against idolatry position also has its defenders. Tom Horner, for example, traces the biblical use of the word 'ebah' = 'abomination' or 'hateful thing' and finds that normally it appears in connection with idolatry.[13] The task of the compilers of the Holiness Code was to purify their nation of the cultic abominations which had led to the disaster of 587 B.C. Homosexual practices was one of these pagan rites.

Letha Scanzoni and Virginia Ramey Mollenkott, in a derivative treatment of this material, make the same kind of claim that Horner does. "The reasons given for these proscriptions involve several factors: (1) separation from other nations and their customs (Lev. 18:1-5), (2) avoidance ofidolatry and any practices associated with it (Lev. 20:1-7), and (3) ceremonial uncleanness."[14]

Whichever of these theories eventually carries the day, there is general agreement that the two texts in the Holiness Code which condemn homosexual practices among males were not a reaction to a widespread problem. More likely, they represented an attempt to either reinforce prevailing societal practices or else prevent a recurrence of cultic types of homosexual acts.

The second question about the texts is what relevance they have for the Christian community. First, they give us our best indication of what Jewish attitudes were about homosexual behavior. There is no doubt that the law condemned such practices. Second, since much of the Holiness Code has been suspended, there is no particular reason why these prohibitions should be carried over. Third, they help explain the silence of Jesus on the matter. Among the Jews homosexuality was not a major issue and sufficient instruction already existed.

In the light of these factors, I conclude that the two verses from <u>Leviticus</u> are important as the best available evidence for ascertaining the established Jewish legal judgment about homosexual activity between men. It can be presumed that this was the position of Jesus and of the early Jewish Christian community. Only with the Pauline mission to the Gentiles did a new experience of homosexuality have to be taken into account.

(3) Romans 1:26-27-

> That is why God has abandoned them
> to degrading passions: why their
> women have turned from natural
> intercourse to unnatural pratices
> and why their menfolk have given
> up natural intercourse to be con-
> sumed with passion for each other,
> men doing shameless things with
> men and getting an appropriate
> reward for their perversion.

Sometimes this pericope is divided into two parts: the first line referring to female homosexual relations and the second to male homosexual relations. But for purposes of convenience I will treat them together.

Romans 1:26 is the only specific reference to female homosexuality in the Scriptures. This could be either because the male writers knew little about it or because the subordinate status of women did not make it into a major issue. In Romans 1:26 the phrase 'para phusin' appears which is usually translated 'against nature' or 'unnatural.' This implies that some basic human mode of living is being violated. "We conclude that Paul speaks of both male and female homosexual acts, and sees them as contrary to God's intention in creation and, thus, in violation of the Old Testament law."[15] Because they have forgotten how to properly exercise their sexual faculty, they have become steeped in sin and death is their proper end.

John McNeill argues that we should not be too quick to presume that we know what Paul meant by 'against nature.' He offers two alternatives. The first possibility is the situation of the hedonistic pagan who continually seeks new forms of sexual pleasure, even going so far as to indulge in homosexual acts against his or her natural inclination.

> Paul apparently refers only to
> homosexual acts indulged in by
> those he considered to be other-
> wise heterosexually inclined; acts
> which represent a voluntary choice
> to act contrary to their ordinary
> sexual appetite.[16]

McNeill claims that William Thompson and
Joseph Fitzmyer have read the verse this way. The
second possibility is that "phusis refers to the
'nature' of the chosen people who were forbidden
by Levitical law to have homosexual relations."[17]
In this case, a recognition of the true God would
entail an acceptance of the Levitical proscrip-
tion. Ultimately, McNeill holds that both interpretations are probably valid.

That Romans 1:26-27 is a clearcut condemnation of homosexual relations between both men and
women is agreed upon by all the commentators.
What is debated is whether the context of lust,
and possibly idolatry, is enough to restrict the
negative judgment to only one kind of homosexual
situation. This problem will reemerge in interpreting the other two New Testament texts.

(4) I Corinthians 6:9-10

> You know perfectly well that
> people who do wrong will not
> inherit the kingdom of
> God: people of immoral lives,
> idolaters, adulterers, catamites,
> sodomites, thieves, usurers,
> drunkards, slanderers, and
> swindlers will never inherit the
> kingdom of God.

The Pauline lists of virtues and vices seems
to have been taken over from the moral wisdom of
the Greco-Roman world. They are illustrative
rather than definitive. What Paul does is adapt
pre-given material to his own purposes. In the

In the Pauline writings and the Pastoral Epistles there are at least thirteen examples of this type of arguemnt.[18]

In I <u>Corinthians</u> 6:9-10 Paul catalogues a series of behavior patterns which are properly identified with the way of evil. Among them are two references to homosexual acts. We do not know how familiar Paul himself was with the various forms of homosexual behavior. Did he choose his descriptive language carefully or was he merely relying on a familiar frame of reference to suggest the general type of conduct he abhorred? The answer to this question has generated some disagreement.

The traditional translation of the two Greek words is: 'passive homosexuals' or 'catamites' for 'malakoi' and 'active homosexuals' or 'sodomites' for 'arsenokoitai.' Horner and Williams, for example, both favor this usage.[19] But John McNeill offers another interpretation. He says that

> the word <u>malakos</u> literally means soft (e.g., <u>Luke</u> 7:25; Mt. 11:8). In a moral context the is normally employed to signify loose, morally weak, or lacking in self-control. There is no justification for applying <u>malakos</u> specifically to homosexuality.[20]

As for <u>arsenokoitai</u>, McNeill pints out that there is no word in classical, biblical or patristic Greek which would be the equivalent of the English word homosexual. There were, however, a variety of names for those who performed homosexual activity. Since Paul did not choose any of the standard Greek words we cannot know for sure what <u>arsenokoitai</u> refers to. Most likely, it has something to do with male prostitution.

McNeill is not primarily interested in defusing the two key words of any homosexual meaning. What he wants to do is to limit the kinds of homosexual situations that are being taken as a form of iniquity. I do not find his arguments entirely convincing, but his overall theological point is not dependent on total agreement with this exegesis. Since we cannot know for sure what level of precision Paul was striving for (especially in light of his adaption of Greco-Roman material), we cannot give any definitive judgment which would rule out the passive partner/active partner meaning.

(5) I Timothy 1:9-10

> Laws are not framed for people who are good. On the contrary they are for criminals and revolutionaries, for the irreligious and the wicked, for the sacriligious and the irreverent; they are for those who are immoral with women or with boys or with men; for liars and for perjurers--and for everything else that is contrary to the sound teaching. . .

This text from a pastoral epistle is most likely taken from the same sort of catalogue of vices that Paul used in I Corinthians 6:9-10. The Pauline authorship of this letter is doubtful, but the spirit of the parenetic passage is consistent with the earlier exposition given of the Corinthian text.

B. The Marginal Texts:

(1) Gibeah (Judges 19:16-26

This tale has many similiarities with the story of Lot in Sodom. A Levite is traveling with his concubine and servants when he stops to rest overnight in the town of Gibeah in the land of Benjamin. An old man, seeing him in the town square, offers hospitality for the night. However, some men from the town come out and ask

197

the old man to surrender his guest so they can 'abuse' him. After refusing the counteroffer of the old man's virgin daughter, they settle for the next visitor's concubine whom they rape the whole night long. The next morning the Levite carries her dead body on his donkey and then cuts her into 12 pieces which he sends around to the various tribes, seeking vengeance on the Benjamites.

It may be that this story was based on some actual sexual offense which led to war against the Benjamites.[21] In any case, it is a shocking account of a brutal heterosexual rape, preceded by the threat of homosexual abuse. Unlike the Sodom story, the deed is actually perpetrated and it leads to the death of the concubine. Once again there is no way of knowing whether this act of lust was part of a general pattern of malevolence by the citizens of Gibeah or whether they were particularly inclined to homosexual practices. The focus of the story is on the violation of hospitality by rape and murder.

(2)   The Relationship between David and Jonathan (I Samuel 13:1-4)-

In various parts of the First and Second broke of Samuel, a description is given of a warm and affectionate friendship between Saul's son Jonathan and David the valiant warrior. Traditionally, this has been interpreted to be nothing more than a good friendship. And nothing is ever said explicitly about a homosexual genital dimension to the relationship. However, this has not prevented some commentators from opening up this possibility, so that in much homosexually-oriented literature the Jonathan-David bond has come to symbolize the beauty and love of the deep homosexual bond which the Judaeo-Christian traditiona has deliberately chosen to neglect.

Recently, Tom Horner has published a book titled   Jonathan Loved David: Homosexuality in Biblical Times in which he argues the case for the homosexual interpretation on exegetical grounds.

198

Horner begins by suggesting that in the ancient Middle East there were three types of homosexual practitioners: aristocratic lovers, homosexual prostitutes, and average citizens. All were married except some of the second category. The Jonathan-David romance would have been an example of the aristocratic or noble lovers tradition. Horner conjectures that Saul discovered the nature of the relationship between his son and David and plotted to kill David. Fortunately, Jonathan was able to warn him in time. Jonathan remained behind with his wife and father after David fled, and eventually father and son were killed together in battle. On hearing of the tragic event, David composed a moving elegy in testimony to his love for the two men (II Samuel 1:19-27). The key verse is 1:26 where David says,

> O Jonathan, in your death I am
> stricken, I am desolate for you,
> Jonathan my brother. Very dear
> to me you were, Your love to me
> more wonderful than the love of a
> woman.

Taken out of context such a declaration seems to offer support for Horner's case. However, since there is no explicit treatment of the matter of homosexuality and since both Jonathan and David were married (David eight times with many children), it is unlikely that scholarly opinion will find Horner's arguments very convincing. The conclusion of D.S. Bailey represents the prevailing consensus, "The homosexual interpretation of the friendship between David and Jonathan. . . rests upon a very precarious basis."[22]

(3) <u>The Relationship between Ruth and Naomi</u> (Ruth 1)-

Horner also explores the possibility of a homosexual relationship between two other Old Testament figures--Ruth and Naomi.[23] Naomi, the long-suffering widow, and Ruth, her widowed daughter-in-law, take a solemn vow never to desert

each other. They even wish to be buried together.
The problem with this kind of tentative probing is
that the characters in the story are not presumed
to be historical figures. As a result, there is
no way of ascertaining a deeper level of truth
beyond what the details of the story allow for.
At best, it can be said that Horner's interpretation has won little, if any, critical support.

C. Conclusion-

I have discussed six classical texts and
three secondary texts as important sources for
contemporary reflection on the biblical attitude
toward homosexuality. While interpretations of
the Sodom story are the most disputed, few
exegetes doubt that both Old Testament Hebrews and
New Testament Christians prohibited homosexual
conduct among their members. Even the absence of
any explicit teaching from Jesus does not counteract this attitude since it is unlikely that homosexuality constituted much of a problem in 1st
Century Israel and there is no indication that
Jesus gave much of a priority to sexual matters in
his preaching. So on one level the Bible seems to
uphold the traditional Christian prohibition of
homosexual behavior.

What recent research has called into question, however, is whether all forms of homosexual
activity and relationship should fall under such a
condemnation. D. S. Bailey in his pivotal work
formulates an argument which has been repeated
many times since. Summarizing the New Testament
Scriptural evidence he says,

> we have decisive Biblical
> authority for censuring the con-
> duct of those whom we may describe
> as male perverts. . .but do the
> Apostle's strictures apply also to
> the homosexual acts of the genuine
> invert, and in particular to those
> physical expressions of affection
> which may take place between two

persons of the same sex who affirm
that they are 'in love?' To such
situations it can hardly be said
that the New Testament speaks,
since the condition of inversion
with all its special problems, was
quite unknown at that time.[24]

John McNeill issues a similar warning about
the limited usefulness of the Biblical texts on
homosexuality when he says (quoting Herman van de
Spijker),

both in the Old and the New
Testmaents, wherever the Bible
clearly seems to refer to homosexual activity, we must recognize
a judgment of condemnation.
However, every text dealing with
homosexual activity also refers to
aggravating circumstances such as
idolatry, sacred prostitution,
promiscuity, violent rape,
seduction of children, and violation of guests' rights. As a
result one can never be sure to
what extent the condemnation is of
homosexual activities as such or
only of homosexual activities
under these circumstances:
Nowhere is there a specific text
which explicitly rejects all homosexual activities as such independent of the circumstances.[25]

A third attempt to point out the difficulty
in interpreting the Scriptural texts for contemporary usage appears in a popular style book by
Letha Scanzoni and Virginia Ramey Mollenkott.

A careful examination of what the
Bible says about issues relating
to homosexuality still leaves us
with many unanswered questions.

201

For one thing, the idea of a life-long homosexual orientation or 'condition' is never mentioned in the Bible. . .furthermore, (it) does not mention the possibility of a permanent, committed relationship of love between homosexuals analogous to heterosexual marriage.[26]

Each of these theorists holds that, although the Bible prohibits the kind of homosexual conduct that was known in the Jewish and Greco-Roman worlds, it is necessarily silent about dimensions of the homosexual experience that have only come to light through the recent research of the natural and social sciences. Homosexuality that is connected with idolatry or rape or promiscuity is surely contrary to Christian values. But it may be, they suggest, that genuine Christian values can be realized in the context of loving and faithful homosexual bonds as well as in heterosexual bonds as well as in heterosexual marriage, singleness and celibacy.

One response to this revisionist claim is to turn to other Scriptural texts or themes to develop a broader focus of analysis. According to this methodological position we should not simply look to those parts of the two testaments where homosexuality is explicitly mentioned, but rather to the fuller context of creation, fall and redemption and to the place of sexuality within this deeper reality.

Karl Barth, for example, in a brief reference to homosexuality in his Church Dogmatics, situates it in relation to the doctrine of creation.[27] For him, the man-women relation is part of the very giveness of things since human existence is social by definition. Out of distinction between the sexes grows the opportunity for covenant, the gift of self in a mutually shared relationship. Barth renders a negative judgment on homosexuality because it is a refusal of openness to the other sex an idolatrous turning in on one's own sex for completion. While Barth's position on homosexuality is very undeveloped, he does show how the Scriptural material can inform an ethical position without being dependent on the classical texts on homosexuality.

A number of other Protestant exegetes, especially those of a Protestant persuasion, tend to trace the evil of homosexual behavior to the doctrine of creation. Don Williams is representative when, following Eichrodt and Von Rad, he pictures Genesis 1-3 as the central passage for a clear judgment on homosexuality. He says, "the primal form of humanity is the fellowship of man and woman. . . The old myths of the androgynous (bisexual and unisexual) Man are rejected and all ambiguity in the relationship between the sexes is removed."28 For him, there is something so basic about the potential for male-female covenanting tht no other sexual structuring can hope to achieve the same kind of appropriate fellowship.

It seems then that there are, at least, three possible positions that have been proposed by which the Scriptures could inform (or determine) the Christian attitude toward homosexual activity. The first points to the six classical texts and finds in them sufficient evidence to sustain the traditional Christian judgment. The second position evolves from an interpretation of the creation accounts in the first three chapters of Genesis (although it usually is coupled with a reference to the classical texts as well). But the third position would limit the Scriptural condemnation to only those more perverse forms of homosexual behavior. At the same time advocates of this last position would hold open the possibility that other kinds of homosexual relationships might be able to express in a satisfactory way the Christian values of love, tender concern, fidelity and self-sacrifice.

If these are the options, how do we decide which one is most adequate to the task at hand?

203

And how important should the Biblical materials be in our overall analysis? To this complicated question I will now turn in Part II.

II. Appropriating the Scriptural Material-

The Bible is the central document for any formulation of the Christian ethical imperative. This truth needs to be asserted strongly, especially in the Catholic ethical community which has not always acted consistent with an appreciation of this reality. But the Bible is also a document of the Church, a church which preceded it in existence, determined its canonicity, and continues to provide a context for theological discourse within which it may be properly interpreted. While we must turn seriously to the Bible in the process of ethical reflection we cannot demand from it more than such a source is capable of providing.

Without pursuing all of the complex questions of how the Christian Screiptures might function in ethical analysis, I will begin by offering a few summary statements which seem to me to capture the most critical points agreed to by many contemporary scholars.[29]

(a) The Scriptures cannot be used in a prooftext fashion-Accordingly it is not sufficient to point to six (or more) texts spread throughout the entire Bible and offer them as some kind of determinative statement which closes the issue forever. On the other hand, the existence of such material cannot be glossed over or neglected. What we need is a close examination of each text in its social and historical setting as well as a reliable determination of the import of the terms used. And all of this must then be placed in the broader theological perspective which organizes and structures the different books of the Bible.

(b) The Scripture contains more than one 'ethic' so that care must be taken in avoiding premature generalizations-The Sodom story (which

204

combines historical and legendary materials), the
Holiness Code (which includes various ritual and
purification laws), and the Pauline list of vices(
which resemble extant moral exhortation from non-
Christian sources) have little in common other
than the references to homosexual behavior. This
should warn us against making these texts fit
together too neatly. And the silence of the
Gospels on the matter of homosexuality requires
further explanation.

(c) The Scriptures must be read as a whole
rather than selectively-It is not sufficient to
have perused the few explicit texts dealing with
homosexual acts. These are only a small part of a
larger vision of the created order and of the
place of sexuality within it. For example, the
recurrent tendency to portray the God-human relationship in terms ofthe bond between husband and
wife in marriage is more enlightening for the perception of a sexual worldview than any passing
reference to sexual misconduct.

(d) The Scriptures are as important for
informing the character of the Christian moral
agent as they are for providing guidelines for
decision-making-It is a mistake to expect the
Bible to function primarily as a source for ethical principles and rules. Many contemproary ethical dilemmas, which were unknown in the ancient
world do not appear anywhere in the Scriptures.
Thus, a Christian answer to nuclear warfare, heart
transplants or the influence of multi-nation corporations must be found by a more complex route of
analysis than simply exegesis of texts. Yet the
Christian who reads the Bible with care and attention, and who hears it read and preached in the
liturgy, can be profoundly affected as a person.
It offers a unique vision of faith. It can establish certain persistent attitudes which dispose
the person toward the good. And it can make
easier the dedicated pursuit of common projects
which transform the life of the community.

One way of expressing all of this is to
suggest that the way that Christians come to an

205

opinion about homosexuality is not through search for definitive rules in the Scriptures but through a process of relating their experience and knowledge of homosexuality to the symphony of values which they have made ther own after a continual exposure to the stories and teaching of the constitutive community text.

(e) The Scriptures propose certain values, themes and virtues that are an integral part of the Christian self-understanding-Any mode of human behavior must be able to be reconciled with the components of a Christian view of the world for it to qualify as acceptable. This applies to homosexual behavior as well. In the Bible these essential components have been expressed in various ways. One approach is in terms of theological themes such as: covenant-response, the kingdom of God, metanoia (change of heart), agape (self-sacrificial love), justification, etc. Another approach uses value and virtue language: love, peace, patience, kindness, chastity, fidelity, etc. Thus, in order for homosexual acts to be moral they would have to satisfy the kinds of requirements generally identified with these biblical themes, values and virtues.

(f) The Scriptures highlight love as the central Christian value and virtue, but ultimately in the context of a realistic anthropology-The so-called Situation Ethics debate revealed the flaws of a direct appeal to love as an applicable standard for all Christian ethical reflection. Homosexuality is no more rendered acceptable by qualifying it as 'loving' than is any other controversial activity. Love is an achievement in time and space of embodied creatures who are capable of violence, hatred and all sorts of malevolence. Love is not self-authenticating in the way that trivial and instinctive expressions of it might suggest. The teaching of Jesus, and the interpretation of Paul and others, pictures love as the most demanding and all-involving sort of human challenge. It is closer to the Cross and to ready forms of difficult service, like the deed

206

of the Good Samaritan, than it is to blissful rapture and arbitrary limitation of the claims of the other. The tests of love are many and some forms of conduct seem more closely related to its achievement than others.

(g) The Scriptures alone are not sufficient for the resolution of most moral issues-The difficult task of developing an integrated set of moral norms, principles and rules is only possible of realization when all resources of the Christian community are taken into account. This means that the Scriptures, as important as they are, are normally not sufficient in isolation. The tradition of Christian wisdom, the knowledge available in the natural and social sciences, the contemporary experience of the faithful, and the insight that comes only through prayer and the anguished searching of a restless heart, are all components of a fuller process of ethical discernment. Therefore, in facing the choice about the morality of homosexual conduct, we do not rest content after exploring the Biblical material, but we move on to relate our Scriptural conclusions to other sources of knowledge and judgment.

With these critical points in mind, let me conclude this chapter by expressing as succinctly as possible what I think the Scriptures have to teach us about homosexuality:

(1) Homosexuality as it was known and practiced in the Judaeo-Christian world of the Middle East was considered as reprehensible conduct for a Christian person.

(2) Since it was not a major problem in the New Testament community of the Church, it receives relatively little attention in the Gospels and letters.

(3) We do not know how Paul (or Jesus for that matters) would have responded to the claim that a particular homosexual relationship was exclusive, loving and permanent. This way of

207

formulating the issue never seems to have presented itself.

(4) The Christian community has inherited a bias, a deep-seated aversion to homosexual conduct, which is expressed in passing in the Pauline letters.

(5) Any defender of the possibility of moral homosexual conduct and moral homosexual relationships among Christians must overcome and explain away an obvious Scriptural teaching against it. In the contemporary discussion, defenders of homosexuality are going against the grain and should not expect a quick reversal of opinion.

(6) The teaching Church (in the Catholic context) continues to interpret the Scriptures as opposed to homosexual conduct. While this does not stop the discussion, it does reinforce a continuation of the traditional condemnation.

(7) It will be in the area of Biblically-rooted values (a more indirect root than restricting oneself to an examination of specific texts) that the whole controversy about sexual ethics (including the morality of homosexuality) will continue on in the foreseeable future. What is at stake in any of these particular forms of sexual patterning and commitment is a whole notion of the limits of Christian discipleship.

Footnotes to Chapter 8-

[1]I will use the translation for the various biblical texts from: The Jerusalem Bible (Garden City: Doubleday, 1966).

[2]D.S. Bailey, Homosexuality and the Western Christian Tradition (London: Longmans, Green & Co., 1955). It should be pointed out that almost all of the revisionists treat Bailey's interpretation as a solidly established fact. He is quoted numerous times in all of the subsequent treatments of the Biblical perspective on homosexuality. Only recently has Bailey's work come in for criticism by other exegetes. It seems strange that such a radical interpretive shift should have gone unchallenged for so long. Perhaps, his work was only noticed by those who already had their minds made up. Having said this, I want to acknowledge that Bailey's book is an indispensable source for anyone who wishes to take the biblical material seriously.

[3]"Linguistic considerations alone, therefore, lend support to Dr. G.A. Barton's view that 'there is no actual necessity' to interpret 'know' in Gen. xix. 5 as equivalent to 'have coitus with.'" Ibid., p. 3.

[4]Ibid., p. 4.

[5]H. Kimball Jones, Toward a Christian Understanding of the Homosexual (New York: Association, 1966), pp. 66-70.

[6]Robert Treese, "Homosexuality: A Contemporary View of the Biblical Perspective," in Loving Women/Loving Men, edited by Sally Gearhert and William Johnson (San Francisco: Glide, 1974), pp. 23-58, esp. p. 30f.

209

[7]John McNeill, The Church and the Homosexual (Kansas City: Sheed Andrews and McMeel, 1976), pp. 43-50.

[8]Tom Horner, Jonathan Loved David: Homosexuality in Biblical Times (Philadelphia: Westminster, 1978), p. 48.

[9]Don Williams, The Bond that Breaks: Will Homosexuality Split the Church? (Los Angeles: BIM, 1978), p. 61.

[10]David Bartlett, "A Biblical Perspective on Homosexuality," in Homosexuality and the Christian Faith, edited by Harold Twiss (Valley Forge: Judson, 1978), p. 25. Cf., also Klaus Bockmuhl, "Homosexuality in Biblical Perspective," Christianity Today, 17, 1973, pp. 488-492.

[11]Bailey, loc. cit., p. 37.

[12]Williams, loc. cit., p. 65.

[13]Horner, loc. cit., p. 73.

[14]Letha Scanzoni and Virginia Ramey Mollenkott, Is the Homosexual My Neighbor? (New York: Harper and Row, 1978), p. 60.

[15]Williams, loc. cit., p. 77.

[16]McNeill, loc. cit., p. 77.

[17]Ibid., p. 56.

[18]Cf. Neil McEleney, "The Vice Lists of the Pastoral Epistles," Catholic Biblical Quarterly, 36, 1974, p. 203.

[19]Cf., Horner, loc. cit., p. 97 and Williams, loc. cit., pp. 83-84.

[20]McNeill, loc. cit., p. 52.

[21]Cf., Bailey, loc. cit., pp. 53-54; Williams, loc. cit., p. 69; Horner, loc. cit., pp. 54-57.

[22]Bailey, loc. cit., p. 56.

[23]Horner, loc. cit., pp. 40-46.

[24]Bailey, loc. cit., p. 157.

[25]McNeill, loc. cit., p. 60.

[26]Scanzoni and Mollenkott, loc. cit., pp. 71-72.

[27]Karl Barth, Church Dogmatics III/4 (Edinburgh: T & T Clark, 1961) p. 166.

[28]Williams, loc. cit., p. 53.

[29]A representative sampling of theologians who have written persuasively on this topic would include: Raymond Collins, "Scripture and the Christian Ethics," in Proceedings of the Catholic Theological Society of America, 29, 1974, pp. 215-241; Nicholas Crotty, "Biblical Perspectives in Moral Theology," Theological Studies, 26, 1965, pp. 574-595; Charles Curran, Catholic Moral Theology in Dialogue (Notre Dame: Fides, 1970), pp. 24-64; Sean Freyne, "The Bible and Christian Morality," in Morals, Law and Authority, edited by J.P. Mackey (Dayton: Pflaum, 1969), pp. 1-38; James Gustafson, "The Place of Scripture in Christian Ethics: A Methodological Study," Theology and Christian Ethics (Philadelphia: Pilgrim, 1974), pp. ; Bruce Birch and Larry Rasmussen, Bible and Ethics in the Christian Life (Minneapolis: Augsburg, 1976).

Chapter 9

Traditional and Contemporary Ethical Arguments

Against the Moral Acceptability of the

Homosexual Way of Life

If the Scriptural teaching on homosexuality is the first source of Christian ethical reflection, the second is the theological tradition of teaching as it evolved through the centuries. In this chapter I will begin with a brief review of different historical accounts of the evil of homosexual behavior as portrayed by major theological figures. Then, in part two, I will examine a representative group of contemporary theologians who argue that the traditional condemnation should be maintained.

I. The Traditional Teaching of the Christian Church on Homosexuality[1]

(a) The Patristic Period and the Early Middle Ages

The general acceptance of the homosexual interpretation of the Sodom story provided a common starting point in terms of which the great theologians of the early Church spoke with one voice. Without equivocation they pictured homosexual acts as depraved and unnatural. Among those who treated the matter were Tertullian, John Chrysostom, Justin, Eusebius, Lactantius, Salvian and Augustine.[2] John Chrysostom, for example, argues that homosexual acts are destructive in two ways: first because they are not open to procreation and second because they lead to hostility between men and women who are no longer motivated to live at peace. Augustine contends, for his part, that homosexual practices violate the Great Commandment of love.

The acts that these authors are referring to seem to be primarily active and passive sodomy. However, in the Epistle of Barnabas fellatio is also condemned.[3] John Chrysostom also makes mention of femal homosexual acts. D.S. Bailey sums up the available evidence in the following terms.

214

Although the matter is never discussed extensively, nor in general otherwise than incidentally, there can be no doubt that the early Church regarded homosexual practices with unqualified disapproval, particularly when committed by men with boys, or with one another.[4]

As I have indicated in my earlier discussion of the history of legal codes prohibiting homosexual behavior, the teaching of the Fathers soon found its ways into canon and civil law. In 300 at the Council of Elvira, pederasts were denied last rites in the first piece of formal legislation. In 390 Emperor Valentian introduced the penalty of death by burning. And in 538 A.D. Emperor Justinian in his influential Code prescribed torture, mutilation, castration and death as an appropriate punishment for homosexuals. This rigorous and severe policy prevailed on through the Middle Ages.

A third way in which the teaching on homosexuality was passed on -- in addition to theological writings and legislation -- was through the penitential books. These guides for confessors were an attempt to standardize policy and practice in the context of the confessional. They provided a handy frame of reference for the relatively uneducated clergy of the early middle ages. In the lists of sexual offenses, penalties are assigned for various classes of homosexual acts. "Generally speaking, clergymen in higher orders are penalized more heavily than those in lower orders, monks and priests more heavily than the laity, and men more heavily than boys, youths, or women..."[5] In the attempt to categorize homosexual acts, for the first time the variety of contexts, ages, and sexes of the participants was taken into account. While the Penitentials are not preoccupied with homosexuality, homosexual practices are always seen as sinful, with some variation in severity of the offense.

215

(b) The Middle Ages

The teaching of the Fathers on homosexuality was treated with great respect and unanimous acceptance in the theological writings of the Middle Ages. The two authors most worthy of note are Peter Damiani (1007-1072) and St. Thomas Aquinas.

Peter Damiani in his Liber Gomorrhianus (1051) levelled a scathing attack on homosexual practices among the clergy, especially in his own area of Europe. He depicted three types of homosexual acts: mutual masturbation, inter-femoral intercourse, and sodomy (in ascending order of gravity). One of the worst abuses in his eyes was the practice of confessing homosexual sins to the person with whom one had committed them. Pope Leo IX received the book, but soon found himself in a storm of controversy occasioned by its publication. Some denied the prevalence of moral decay among the clergy and others found his style interperate and unhelpful. Eventually, the furor died down, but with what long-range effect we do not know.

St. Thomas Aquinas takes up the issue of homosexuality in his Summa Theologica in the course of a discussion of the virtue of temperance.[6] In balanced tones he argues that sexual acts can be 'according to nature' or 'against nature.' By 'nature' is meant conformity to right reason which discerns the proper finality of all human acts. Thus some sexual acts impede the achievement of the proper end of sexual intercourse which is the procreation of children. Sexual sins 'against nature' have as their goal the pursuit of venereal pleasure for its own sake, without reference to procreation. Thus, bestiality, sodomy, and masturbation are sins against nature. Thomas condemns homosexual acts between men and between women, although he does not explicitly discuss each form of homosexual act.

216

Thomas begins with the premise that the primary purpose of the sexual organs is pro-creation. In terms of this standard, all homosexual acts are unnatural and sinful.

(c) Subsequent History

From the time of St. Thomas Aquinas to the contemporary period, theological discussions of homosexuality have tended to be literal restatements of the arguments from Scripture and from natural law. It has been primarily canon and civil law which have functioned as the forum for arguments about the appropriate response of the Church and the civil authorities to the social disruption that prevalent homosexual practices might cause.

> Generally, it seems that in practice homosexual offenders only became liable to the severity of the law if their behavior was attributable to heretical ideas, or if immorality in conduct was accompanied by grave error in belief.[7]

The outbreak of the Albigensian heresy gave some grounds for connecting heterodox opinion with immoral practices, but it is not clear how widespread the problem was. In any case, by the time of the Inquisition, the same punishment was meted out for heresy and homosexuality and, at least linguistically (e.g. faggot) they came to be equated in the popular imagination.

The Protestant Reformation for all of its airing of the issues of celibacy and marriage did not deviate at all from established Catholic teaching about the morality of homosexuality. Up until the modern era, this unanimity of opinion prevailed in the Catholic, Orthodox, and Protestant theological traditions.

217

II. The Non-Revisionists: Contemporary Christian Arguments

Most Catholic authors, and some Protestant ones, who consider homosexual activity to be immoral adopt some form of natural law reasoning. They make the judgment that there is an order or structure of finality built into the human creature which can be discovered and brought to consciousness. In the sexual realm this pre-given disposition is determined both by our status as embodied selves and by the constitutive element of gender identity which affects all of the dynamics of human relatedness.

What this entails is that human meaning is a function of more than intentionality. The human being is not capable of achieving certain desired states or ends when these require the violation of proper human processes. For example, the desire for the sharing of love with another person cannot realize itself in a vacuum, oblivious to the centrality of the physical and social limits of sexual possibilities.

This natural law position claims that our created nature as sexual beings encompasses both mutual affection and generativity. These dual values can best be protected when a stable context for nurturance of each other and of the fruit of one's sexual union is provided for. Only the mystery of differentness is sufficient to maintain both the allure of the unknown and the complementarity of the revealed. Man and woman, in this sense, were made for each other and no other form of sexual sharing is adequate to the interpersonal and cross-generational institution that we call marriage and family.

According to natural law theory, homosexuality is wrong because

(i) it is contrary to the procreative purpose of sexual intercourse.

218

(ii) it is an attack on the basic unit of society -- the family

(iii) it is deficient in the potential for complementarity between the partners

(iv) it is a deliberate pursuit of sexual pleasure in the absence of a stable framework for mutual growth and sharing.

This natural law approach is quite standard in non-revisionist writings on homosexuality. In order to clarify what are the central points in the steps of the argument I will concentrate on three recent expressions of this position.

The first author, John Harvey, is probably the most prolific Catholic authro on the subject of homosexuality. In a series of articles and parts of books, he has reiterated a strong natural law defense of the traditional prohibition against homosexual behavior.[8] He says,

> By their nature homosexual acts exclude all possibility of pro-creation of life. Such acts are, therefore, inordinate uses of the sexual faculty...Furthermore, it is argued that sexual acts between memebers of the same sex are contrary not only to the primary purpose of the sexual faculty, namely, procreation, but also to the secondary purpose, which is to express mutual love between husband and wife...The goals of human sexuality and personality demand that the sexual faculty have its proper function within the family framework.[9]

Harvey asserts that, according to this natural law view, the only true option for a confirmed homosexual person is a life of continence, made possible by a rigorous program of prayer and spiritual direction. Neither heterosexual marriage or homosexual bonding are adequate alternatives. And a promiscuous exercise of one's homosexual tendencies is ruled out altogether. Harvey believes that a chaste homosexual life must be founded on an ascetical plan which might well include the following elements: daily meditation, frequent mass and communion, daily examination of conscience, systematic reading of Scripture, regular confession, and habitual practice of acts of charity.[10]

Harvey's approach has the appeal of consistency. Just as all heterosexual individuals before marriage must foresake the ultimate forms of sexual expression, so must homosexuals. The only difference is that with homosexuals there will never be a time when such activity will be morally acceptable. The homosexual, for Harvey, must strive to live by a moral standard which will place him or her outside of the institutions of the gay world. It is an either/or situation. There is no way of reconciling any form of overt homosexual relationship with Christian ethical standards.

A more nuanced version of natural law theory as applied to homosexuality can be found in a recent book by Philip Keane.[11] First, he takes issue with the attempt to limit the significance of the Biblical teaching about homosexuality. Instead, he concludes that

> the Scriptures do take a general or universal-level stand to the effect that homosexual activity always involves evil, even though we may have to very sensitively define just what this evil means in particular cases...The Scriptures' concern about homosexual acts is a basic concern rather than something only relevant to few isolated types of homosexual activity.[12]

220

From this starting point, Keane goes on to find in the Catholic tradition a constant teaching that there is some type of evil present in homosexual acts. What this entails is best expressed in terms of the priority of the marital bond as the paradigm instance of sexual expression. Homosexual acts are always evils in the natural order despite the fact that mitigating circumstances may limit their evil in the moral order.

> The positon taken herein (and I believe in the best of the Christian tradition) is that there is a priority or normativity to heterosexual acts and relationships that cannot be dismissed in any theology of homosexuality... Homosexual acts always involve a significant degree of ontic evil because of their lack of openness to procreation and to the man/woman relationship as it functions in marriage...There are cases in which the ontic evil of homosexual acts does not become an objective moral evil because in the circumstances germane to these cases it is truly proportionate for the homosexual acts to be posited...These acts are ontically evil in what they lack, but not morally evil in the actual concrete totality in which they exist.[13]

Unlike Harvey's either/or approach which attempts to preserve the incommensurability of good and evil in the objective order, Keane describes a social context in which an ambiguous gray moral world can be related to a firm conviction about the difference between moral value and moral disvalue, between that which is meant to be and that which is only tolerated.

On the one hand, Keane employs natural law languate to indicate the priority of marriage and openness to procreation as the basic presupposition for all evaluations of sexual conduct. On the other hand, he wants to allow for the diversity present in a human world fractured by sin. Thus, even though homosexual relationships can never adequately realize the highest Christian sexual values, in some instances the degree of moral guilt attached to them is considerably reduced, or possibly even balanced off. From Keane's point of view, the subjective factors of the person's concrete situation must always be taken into account before an accurate assessment can be given of the moral evil involved.

The distinction between ontic evil (described solely in terms of the objective, pregiven structure of human createdness) and moral evil (described relative to all of the subjective, inter-personal, and temporal factors as well) has become a popular methodological distinction in recent Catholic moral theology.[14] It is one way that natural law thinkers have tried to preserve the objectivity of morality without succumbing to an implicit legalism which neglects the uniqueness and irreducibility of each person and of the significance of the motives, intentions and consequences which accrue to moral decision-making. Those who are comfortable with this type of distinction will find Keane's exposition helpful.[15] But others will want to challenge either the normativity of heterosexual marriage as a starting point or the acceptability of stable homosexual unions as a proper accommodation to the sinful human condition.

A final instance of natural law argumentation appears in the Declaration on Sexual Ethics which was issued by the Vatican Sacred Congregation for the Doctrine of the Faith in 1975. As an official response to the controversy over sexual ethics that had broken out after the Second Vatican Council, the Declaration tried to combine tradition doctrine which pastoral sensitivity. In

222

the key passage of the section on homosexuality,
it says,

> In the pastoral fields, these
> homosexuals must certainly be
> treated with understanding and
> sustained in the hope of over-
> coming their personal difficulties
> and their inability to fit into
> society. Their culpability will
> be judged with prudence...For
> according to the objective moral
> order, homosexual relations are
> acts which lack an essential and
> indispensable finality. In Sacred
> Scripture they are condemned as a
> serious depravity and even pre-
> sents as the sad consequence of
> rejecting God. This judgment of
> Scripture does not of course
> permit us to conclude that all
> those who suffer from this anomaly
> are personally responsibile for
> it, but it does attest to the fact
> that homosexual acts are intrin-
> sically disordered and can in no
> case be approved.[16]

This sort of presentation is really in the
form of an argument from authority and consequently is much stronger on assertion than on
argumentation. But ultimately, it presupposes the
validity of the traditional position of the
Catholic Church on homosexuality. The intent is
not to say anything new but to counteract the
tendency to consider the older approach outdated
or controverted by new evidence.

(b) Criticisms of the Natural Law Argument

Despite its longevity as an stablished metho-
dolgy for ethical analysis, natural law theory is
not without its critics, both within and without
the Roman Catholic tradition.[17] It has been
accused of being static and unhistorical,

philosophically inconsistent, excessively physicalist, and preoccupied with negative moral absolutes.

In response to this challenge, defenders of natural law have attempted to reexpress its claims in language that is more general, biblically-informed, personalist and developmental. This modified version of natural law is more concerned with describing the fundamental structures of human existence than with specifying the proper form of moral conduct in an interlocking series of propositions. Only if human actors know their ontological limits will their efforts at creativity be capable of realization. Any form of endeavor which violates these natural paramenters will be destructive of basic human values no matter what level of success seems to have been achieved.

In the area of sexuality, the biggest problem for natural law theories is how to preserve the heterosexual-marital-procreative paradigm once the procreative component is minimized. Contemporary discussion of the issue of contraception has brought this difficulty to the surface.[18] There has been a progressive deemphasis on the pro-creative end of marriage from the time of St. Augustine to the Second Vatican Council. Even Pope Paul VI in Humanae vitae assumed the parity of the procreative and unitive ends of marriage. But the real stumbling-block comes when Catholic and Protestant ethicists declare that every act of sexual intercourse does not have to be open to the possibility of fertilization and that there are legitimate reasons for foresaking this goal either temporarily or more permanently through sterili-zation. Once this shift in the orientation of the heterosexual couple takes place, it can be asked how their situation differs from that of the homo-sexual couple.

John McNeill makes bold to challenge the viability of the traditional natural law teaching on these very grounds. He says,

From the moment the Church granted
the morality of the rhythm method,
for example, as a natural form of
birth control, and justified
sexual activity as still
fulfilling the 'secondary' aims of
mutual love and fulfillment, there
was a serious reason to reconsider
the traditional position that all
homosexual activities are necessarily wrong on the ground that
they cannot lead to procreation.[1]

But McNeill does not rest content with this formulation of his challenge to the traditional
teaching. He goes on to claim,

The genuine homosexual's situation
is more comparable factually to
that of a heterosexual couple
incapable of having children than,
for example, to the situation of
those who practice birth control,
since it is not through a free
choice within their control that
homosexuals eliminate the possibility of procreation from their
sexual life.[20]

I think that a natural law rejoinder to
McNeill's criticism would run along the following
lines. Those who consider artificial contraception to be immoral would preserve the notion of
genital finality and argue that utilization of
infertile periods in the menstrual cycle does not
violate the procreative intent. However, those
who allow for conscientious choice of artificial
contraceptive means would want to separate the
morality of the overall procreative disposition of
the marital couple from the requirement that each
act of sexual intercourse fully express this
intent. Thus, for example, openness to fertility
would be only one of the possible goods in a
marital relationship. Its complete absence would
seriously call into question the status of the

225

sacramental bond. But there could be a wide range of reasons why, for periods of time, it would not be evident in the sexual act itself. Further, it could be argued that the fertility of the marital relationship could be adequately realized by the adoption of children and/or by a life of dedicated service to others. In these cases, the symbolism of the heterosexual genital act would be upheld even though in a more indirect and non-biological fashion. The key difference in the homosexual situation would be that the genital acts that focus and express a particular homosexual relationship would never symbolize at the proper level of enbodied meaning the procreative goals of the partners.

I think that McNeill's point is well taken, yet it does not require that we accept his conclusions. It is still possible to defend the morality of some instances of contraceptive behavior without equating the situation of the deliberately infertile couple with that of the homosexual couple. What is ruled out in this natural law explanation is the permanent, deliberate absence of any procreative dimension to the relationship. However, we might describe such a heterosexual pairing, it would not, in Christian terms, be a marriage. In contrast, the problem with homosexual sexual sharing is that, even with all the best intentions, the acts themselves cannot achieve either the creation of another human being or the effective symbolization of such a possibility.

Proper reflection on the essential dimensions of the natural law argument disallows the kind of claim that some homosexual spokespersons sometimes make that homosexuality is 'natural' for those with that particular orientation. They claim that to ask such people to seek a heterosexual adjustment or to refuse to grant then the moral right to engage in homosexual acts of any kind is tantamount to requiring them to act 'unnaturally.' The logic of this homosexual apologia in natural

226

law terms could be expressed, 'This is what I am, therefore this is how I should be able to act.'

What this sort of appeal does is to collapse the full dimensions of the sexual possibility into a matter of attraction and erotic drive. There is in the human species a wide varity of sexual objects toward which certain kinds of people are inclined. In addition to the basic heterosexual alternative and the genital homosexual relationship, some percentage of the race would prefer to act out with children, animals, inanimate objects, corpses and, if they could, themselves. While we may classify many of these conditions as a sign of mental instability or illness, there is no contradicting the fact that for the persons involved, a certain kind of natural disposition is at work. Because such sexual propensities are in need of a fuller analysis relative to some theory of sexual fulfillment, we hesitate to consider them 'natural' in the sense of appropriate or happiness-inducing or reasonable. The natural law thinker says the same kind of thing to the homosexual. What the homosexual advocate proposes is only natural in a restricted sense of the term. The choice about the specifics of one's life as a sexual being should take into account the experience and wisdom of the whole human community which has persistently refused to consider non-generative sexual relationship a proper realization of the natural species-affirming sexual finality.

Having examined the current criticisms of traditional natural law theory as applied to homosexuality, I would like to examine the modified version of natural law as illustrated in the work of Philip Keane and others. These authors make the claim that there is a significant difference between ontic evil and moral evil. Homosexuality alway partakes in ontic evil, but in some limited contexts, the degree of moral evil may be considerably reduced or perhaps not existent at all.

The advantage of this distinction is that it seems to preserve a consistent moral theory while at the same time allowing for compassionate pastoral latitude. There is always something missing in homosexual activity. But since some homosexuals are at least trying to make the most of an abbreviated range of possibilities, we should encourage them to incorporate as many Christian values into their relationship as they are capable of embodying. We judge the act (in a general way) but remain agnostic about the moral status of the well-meaning participant.

It seems to me that the central weakness of this version of natural law is that it weakens the teleological (end-oriented) dimension of the description of human sexuality without enhancing the deontological (rule-guided) dimension. In other words, once it is posited that homosexual persons need not be expected to achieve pro-creative ends, it is progressively more difficult to arrive at standards by which the exchange of pleasure between the partners in a homosexual relationship can be tested for depth and authen-ticity. Formerly, we fell back on norms such as the following -- marriage should be exclusive and permanent because this is the best way to provide a stable and loving home in which children can be raised to maturity. The teleological criterion functioned to help articulate deontological principles and rules. The trouble is that once the clarity about the proper end of a particular kind of sexual relationship (e.g., the homosexual couple) is uncertain (and this is what seems to happen in an ontically-evil but morally good homo-sexual situation) then the normative principles and rules become excessively arbitrary and undifferentiated.

Keane himself is extremely chary of allowing his formulation to be used to support Church cele-bration of homosexual relationships (as in marriage) or to promote a change in civil law to permit adoption of children by homosexual couples.[21] But I do not see why this reserve has

228

to follow from Keane's moral distinctions. As long as some overt homosexual relationships can be free of moral evil then it is not clear why either Church or society should feel constrained to prohibit a full exercise of the couples' prerogatives. Such considerations make me wonder how helpful the distinction between ontic evil and moral evil really is when applied to homosexual behavior.

(c) The Argument from Psychological Symbolization

Most versions of a natural law prohibition against homosexuality concentrate on the physical structure of the sex act and its ability to establish a procreative context for love-making. Even those proponents who allow for a moral use of contraceptive intervention want to highlight the ultimate centrality of the physical complementarity of man and woman. Just as the sperm and the egg can fuse to create a new being so these unique persons of separate gender identity can become 'one flesh.'

The argument to be discussed in this section resembles the natural law approach (and in many ways it makes the same kind of primordial structural claim). However, in this case the stress is on the psychological relatedness between the sexes.

Ruth Tiffany Barnhouse, whom I have discussed in the chapter on psychological theories, brings together a Jungian psychoanalytic framework with certain normative judgments about the proper kinds of sexual participation. For her, homosexuality involves a retarded stage of psychological development. It is a form of immaturity. In this, it is not unlike other kinds of personal immaturity. But to project it as a normal alternate lifestyle is to go against the evidence.

229

Out of this psychological perspective, Barnhouse fashions an ethical position which she thinks does justice to the demands of the Christian Gospel. According to her,

> the true religious goal of human sexuality can thus be seen not as satisfaction, but as completeness. Without this goal of completeness, satisfaction pursued as an end-in-itself deteriorates into lust.[22]

She goes on to relate this understanding of need for integration of opposites to certain Christian conceptions of God.

> The wholeness of the sacred order is neither symbolized nor approximated by sexual practices which are thus grounded in the denial of half of the image of God. Some measure of physical or partial emotional satisfaction may be achieved but the Christian goal of completeness is not.[23]

Ultimately, according to Barnhouse, homosexuality is a symbolic confusion.

A second commentator, Michael Novak, also argues in terms of symbolization. He says,

> What is at stake in the argument over homosexuality is the value we place upon sexuality....Overt homosexual acts, even in the context of permanent commitment and perfect mutuality, do not symbolize this Catholic sense of earthiness and harmony...They represent, at best, the overflow of friendship -- the expression of friendship through sexual demonstrativeness.[24]

230

Novak thinks that more is at stake in our reponse
to the platform of the gay liberationists than
first meets the eye. "'Gay liberation' is not a
form of genuine liberation, not a form of human
progress. It is one more false god, one more
false prophecy, against which it our vocation to
offer the dignity of resistance".[25]

Thus Novak and Barnhouse agree that the
central issue is whether homosexual love-making
can effectively symbolize the kind of completeness
and harmony that is part of the Christian vision
of creation and reconciliation. In a disjointed
world, where even our sexual differentiation is a
sign of contradiction, we are held out a promise
that the many can become one, that opposition can
turn into a transcendent unity and peace. Heterosexual intercourse (under the proper conditions)
can both effect a semblance of such unity and
foreshadow the fuller experience that is yet to be
achieved.[26]

A third version of this basic argument
appears in an essay by William Muehl. He considers the traditional Christian reluctance to
ratify homosexual conduct as based on a community
perception that momentary experiences of pleasure
and overarching appeals to a loving will are not
sufficient to validate sexual relations between
persons of the same gender. People can be hurt in
slow and subtle ways. Indeed, hatred and
agression can for a time resemble the ecstasy of
true love. Christians have yet to discover what
it is that is symbolized by the homosexual
partnership. Until they do and until they are
convinced that this is compatible with Christian
values, they will beg off celebrating the bond.
By way of a summary statement, Muehl gives the
following assessment.

> Homosexuality ought not to be
> treated as the manifestation of
> some special depravity whose
> practitioners should be driven
> from the church and harassed

231

at law. But neither can it be defined as an appropriate expression of Christian love in interpersonal terms. The gay relationship is one form of sexual irresponsibility among many and no more reprehensible than most.[27]

(d) Criticisms of the Psychological Symbolization Argument

The first point in dealing with the issue of sexual symbolization is divorcing this approach from any particular psychological school. You do not have to be a Jungian (as Barnhouse is) to recognize a kind of transcultural referent in the uniting of male and female. In many religious traditions, the sexual congress of gods and godesses is presented as the source of the created order. And this archetypal act is replicated in temple rites where female prostitutes are available to the petitioning adherent. Fertility of the crops and animal life, a proper regulation of the seasons, and the balance of sun and moisture are often correlated with some operative principle which is explained in sexual terms.

In the Judaeo-Christian tradition God is a faithful husband who continues to welcome back his unfaithful wife (as in the story of Hosea and Comer). And Christ is the bridegroom who takes the Church as his bride. The imagery of the 5th Chapter of Ephesians correlates the Christ-Church relationship with the human bond of heterosexual marriage. Nowhere in the Scriptures is God or Jesus depicted as a homosexual lover or is same sex friendship considered to be able to effectively convey the intimacy of the religious relationship. As John Noonan so insightfully argues,

No homosexual is a hero in either Testament. David can be an adulterer, repent, and be forgiven. But no prophet, priest

232

or king of Israel is stigmatized
as a sodomite. In the New
Testament Jesus selects a band of
men to live with him, to be his
followers, to become his friends,
to share his most intimate love.
No one who has read these passages
describing Jesus and his friends
can suppose that homosexual
genital acts are permitted in his
circle... This primordial
Christian fellowship offers a
pattern that has been repeated for
nineteen hunred years--intimacy
between persons of the same sex
without a genital relation.

Ultimately, genital sex is the social symbol
of the union of opposites, of the integration of
the unlike. Starting with the obvious difference
between male and female genitalia, as well as
their suitability for complementary sexual
activity, the human race seems to have abstracted
from this physical giveness to allow (in story and
song) the sexual distinction to serve as a symbol
for the deep human drive to maintain individuality
and separateness at the same time that fusion and
mutual transcendence are acheived.

In a way, there is no counter argument which
can disqualify the structure of meaning of this
social symbol for those who recognize it. Could
not the male-male or female-female union do the
same thing? Perhaps, but most people seem to be
unable to recognize such a resonance in their
experience. It has been pointed out that same-sex
friendships seem easier to establish and maintain
through most stages of life than other-sex friendships. This may be a function of cultural traditions, but I suspect that the genital component
of the relationship is the prime determinant. In
same-sex groups, the sexual dimension of the
relationships is minimized and therefore many
sources of tension and competitiveness are
defused. However, once genital possibilities are

233

raised in same-sex groups, the dynamics are considerably altered. Every decision about friendship is also a decision about the fuller possibility of sexual intimacy. Despite the critics of marriage who see it as a bourgeois invention, many married people know a new sense of personal freedom in relating to both men and women. The spousal sharing provides for one level of need, but the whole range of non-genital relationships with others is often equally important.

Like mated to like seems too commonplace and easy of achievement to capture the yearning of the species for completion and fulfillment. If, as some suggest, the homosexual genital act is an exercise in narcissism it would constitute not a symbol of extension and mutual expression but a monadic abuse of the other as object. But even if this is not the case, the very similarity between the participants, not only the physical resemblance but the psychic, would seem to breed boredom and dissatisfaction. It seems that only the mystery of the other, especially when rooted in gender specificity, can sustain the ongoing task of self-giving and mutual domestic responsibility.

I am persuaded that the argument from psychological symbolization is a powerful one. It is based upon certain physiological realities, but it goes beyond these to describe male and female in the fuller dimension of their contrapuntal existence. The effective union of opposites in heterosexual intercourse symbolizes the human and religious desire for shared intimacy in a way that same sex genitality is not able to. Those who think that such symbols can be facilely transposed run counter to the available evidence.

(e) The Analogy with Alcoholism

A third type of argument about homosexuality compares it with certain destructive human propensities, such as various sorts of addictive behavior.[29] Homosexuality has in common with these addictive states, it is asserted, the following characteristics: the causal explanations are controverted; the accusation of sinful conduct seems unable to effect a change; and most people cannot overcome their difficulty without outside help. In each of these dilemmas, it is presumed that genuine happiness is only possible after the conduct in question is brought under control.

The analogy with alcoholism and other addictive patterns presupposes that there is something both deficient and destructive in the relatedness abilities of most homosexuals. As long as they immerse themselves in the gay subculture, they will be aware of no better alternative. But if they can only step back and take a closer look at themselves, a clearer judgment can be made about how their sexual orientation can be properly directed. To achieve this goal, personal counseling and support groups are essential components in a therapeutic process. The aim is not so much effecting a 'cure' as it is abstaining from promiscuous sexual activity. Just as it is critical that the alcoholic be able to admit his or her alcoholism in a public way, so the homosexual must make the same transition. The more deeply rooted the urge to homosexual behavior, the longer the process of personal adjustment will probably take.

In the Christian context, such an approach tries to avoid moralism at the same time that it defends the final call to moral responsibility on the part of the homosexual. It says, 'Even though you cannot change who you are as a sexual being, you can organize your life in such a way that the Christian values of chastity and self-giving love are more effectively realized.' It holds out continence as a manageable goal, but only when the broader need for personal and social support is provided for.

(f) Criticisms of the Alcoholism Analogy

The main weakness of the alcoholism analogy is that it promotes a sickness model of interpretation of the homosexual condition. As I indicated in Chapter 6, while some homosexuals may be mentally ill, I do not think that this is typical. In fact, some homosexuals may be blessed with a fairly high level of personal functioning. In addition, homosexual behavior does not seem to be any more compulsive than heterosexual behavior. Some homosexuals have a strong sex drive and some do not. Some homosexuals can remain continent for long period of time (even out of personal, nonmoral motivation) and some cannot. Homosexuality does not seem to be so much an addiction as a self-conscious way of relating to others. While I think that there is considerable evidence to prove that the homosexual way is more difficult and less fulfilling for a higher percentage of participants than the heterosexual way, I do not wish to overlook the positive features of some instances of homosexual adjustment.

The big difference between homosexuality and alcoholism is that homosexuals have a greater degree of freedom in fashioning their style of sexual behavior than alcoholics do in handling intoxicating beverages. However, the healthy homosexual is not one who indulges his or her erotic desires moderately, but (in the Christian context) one who forsakes genital expressiveness for other kinds of relatedness. To this extent, there are some obvious parallels with the nondrinking alcoholic. Yet, it is more helpful, in my opinion, to focus the discussion on Christian ethical criteria which presuppose a relative freedom of self-disposition than on sickness criteria which are arbitrary and very much culturally-conditioned.

III. Conclusion

The contemporary defenders of the traditional Christian prohibition of homosexual behavior have

gone in three main directions. As I pointed out
in the last chapter, one group, mainly Protestant,
argue in terms of a textual and thematic reading
of Scripture. From Karl Barth to Carl Henry they
assert that the Genesis account of creation
reveals the fundamental importance of the male-
female covenant of marriage as the prototype of
all sexual relatedness. The specific condemnations that are found in both the Old and New
Testaments (context-dependent that they might be)
are still witnesses to the firmly held opinion of
the Judaeo-Christian community. This teaching
admits of no change because it is a form of
revelation describing the constitutive order of
God's universe, including the function of
sexuality within it.

A second group, mainly Catholic, offer
various formulations of natural law theory to
highlight the significance of the procreative
dimension of sexual intercourse. They reason from
a particular understanding of genital finality to
the need for stable structures of ongoing com-
mittedness.

The third group appeals to a common experience of sexual symbolization. The masculine-
feminine polarity of sexual differentiation (and
the concomitant desire to achieve union between
opposites) is so basic that the loving act of
heterosexual intercourse in a context of faithful
relatedness is the best image we have for
expressing the deepest human yearnings. No same
sex pairing is able to adequately represent this
same transcendent aspiration.

Finally, a fourth approach draws upon the
analogy with alcoholism to picture homosexuality
as self-destructive on psychological grounds.
Here it is more a matter of sickness rather than
of moral fault. When homosexuality is considered
an addictive illness rather than a freely chosen
sexual life style, the proper therapeutic route is
abstinence.

237

Each of these positions has its defenders and critics. I have found the sexual symbolization argument the most persuasive, although I think there is merit in some modified natural law positions as well. I suspect that the arguments from authority which simply refer to these views without arguing consistently from them will not carry the day in the Christian discussion of this issue.

Footnotes for Chapter 9

¹The best reviews of the historical material may be found in: Arno Karlen, Sexuality and Homosexuality: A New View (New York: W.W. Norton, 1971); D.S. Bailey, Homosexuality and the Western Christian Tradition (London: Longmans, Green and Co., 1955); and John McNeill, The Church and the Homosexual (Kansas City: Sheed Andrews and McMeel, 1976).

²Tertullian, De. pucic, iv; John Chrysostom, In epist. ad Rom., iv and In epist. ad Tit, v.4; Justin, I Apol. xxvii; Eusebius, Theoph. ii, 81 Demonstr. evang. iv, 10; Lactantius, Instit., v, 9; Salvian, De gubernat. Dei, vii, 7; Augustine, Confessions, viii, 1-15 and City of God, III, xvi, 30.

³Epist. Barn., x, 8.

⁴Bailey, loc. cit., p. 85.

⁵Ibid., p. 102.

⁶Summa Theologica, II-II, q. 153 art. 2, q. 154 arts 1, 11 and 12.

⁷Bailey, loc. cit., p. 136.

⁸Cf. John Harvey, "Homosexuality as a Pastoral Problem," Theological Studies, 16, 1955, pp. 86-108; "Homosexuality," The New Catholic Encyclopedia, vol. 7, 1967, pp. 116-119; "Morality and Pastoral Treatment of Homosexuality," Continuum, 5, 1967, pp. 279-297; "The Controversy Concerning the Psychology and Morality of Homosexuality," American Ecclesiastical Review, 1678, 1973, pp. 602-629.

⁹John Harvey, "Morality and Pastoral Treatment of Homosexuality p. 289.

[10]John Harvey, "Pastoral Responses to Gay World Questions," in Is Gay Good?, edited by W. Dwight Oberholtzer (Philadelphia: Westminster, 1971), pp. 134-135.

[11]Philip Keane, Sexual Morality: A Catholic Perspective (New York: Paulist, 1977).

[12]Ibid., p. 80.

[13]Ibid., p. 87.

[14]For a fuller discussion of the issues involved, see: Richard McCormick, Ambiguity in Moral Choice (Milwaukee: Marquette U. Press, 1973); Peter Knauer, "The Hermeneutical Function of the Principle of Double Effect," Natural Law Forum, 12, 1967, pp. 136-162; Cornelius Van der Poel, "The Principle of Double Effect," in Absolutes in Moral Theology, edited by Charles Curran (Washington: Corpus, 1968), pp. 286-210; Joseph Fuchs, "The Absoluteness of Moral Terms," Gregorianum, 52, 1971, pp. 415-458; Donald Evans, "Paul Ramsey on Exceptionless Moral Rules," The American Journal of Jurisprudence, 16, 1971, pp. 184-214; Richard McCormick, "Norms and Conscience," Theological Studies, 38, 1977, pp. 70-84; Louis Janssens, "Norms and Priorities in a Love Ethic," Louvain Studies, 6, 1977, pp. 207-238.

[15]Lawrence Reilly employs the same terminology as Keane when he says, "Even though homosexuality is an ontic evil and homosexual acts usually have disproportionate amount of ontic evil, homosexual persons are not evil persons...There are circumstances -- perhaps more common than we were wont to believe in the past -- in which the ontic good of a stable homosexual union outweighs the ontic evil inherent in the union." In "A New Sexuality? Reaction to John McNeill's 'The Church and the Homosexual,'" Louvain Studies, 6, 1977, pp. 297-298.

[16]Sacred Congregation for the Doctrine of the Faith, _Declaration on Sexual Ethics_ (Washington: USCC, 1975).

[17]For a fuller discussion of this matter, see my article: "The Problem of Methodology in Contemporary Roman Catholic Ethics," _St. Luke's Journal of Theology_, 22/1, 1978, pp. 20-42, esp. pp. 20-25; Also see: Michael Crowe, "The Pursuit of Natural Law," _Irish Theological Quarterly_, 44, 1977, pp. 3-29.

[18]There is a huge literature on contraception. I would especially recommend: John Noonan, _Contraception_ (New York: Mentor, 1965); Charles Curran (ed.), Contraception: _Authority and Dissent_ (New York: Herder & Herder, 1969); Daniel Callahan (ed.), _The Catholic Case for Contraception_ (New York: Macmillan, 1969); Norbert Rigali, "The Historical Meaning of the Humanea Vitae Controversy," _Chicago Studies_, 15, 1976, pp. 127-138 and 16, 1977, pp. 299-308; Joseph Selling, "Moral Teaching, Traditional Teaching and Humanae Vitae," _Louvain Studies_, 7, Spring '78, pp. 24-44; and John C. Ford and Germain Grisez, "Contraception and the Infallibility of the Ordinary Magisterium," _Theological Studies_, 39, 1978, pp. 258-312.

[19]John McNeill, _loc. cit._, p. 100.

[20]_Ibid._, p. 101.

[21]Keane, _loc. cit._, p. 89.

[22]Ruth Tiffany Barnhouse, _Homosexuality: A Symbolic Confusion_ (New York: Seabury, 1977), p. 172.

[23]_Ibid._, p. 174.

[24]Michael Novak, "Gay Is Not Liberation," _Commonweal_, 100, 1974, p. 304.

[25]_Ibid._, p. 319.

[26]Gerald Coleman states the case in similar language. "Homosexual union cannot fulfill this masculine/feminine mutuality, although I have no doubt that there can be homosexual unions that have beauty and mutual commitment and are spiritual in motive...The homosexual encounter is inevitably a confrontation of two like personalities with no hope of ultimate oneness through sharing what is opposite but complementary. Thus it is probably more accurate to speak of a Homosexual _pair_ rather than a homosexual _couple_...'a pair of friends.' In _Homosexuality -- An Appraisal_ (Chicago: Franciscan Herald, 1973), p.

[27]William Muehl, "Some Words of Caution," in _Homosexuality and the Christian Faith: A Symposium_, edited by Harold Twiss (Valley Forge: Judson, 1978), pp. 86-87.

[28]From a soon to be published essay titled "Genital Good."

[29]William Muehl, for example, defends the validity of this comparison. Cf., "Some Words of Caution," p. 82. I have heard this analogy used many times in public discussions of homosexuality.

Chapter 10

The Ethical Revisionists: Arguments for the Moral

Acceptability of the Homosexual Way of Life

Among all the calls for reform of Christian sexual morality, the most emotion-laden one of all may be the advocacy of the moral legitimacy of adult homosexual relationships. How could such a universally-held and long-lived Christian ethical teaching be the subject of any doubt? Can a change in such a fundamental teaching really be the goal of anyone who wishes to take the Gospel seriously? There are some thinkers in both the Protestant and Catholic Churches who have indeed argued that a reformulation of the Christian teaching on this matter is long overdue. But there is quite a bit of variety in the form of their argumentation and in the degree to which they think the condemnation of homosexual acts can be lifted.

I will divide this chapter into two major sections. In the first, I will present the opinions of the so-called moderate revisionists. Most of these theologians are concerned with developing an ethic for homosexual relationships which resembles that applied to heterosexual couples. In the second section, I will deal with the radical revisionists. These theorists consider the Christian sexual ethic to be no longer tenable and they proceed to offer various alternatives.

I. The Moderate Revisionists--

This group of thinkers have in common that they are prepared to modify what they take to be the excessive rigor of the Christian ethical teaching on homosexuality. At the same time, they do not wish to abandon the central values of the Christian sexual ethic. In various ways, they modify the traditional judgment, but remain under its central influence. For the sake of convenient exposition, I have divided them into four main categories.

244

(a) <u>Homosexuality as a linguistic problem</u>--

As I illustrated in Chapter 1, the language of homosexuality is sometimes elusive. There is no conceptual definition of what constitutes homosexuality that has won general acceptance. As a result, it is possible to so alter the traditional meaning of words that a common frame of reference becomes more difficult. Just as the term 'love' can be debased by being applied to personal response to inanimate objects and products, so the term 'homosexual' can be made to refer to all same sex emotional interaction.

In a widely read book that focuses on the psychological dynamics of committed celibate relationships, Donald Goergen devotes a chapter to the problem of homosexual feelings and genital arousal patterns. He begins by acknowledging that he will employ a familiar vocabulary in an unconventional way.

> Heterosexual and homosexual relationships are two kinds of interpersonal relationships. I am using the word homosexual here in a positive way and in a way different from its ordinary usage. I distinguish between healthy and unhealthy homosexual relation-ships, but I do not consider the word <u>homosexual</u> to necessarily imply <u>that which</u> in itself is unhealthy.[1]

The reason this is so is because homosexual relationships are not, of necessity, homogenital relationships. What Goergen wants to suggest is that men and women need to be open to same-sex relationships (which will always have some erotic dimension) as well as opposite-sex relationships. A healthy individual should be capable of both kinds of relatedness. What would be pathological for a homosexually-oriented person would be the

245

blocking of heterosexual affective relationships altogether.

From this relatively uncontroversial starting point, Goergen goes on the employ his terminology is such an ambiguous way that it is not clear what he intends to express. For example, he says,

> Homosexual friendships are an important dimension of any person's life. Celibate homosexuality, in the positive sense of that word, remains nongenital. . . Friendship between people of the same sex involves affective and erotic aspects. Limitations need to be placed on homosexual friendships lest they too become genital.[2]

What this seems to mean is that homosexual individuals who have a vowed commitment to a celibate life should exercise the same restraint as heterosexual celibates. With this, there is little argument. But it could also mean that, in the absence of such a formal self-engagement, it is desirable that same sex friendships include a genital dimension. This latter interpretation is reinforced by the absence of any ethical analysis in Goergen's book and by one cryptic sentence where he allows the matter to rest. "The so-called traditional Christian attitude towards homosexuality is beginning to change. There is pluralism in this regard. . ."[3] Surely, there is pluralism. But what remains in doubt is whether Goergen's deliberate shift in definition of standard vocabulary does not contribute to the confusion.

Goergen has made the word 'homosexual' mean so many things that we cannot be sure where he comes out ethically. This difficulty is compounded by his focus on the situation of religious celibates. For if those who have foresworn genital involvement with either sex are encouraged

to pursue the affective dimension of all relationships indiscriminately, how much more might
homosexually-oriented non-celibates feel so
inclined.

If Goergen remains unsatisfactory because of
all the questions he leaves unanswered, Roger
Shinn can be included in this category because he
thinks the methodological uncertainty makes any
answer extremely restricted in its applicability.[4]

Shinn believes that Christian judgments on
matters of human conduct and behavior are mutable,
especially when our knowledge of the factors
involved becomes more precise and trustworthy.
Most contemporary dilemmas are more complex than a
biblical fundamentalism or an uncritical devotion
to received tradition would allow for. There are
no automatic answers available. Therefore, in
those cases where our present-day knowledge is
insufficient (and thus where our linguistic
categories are deficient), we must humbly accept
our limitations and not pretend to have more
certainty than we do.

For Shinn, however, "the renunciation of an
ethic of condemnation has not led to an ethic of
endorsement."[5] Heterosexual love continues to
have a normative place in Christian theology. Yet
there is always the possibility that authentic
sexuality and genuine love may appear in other
forms of sexual relationship. No legal boundaries
can be exhaustively set out.

There is a great deal of hedging in such a
formulation of the problem. Shinn wants neither
to ratify nor to condemn apodictally homosexual
love. His alternative is to speak in muted tones
with full recognition of the diversity of extant
opinion in the social scientific judgment,
although his basic sympathies are with the tradition.

(b) <u>Homosexuality as a questionable condition</u>
<u>which can be responsibly structured</u>--

In a highly nuanced theological presentation,
Helmut Thielicke has spoken of the homosexual
situation as contrary to the order of creation but
capable of being raised to the point where
ethically responsible decision-making is possible.
He begins by laying out his theological anthropology.

> For biblical thinking and the
> Christian thinking which follows
> biblical thought, it is impossible
> to think of homosexuality as
> having no ethical significance, as
> being a mere 'vagary' or 'sport'
> of nature. The fundamental order
> of creation and the created
> determination of the two sexes
> makes it appear justifiable to
> speak of homosexuality as a
> perversion'. . .(it) implies no
> moral depreciation. . .it is used
> purely theologically in the sense
> that homosexuality is in every
> case <u>not</u> in accord with the order
> of creation. . .In this sense
> homosexuality falls on the same
> level with abnormal personality
> structure (psychopathy), disease,
> suffering, and pain, which like-
> wise are generally understood in
> the Bible as being contrary to
> God's will in creation.[6]

Because there is something deficient in the homosexual's very makeup, he or she must be willing to
undergo therapy if this has any promise of
success. The goal would be to reintegrate the
person into the order; as a heterosexual being.

But Thielicke is realistic enough to
recognize that some percentage of homosexually
active individuals may be incapable of change. If

that is the case, then the question remains of
what kind of counsel the Church might be able to
give such people. He says,

> Perhaps the best way to formulate
> the ethical problem of the
> constitutional homosexual, who
> because of his vitality is not
> able to practice abstinence, is to
> ask whether within the
> coordinating system of his con-
> stitution he is willing to struc-
> ture the man-man relationship in
> an <u>ethically responsible</u> way.[7]

Thielicke thinks that several factors work against
this taking place. First, there is no supportive
context like marriage. Second, the prevalence of
promiscuity in the homosexual world is a handicap.
Third, being part of an outcast group brings one
in contact with people of questionable character.
And finally, the threat of discovery creates a
degree of personal tension.

Notwithstanding these inhibiting features of
gay life, Thielicke does not want to rule out some
positive Christian standing for the ethically
sensitive homosexuals. His concluding opinion is
expressed in the following way.

> The 'homosexual constitution'
> lived within the limits we have
> defined, is not even to be
> <u>ethically</u> disqualified <u>a limine</u>
> but is capable of realizing rela-
> tive ethical values within the
> questionable framework of this
> disposition and it is possible for
> it to be a relative ethical order,
> even though in principal it is
> contrary to the order of creation
> (understood in the theological
> sense!).[8]

Thielicke's theological-ethical methodology is very Lutheran in its orientation. As the most prolific of modern moralists, he has subjected a wide range of issues to analysis with a 'two kingdoms,' 'law-Gospel' framework. In his tentative response to the dilemma of confirmed homosexuals, he tries to allow some room for the Gospel to penetrate through to this component of the fractured human community. Since the full Word cannot be heard without significant healing (and this is not possible in the here and now), a partial Word will have to suffice. Justification is never a human achievement so even the well-intentioned heterosexual (operating within the order of marriage) must struggle to disentangle the purity of the Word directed to them from their fragmented experience of personal sexual responsibility.

Is such a description of the homosexual condition going to win adherents? Thielicke seems to consider homosexuals as second-class citizens in the Christian community with a considerably less demanding ethic as their moral lot. To some this position will seem patronizing and offensive. To others it will seem a reduction of the full Gospel demand which is addressed to all human creatures equally. Thielicke has tried to adapt the tradition in such a way that attributions of personal sin (as contrasted with participating in a sin disturbed condition) would not necessarily accrue to all homosexuals. I doubt that many will find his formulation satisfactory.

A second theologian who argues in basically the same mode as Thielicke is H. Kimball Jones.[9] He asserts that the heterosexual disposition is the God-intended state of nature. A relationship of love between a man and a woman is the only way to completely fulfill their sexual needs. As for homosexual persons, they must first of all appreciate that they are loved by God. Then they must order their lives in such a way that this love can be somehow reflected in their relationships.

The two routes traditionally suggested by the Church for the homosexual, namely, continence and sublimation, have proven inadequate. What is needed is a bolder response. And this is what Jones proposes.

> We suggest that the Church must be willing to make the difficult, but necessary, step of recognizing the validity of mature homosexual relationships, encouraging the absolute invert to maintain fidelity to one partner when his only other choice would be to lead a promiscuous life filled with guilt and fear. This would by no means be an endorsement of homosexuality by the Church.[10]

Against the possible charge that this would glorify the homosexual way of life, Jones responds.

> However creative and fulfilling it may be (and it may be quite creative and fulfilling), it nevertheless remains an unnatural expression of human sexuality. . . The problem here is one of distinguishing between acceptance and sanction.[11]

The similarity between Thielicke's position and Jone's should be evident. But it comes to light even clearer when Jones sums up his ethical judgment of how the homosexual person might be embraced by the Church.

> Consequently, we assert that the homosexual who cannot change must be accepted for what he is and encouraged to live responsibly within his given sexuality; at the same time, we should surely see his position as being unenviable

251

and his way of life as one not to
be recommended as being desirable. . .He is a sexually-
handicapped person, and there is
no getting around this; but, by
the grace of God, his handicap can
become a creative force in his
life.[12]

The balance and pastoral sensitivity of this
type of approach is surely appealing. It seems to
give the Church breathing room and time to rethink
the long-range implications of a change in
teaching. It is not condemnatory of individuals
but only of certain ways of living out one's homosexuality. Yet as a final solution it is
inadequate because it begs the question of what
'responsible homosexual living' might look like.
Presumably, it would resemble a marital commitment
pattern as Jones suggests in a later contribution.[13] But there is no attempt to estimate what
percentage of homosexuals might be capable of such
stable relationships and it gives no guidance to
those who are not. Ultimately, I have the sense
that Jones is hoping against hope that healthy
homosexuals will responsibly couple in sufficient
numbers to give the Church something to say on the
matter.

(c) Homosexuality as an instance of Christian
compromise--

Charles Curran has popularized the terminology of a 'theory of compromise.' It is designed,
in this instance, as a way of giving guidance to
those troubled by the ineffectiveness of
established Christian pastoral strategies for
ministering to the homosexual. In looking at the
various ethical options on homosexuality, Curran
suggests that there are three main approaches
taken to the issue in the recent literature. The
first group, represented by the defenders of the
tradition, see homosexual acts as intrinsically
immoral. A second group see homosexual acts as in
themselves neutral. A third group, within which

252

Curran places himself, do not celebrate such acts but on the other hand they do not always condemn them either.

According to Curran, it is the infecting power of sin which militates against the achievement of a proper sexual adjustment. The homosexual is in an anomalous position since, without personal fault, he or she is different and once this self-knowledge is gained, the range of available options is considerably reduced. It is at this point that Curran claims that the Church must have something comforting to say to such an individual. And he finds the proper word in his own theory.

> Homosexual behavior well illustrates the theory of compromise. In general, I accept the experiential data proposed by the other mediating positions. The homosexual is generally not responsible for his condition. Heterosexual marital relations remains the ideal. Therapy, as an attempt to make the homosexual into a heterosexual, does not offer great promise for most homosexuals. Celibacy and sublimation are not always possible or even desirable for the homosexual. There are many somewhat stable homosexual unions which afford their partners some human fulfillment and contentment. Obviously such unions are better than homosexual promiscuity. . .In many ways homosexuality exists as a result of sin. . .Homosexuality can never become an ideal.[14]

Several things can be said about Curran's approach. First, it will not satisfy anyone from the mainstream of the gay movement who refused to accept the imputation of a sin-wrought origin for the homosexual condition. Second, it seems to confuse ethical judgment with pastoral sensitivity. Third, it makes no attempt to probe the situation of the 'stable homosexual union.' It simply presupposes that this exists and that it is self-validating. Fourth, it overlooks the import of the traditional insight that we become that which we do. This suggests that our character is as much a product of our concrete way of acting in the world as it is a matter of purified intention. Until the form of the homosexual relationship is proven capable of realizing Christian values, it should not be presumed to be the case. Finally, it renders no explicit judgment on the wide variety of homosexual relatedness patterns outside of the stable couple.

A second theologian who moves in the direction of compromise is Ralph Weltge. Under the strong influence of Karl Barth, he forges an answer to the Church's perplexity about homosexuality which refuses to say 'yes', but in the same breath avoids uttering a definitive 'no.' In the overarching context of human existence before God, one's sexuality has a subordinate place. Therefore, to make too much of a particulaar sexual orientation is a kind of self-idolization. However, the Gospel offers guidance for all facets of life in society so that we must search for a measured response to the homosexual condition.

Weltge reads the available evidence in the following way.

> I am convinced that the homosexual is justified, but justified by God's grace and not by homosexuality. . .There are some things the homophile community cannot expect from the church. One is the abandonment of the norm honoring the goodness of creation in the paradox of man and woman . . .Realism and strategy suggest that achieving a suspended

254

judgment or even apathy from the church is a more sensible goal for the homophile movement. As a corollary, the church is not about to sacralize homosexuality. . .All the church can offer is a continuation of the present arrangement of 'living in sin without benefit of clergy.'[15]

But this is not all that Weltge has to offer. Having given due reverence to the values at stake in the controversy, an affirmation that clearly reflects his own leaning, he then tries to push the discussion one step further. Finally, it is the silence of the common lot of sinners, expectantly awaiting the return of the Lord, which equalizes the status of people of all sexual persuasions. "The Church is not required to pronounce God's no on the homosexual and abandon him in condemnation. Neither is it supposed to justify him with some improved and better human yes. . . 'Mercy triumphs over judgment' (James 2:13). That is the first and last word."[16]

Weltge does not even get as close as Curran to an 'ethic for homosexuals.' Instead, he chooses to represent the tradition in encouraging the heterosexual part of the Christian community to refrain from playing God and equating homosexual behavior with a sin-condemned standing before God. While the Church in this world must continue to uphold the self-evident priority of the man-woman relationship, there is no necessity to go to the extreme of abhorring those who violate this mandate. Weltge stands and speaks out, rather than to, the homosexuals in the community.

My reaction to Weltge's position is that he leaves more unsaid than he actually covers in his analysis. At best, it is a propaedautic to systematic ethical reflection about the function of active sexual behavior in the life of the homosexual. He reminds us well about sitting in judgment of persons, but that does not eliminate the need for critical appraisal of a whole way of life.

Weltge chooses to avoid confronting some of the more important dimensions of the issue of homosexuality. I think the same can be said for two other thinkers who also move in the direction of a compromise position.[17] John von Rohr, for example, falls back on the Protestant stress on the universal sinfulness of the human species. Once again he presumes the normative status of the loving heterosexual relationship. To that extent homosexuality is 'unnatural.' If it is possible, one should pursue a heterosexual life style. However, for some, this will be an unrealizable goal. When this is the case, the key operative value that should guide the homosexual relationship is the same one as in a heterosexual relationship-deep and abiding personal love. Thus, the challenges are the same. Von Rohr concludes, "the sinfulness of homosexuality is not to be found in the fact that it is homo-sexuality, but rather in the fact that it is homo-sexuality in the midst of man's disordered state, where all sexuality becomes an instrument of his lust as well as of his love."[18]

A second thinker, Theodore Jennings, also focuses on the sin-touched quality of human sexuality. Jennings follows Barth in making two claims: (i) heterosexuality is a fundamentally superior form of sexuality than is homosexuality (ii) no natural human condition is intrinsically justified. What this starting point leads him to is the quieting of the Christian furor over the issue. Better to be silent or hesitant to speak than to contribute to the climate of prejudice and oppression under which many homosexuals are forced to live. Jennings cautionary note is phrased in this fashion. "We certainly cannot argue that because homosexuality (as a permanent and exclusive sexual pattern) precludes marriage and family, it must be ruled out a priori as unchristian."[19] If that is so, then what can we say? According to Jennings, we can portray

256

certain characteristic forms of homosexual temptation. These would include: relational
irresponsibility; irresponsibility toward oneself;
being closed to the genuine otherness of another;
and reducing relationships to a physical, genital
encounter.[20]

Neither von Rohr nor Jennings goes beyond
some of the theologians upon whom they have drawn.
The criticisms I have applied to Curran and Weltge
would apply equally well to them. What strikes me
the most about this set of theologians is that
they have the heart of a pastor and the training
of an ethicist and they are not quite sure how to
bring them together. Perhaps they unconsciously
wish for the issue to go away. It is unlikely
that they will move to a more militant standpoint,
but they are not convinced either that the traditional prohibition is much help in the concrete
circumstances of Christian homosexuals.

(d) Homosexuality as perversion and as inver-
sion--

I have already given considerable attention
to the work of D.S. Bailey on the exegesis of the
biblical passages on homosexuality and on the
evolution of the Church teaching. Now I want to
turn to the personal conclusions that Bailey
arrives at insofar as he wishes to influence contemporary Christian opinion about the matter.

The basic distinction that Bailey proposes,
which has since been adopted by a number of
others, is that between a pervert and an invert.[21]
A pervert is not a true homosexual but a heterosexual who engages in homosexual practices. An
invert, on the other hand, is a true homosexual.
If this is an accurate division of those who
participate in homosexual acts, then the question
posed to the Christian teaching is whether there
is a moral difference in the two situations.
Bailey argues that

we have decisive Biblical
authority for censuring the conduct of those whom we may describe
as male perverts. . .but do the
Apostle's strictures apply also to
the homosexual acts of the genuine
invert, and in particular to those
physical expressions of affection
which may take place between two
persons of the same sex who affirm
that they are 'in love?' To such
situations it can hardly be said
that the New Testament speaks,
since the condition of inversion,
with all its special problems, was
quite unknown at that time.[22]

Of the Scriptural and theological condemnation of perversion, in both its homosexual (and
heterosexual) forms, there can be little doubt.
Perversion destroys the social fabric and eats
away at the stability of marriage and family life.
And by some ineluctable process, perversion has a
way of perpetuating itself in the next generation
by corrupting the innocent and the young. Despite
the mixed evidence, Bailey hypothesizes that
sexual inversion is probably a product of some
distortion in the parental-child dynamic so that
it is an inter-generational construct.

Whatever the origins of homosexual inversion,
the Church still has an obligation to give some
ethical guidance to true inverts. But when it
looks at the sources of its teaching it finds itself in a quandary since only perversion is
explicitly known in the Scriptures. For this
reason a new tack must be taken. Bailey sums up
the problems with receiving the inherited teaching
in our day in history when he says, it is evident
that this tradition is (a) erroneous, insofar as
it represents the destruction of Sodom
and Gomorrah as a Divine judgment upon
homosexual practices (b) defective in that: it is
ignorant of inversion as a condition due to biological, psychological, or genetical causes; and

consequently of the distinction between the invert and the pervert; it assumes that all homosexual acts are, so to speak, 'acts of perversion;' takes little account of female homosexuality; it unjustifiably regards male homosexual offenses as both intrinsically and socially more serious than heterosexual offenses; it tends to think too exclusively in terms of the act of sodomy; by invoking capital punishment has imposed a disproportional penalty; and is strongly influenced by emotional factors.[23] The conclusion that he draws from these points of criticism is that "the tradition can no longer be regarded as an adequate guide by the theologian, the legislator, the sociologist, and the magistrate."[24]

As I have already indicated, I think there are legitimate grounds for questioning Bailey's exegesis of the biblical texts. Still, he does accurately point out the limitations in using the Scripture for deciding this matter to the neglect of other kinds of data and theory. It is the living Church as it has interpreted the prohibition aganist homosexuality through the ages that is the proper source of contemporary reflection. Today this requires a more sophisticated analysis of the diversity of the world of the invert (it is not a monolithic society as Bailey seems to imply) and a correlation of these different structures with the demands of a Christian life of discipleship. Bailey begs off doing an ethic for the invert once he has made the case that the Scriptures are not applicable. Since I remain unconvinced that the Scriptures have nothing of relevance to say about the matter, the basic problem with Bailey's thesis is that it does not finally offer any positive directions, except to call for reform of the civil law.

Another proposal on what the Christian churches should say or not say about homosexuality, one which has the same agnostic ethical flavor as Bailey's, is rendered by W. Dwight Oberholtzer.[25] He too believes that what the Scriptures refer to as homosexuality, does not

259

encompass the same range of phenomena as that studied by the modern social sciences. In our time, we have had to take into account the following data. Homosexuals as a group (abstracting from their sexual behavior) are no more moral or immoral than heterosexuals as a group. In fact, they have more in common than they realize. It seems evident that true homosexuals cannot change. For such persons, joy, beauty, and other good things can be found in the gay world. Because both gay and straight life pose many of the same challenges, any ethic proposed for one should be directly relevant for the other as well.

In the long run Oberholtzer pictures the need for starting from scratch in developing a viable Christian ethic for homosexuals. We have learned too much of late to be content with defending an outdated version of sexual legalism. What we need are many ethics of gay life, all of which will attempt to express a symmetrical application of the same moral values that have been used to focus heterosexual life.

Like Bailey, Oberholtzer tells us more what we need than how to get there. By starting anew he seems to expect that we will make better progress than if we subbornly tried to keep alive an inapplicable tradition. Yet I never sense that Oberholtzer is impatient or inclined to play iconoclast. He is a moderate revisionist in the same way that Bailey is. They believe they have discovered a glaring gap in Christian sexual teaching. But the tradition has much to offer and time will allow sufficient experience and chance for debate so that homosexuals too may be included in a workable Christian moral catechesis. Since I disagree with Oberholtzer's estimate of the impoverishment of the Christian sources, I find his article to be unproductive. He has more faith in the reliability of the social sciences than he does in the cumulative wisdom of the faith community. With such a predisposition, it is not surprising that he points us in a direction but provides no solid theological clues for arriving at our destination.

(e) Conclusion--

In this first section of the chapter, I have examined the ethical methods of representative figures among the moderate theological revisionists. What these thinkers have in common is a love of and respect for the Church and its traditional teachings. They are not prepared to abandon entirely the inherited sexual ethic. Yet each in his own fashion has argued the case for some accommodation of this ethic to the needs and possibilities of the confirmed adult homosexual. Some explain the need for this change in terms of the sinfulness of the human condition. Others believe that the category of healthy homosexual was unknown in previous generations and therefore outside the ban.

Another thing that these theologians share in common is a conviction that a harsh word of condemnation to a person who cannot change is cruel and unfeeling and in conflict with Jesus' compassion and understanding. Since they do not envisage the possibility of homosexual continence (for many), they choose tolerance and/or some type of acceptance over exclusion and negative judgment. Especially in an age when heterosexual patterns of relatedness among Christians have gone through many changes, it seems hypocritical to preserve a pristine ethic for one minority group alone.

Moderate revisionism is appealing to anyone who finds the nonrevisionist position unacceptable. Moderate revisionism seems open-minded yet balanced. As a _via media_ it seems a steady path between the two extremes. Yet, as I have tried to point out, in its present form moderate revisionism really has no concreteness or specificity. It renounces one consistently drawn and integrated ethic and replaces it with a wish, with a project for the future. In the meantime, having sufficiently chastened the defenders of the tradition, it capitulates to the new without any sure idea of where it is leading. Since the social scientific data is used selectively, the moderate revisionists continually imply that eventually, once societal strictures are broken down, the majority of homosexuals will settle down into comfortable, stable, loving relationships much as hetersexuals do. In the absence of any proof that this is likely to occur, I must suggest that at its deepest core, moderate revisionism is fashioned from a vestigial liberal romanticism which presumes that if our intentions are right, and we are sufficiently well educated to be in favor of all good things, the ultimate story of our life will be self-fulfillment and happiness no matter what the parameters of our existential condition.

But moderate revisionism does not exhaust the ethical possibilities. Some Christians think that only a more radical stance will suffice. In this next section I will concentrate on this alternative.

II. The Radical Revisionists--

The common bond among those thinkers I have titled the 'radical revisionists' is a deep dissatisfaction with the traditional Christian teaching on homosexuality. Some have arrived at this conclusion after prolonged study of the Scriptural and theological texts. Others speak out of their own experience as homosexuals who have known discrimination and hardship in the Church. Still others have considered the Christian sexual ethic in general to be inadequate to the complexity of contemporary social life and, as a result, have used the homosexuality question as one example of a broader dilemma.

While the sheer existence of such radical challenges within the Christian community has been upsetting to many among the faithful, there is

262

still a spectrum of opinion even within this advocacy group. I will focus on three basic types of argument. The first and largest contingent pictures all forms of sexual behavior as morally neutral in the physical order. The second category wishes to promote integration of homosexuals within the mainstream of Church life by foreswearing the ethical question altogether. A third and final type is more anarchistic in orientation. After describing each of these types, I will offer some concluding criticisms.

(a) The Ethical Libertarians--

If the quotient of pain and suffering in the world is already too high, why would Christians, who profess a Gospel of peace, mercy and understanding, wish to contribute to the hardship of many Christians and non-Christians who are homosexual? Wouldn't a better strategy be to ask homosexual persons to attempt to integrate into their lives, including the sexual dimension, the same values that heterosexual people are asked to live by? Even more, if gays have always been active in Church congregation sometimes even in leadership roles, (even if always clandestinely), wouldn't it make better sense to welcome them formally and encourage an even fuller level of involvement? If the plight of unmarried couples, and divorced and remarried partners, and unhappy celibates, has drastically changed Church theory and practice, doesn't it seem consistent to extend the same privilege to gays? These and other challenges are presently being raised against the historical condemnation. By examining the arguments of some leading spokespersons, we may get a better idea of the nature of their theological positions.

Norman Pittenger is an Anglican theologian who operates out of a process theology model. He was one of the first Christian thinkers of note who publicly advocated a full acceptance of homosexuality as a viable moral choice for a

Christian.[26] As a consequence of this straight-forward expression of opinion, his work has been much quoted and has exercised considerable influence in his own denominational communion.

Pittenger begins by asserting that homo-sexuality as a state or habitual orientation is fully 'normal' and 'natural.' At the level of the givenness of their sexual self-definition, nothing of significance distinguishes gays from straights. Both types seek love and both normally engage in certain sexual acts as a way of manifesting this love. To ask either group to foresake physical expression forever is barbaric and cruel.

True love can be known by the presence of certain characteristics: commitment; mutuality in giving and receiving; tenderness; faithfulness; hopefulness; oneness.[27] Only the wrong inner spirit and the wrong intentionality can transform physical gestures of love into sinful signs of duplicity and abuse. It is the intention which is most important of all the human factors that make up an act. Promiscuity is out, because by defini-tion this is a disproportionate failure to invest oneself as a person in a series of casual liaisons. But it is hard to say how much can be expected of a homosexual Christian.

In an attempt to provide a semblance of an answer, Pittenger goes on to list 6 propositions which might form the basis of an ethic for homo-sexuals:[28]

(i) Nobody should simply accept his homo-sexuality without questioning it.

(ii) If a person recognizes that he is a homosexual, he ought to accept the fact as well as recognize it.

(iii) God still loves him just as he is.

(iv) He should be a responsible person.

264

(v) He should try to develop close friendships with persons he esteems and likes.

(vi) If a relationship develops, problems may
arise.

It is just in this area of relationships of
varying degrees of commitment and longevity that
Pittenger hopes to keep all of the options open.
First, he is against promiscuous behavior, but
even when it occurs over a long period of time, he
sees no cause for undue alarm. Second, fidelity
does not demand exclusivity, even though that
would be a proper goal. Third, one-to-one
relationships are the best places to foster an
ability to love. Fourth, if love is present in
the relationship, physical acts should express
one's true feelings, respect the desires of the
other and lead to a deeper reciprocal bond.

As far as the Church status of such loving
homosexual relationships is concerned, Pittenger
is opposed to homosexual marriages.

> A homosexual relationship does not
> constitute a 'family;' the absence
> of children would be sufficient
> evidence of this. A homosexual
> partnership is something differ-
> ent; that does not mean that it
> must be something worse. . .even
> if some such 'service,' with a
> blessing, is not now readily
> possible in most churches, there
> is surely no reason why such
> persons as I have in mind should
> be refused the sacraments of the
> church unless they agree to give
> up all physical relations and
> promise to be celibates.[29]

There is thus a lack of symmetry in trying to com-
pare a homosexual couple with a married heterosexual couple. But this should not prevent the
Church from recognizing the validity of both forms

of relatedness. As Pittenger expresses it in his concluding statement, "the homosexual who decides for a long relationship, as he may hope a lifelong one, with another of his own sex, is almost certainly doing the very best thing that is open to him. Nor do I have the slightest doubt that God can and does bless that relationship."[30]

Pittenger's theological argument hinges on our acceptance of the following points:

(i) that heterosexuality and homosexuality are of equal worth in the natural order

(ii) that sin is constituted by intention

(iii) that love is known by focusing on the pair rather than on the society as a whole

(iv) that fidelity in love does not demand exclusivity

(v) that to be moving in the direction of love is a sufficient norm for sexual activity in a relationship.

Since I have problems with each of these claims, I find Pittenger's presentation the most facile kind of liberal apologetic. If we were disembodied creatures who could achieve happiness simply by willing it, such an approach might stand the test of time. However, since we are sinful creatures who continue to harm ourselves and others, we have to take sufficient account of the structures and limits of human relationships.

Our second representative of ethical libertarianism created a sensation when his long-suppressed manuscript was finally released for publication.[31] John McNeill, a Jesuit priest, had accepted the orders of his religious superiors in the interim between the initial trouble and the time of publication, but he had continued to appeal to the scholarly community for criticism and support. In the long run, such attempts at

266

silencing have proven less effective than the post-publication response from other moral theologians.

McNeill devotes the first half of his book to an analysis of the evidence on homosexuality in the theological tradition and in the human sciences. Basically, he ends up debunking the standard theological positions as insufficiently comprehensive and outdated relative to recent humanistic research. For instance, he suggests that there are present in society many happy and healthy homosexuals living in stable relationships. This data gives promise of a whole new perspective on the possibilities of such encounters. Once these homosexual couples are given a chance to flourish then the inherent prejudice of the classic moral and psychological theories, which presupposed the normativity of the heterosexual bond, will be exposed for what it is.

In his criticisms of the Scriptural material, McNeill follows D.S. Bailey's distinction between an 'invert' and a 'pervert' and claims that the biblical authors knew nothing of the permanent homosexual condition nor did they envisage the possibility of stable gay relationships. Therefore, the biblical foundation of the condemnation is undermined, at least insofar as it applies to self-conscious adult homosexuals. Furthermore, the second foundation of the classic prohibition, namely, the natural law argument, was based upon a Stoic view of nature which stressed rationality and static structures and which demeaned the importance of the physical order, particularly sexuality. A more developmental and personalist view of natural law cannot rest content with such a formulation. Finally, the previously unstudied world of the healthy homosexual has been brought to public attention and exposed the narrowness and selectivity of the prevailing psychological theories. For all of these reasons, the ethical condemnation of homosexual activity needs to be reexamined.

way. McNeill summarizes his own position in this
way.

> Given, as I believe, (1) the
> uncertainty of clear scriptural
> prohibition, (2) the questionable
> basis of the traditional condemna-
> tion in moral philosophy and moral
> theology, (3) the emergence of new
> data which upset many traditional
> assumptions and (4) controversies
> among psychologists and psychia-
> trists concerning theory,
> etiology, treatment, and so on,
> there obviously is a need to open
> up anew the question of the moral
> standing of homosexual activity
> and homosexual relationships for
> public debate. . .it would appear
> to follow that the same moral
> rules apply to homosexual as to
> heterosexual attitudes and
> behavior. Those that are
> responsible, respectful, loving,
> and truly promotive of the good of
> both parties are moral, those that
> are exploitive, irresponsible,
> disrespectful, or destructive of
> the true good of either party must
> be judged immoral.[32]

What this position does is make the physical and
psychological factors unimportant since sexual
gender identity is not determinative of one's
sexual possibilities. All theories of sexual
complementarity are downplayed. It is implicity
suggested that two homosexual males or two homosexual females can find the same kinds of fulfillment and completion in each other that heterosexual males and females ordinarily find in
members of the opposite sex.

Rather than settle for the simple acceptance
of the worth of homosexual relationships, McNeill
goes on to suggest that gays have a special

268

calling within the Christian community. For they can overturn the partriarchal male-female model which has predominated in Western marriage (to the detriment of the woman) and replace it with a friendship-equality model in which the partners seek only the good of the other person. A further challenge for male homosexuals, according to McNeill, is to transcend the 'macho,' power- and violence-oriented role for men with a more characteristic expression of warmth, tenderness and care. Thus, he says, "the homosexual, by escaping the confines of the male image, is relatively free to develop a sensitivity to the true values of the past, and his isolation from normal structures forces him to attempt new incarnations of these values."[33]

At the pastoral level, such an ethical position requires the Church to minister to the homosexual minority in a new spirit of openness. No longer can it be held that a life of celibacy and sexual sublimation is the proper route for all homosexuals. While excessive promiscuity and exploitation are ruled out, the form that love will take cannot always be described in advance. The long-range goal of a relationship is the achievement of mutual commitment and reciprocal love. Yet the fragility of particular relationships and the growth process of the individuals involved may not allow for full realization of these proper ends. This is further complicated by the absence of legal and social support structures. As long as the Church continues to support structured social injustice against homosexuals, it can hardly expect the kind of stability in gay couples that even married couples are having a harder time achieving. Beyond the general statement that norms such as mutuality, fidelity, and unselfishness are operative in all human relationships, McNeill thinks that more time must pass before anything further can be said. "Beyond these general principles I believe it is impossible for me at this point to define more clearly or to lay down a priori what the nature of

269

an 'ethically responsible homosexual relationship' should be."[34]

In the final analysis, McNeill has made the following claims:

(i) The Biblical and theological interpretation of homosexuality are inconclusive.

(ii) The social sciences give us new data and refute some previously held generalizations, especially as found in the psychiatric literature.

(iii) There is no reason for denying the fundamental equality of heterosexual and homosexual relationships.

(iv) The stable, loving, healthy homosexual relationship is a goal which is realizable, as seen in the lives of a significant percentage of gays.

(v) In this time of transition many gays will only approach this goal slowly and with great difficulty.

(vi) The Church should not place an intolerable burden on Christian homosexuals by asking for a celibate adjustment. Instead it should preach and teach about those moral values such as mutuality and fidelity that should govern all human affective bonds.

(vii) A full ethic for Christian homosexuals has yet to be worked out.

McNeill's position is a logical outflow from his presuppositions. If in fact the Christian theological sources have nothing of worth to say about homosexuality, then full acceptance seems to be the humane thing to do. However, I have already expressed my disagreement with McNeill's use of the Scriptural and other material in previous chapters. He leaves out of account the function of the ongoing life and moral experience

270

of the Christian church. He would have us adopt
an ethic which is almost saccharine in its
optimistic picture of the homosexual possibility.
He never engages in a realistic discussion of the
forms of homosexual life nor of the negative
characteristics that can be found in much of it.
Instead, he instinctively appeals to the latent
desire in the progressive heterosexual population
that somehow, once the barriers are dropped, most
homosexuals will settle down into stable domestic
pairs with all of the basic qualities of marriage.

I believe that McNeill's book is a poorly
constructed attempt to justify homosexual
relationships by selectively presenting the
evidence about the nature of the homosexual way of
life. At best, his ethic would apply to a small
percentage of gays. At worst, it may delude the
Church into thinking that the structures and
embodied forms of sexual existence have no
significance. If the homosexual condition is
according to the will of God, as McNeill asserts,
then we need a better explanation of what its
unique contribution might be than is provided in
this book.

Pittenger and McNeill have given the longest
presentations of the sexual libertarian point of
view. But there are a number of other theologians
who have added their voices to the call for a
change based on the moral neutrality of sexual
orientation and activity. Most of these appear as
parts of books or in the periodical literature. I
will now give a brief exposition of some of these
versions.

In the much maligned book <u>Human Sexuality</u>,
the authors treat homosexuality as one instance of
ethical controversy.[35] In a move that they make
throughout the study, they claim that since the
empirical evidence is inconclusive, any ethical
position must be tentative and provisional. This
is buttressed by the further judgment that the
Christian tradition has only condemned homosexual
'perversion' and not necessarily all forms of

homosexual relatedness. As a result of this sharp variation in contemporary opinion, four approaches are presently proposed:[36]

(i) homosexual acts are 'intrinsically evil'

(ii) homosexual acts are 'essentially imperfect'

(iii) homosexual acts are to be evaluated in terms of their relational significance

(iv) homosexual acts are essentially good and natural.

Consistent with their methodology, they opt for the third approach as the most reasonable.

Since it is the relational factors that are most important, the book presents a number of qualities which generally ought to be present in sexual relationships.

> A pastor or counselor should attempt to help a homosexual make a moral judgment upon his or her relationships and actions in terms of whether or not they are self-liberating, other-enriching, honest, faithful, life-serving and joyous.[37]

There is not indication anywhere in the book that these qualities must all be present nor that they should be rated by any scale of importance. Thus the attitudinal context of human sharing is the key. The authors conclude their excursus with the optimistic judgment,

> There is much that is uncertain and provisional about the subject of homosexuality. . .where there is sincere affection, responsibility, and the germ of authentic human relationship-- in other

words, where there is love--God is
surely present.[38]

This book has a number of major flaws which
depreciate the value of its analysis of particular
issues.[39] In regards to homosexuality, it is
extremely derivative and accepts arguments already
objected to in previous sections of this book.

Another version of radical revisionist
thought is given by Neale Secor.[40] He objects to
the standard argument of Protestant theologians
who turn to the Creation accounts of Genesis to
situate the male-female relationship. They then
see the homosexual condition as a result of the
Fall. On the contrary, other cultures and relations have said 'Yes' or 'maybe' to the status of
the homosexuals among them. With the availability
of such comparative perspectives, and with the
exposure of the fallibility of psychiatric
theories, all previous ethical conclusions must be
considered hypothetical and potentially
unreliable.

In answer to the question--what can a
Christian ethicist say about homosexuality?--Secor
offers three working hypotheses:[41]

(i) All human sexual identifications and
behavior patterns, irrespective of gender object,
are morally neutral.

(ii) No matter what the particular sexual
behavior (hetero, homo, mono), the test for sin is
whether or not that behavior meets presently
understood and approved Christian standards (what
God wills for man) for all human relational
behavior.

(iii) Christian ethical concern for the homosexual exists not because he has a certain sexual
proclivity but because he is a person.

In the same volume, Lewis Maddocks proposes a
similar view.[42] The sine qua non for Christian

273

membership is professing the lordship of Jesus Christ. Sex acts are not a fitting test since, in themselves, they are neither moral or immoral. What the Church is called to do is to make explicit what is already the case de facto, i.e., it must open its ranks to full homosexual participation including ordination.

Other voices that repeat this same theme that all sex acts are morally neutral and should be judged by the same standards include:

(1) Clinton Jones-- who teaches that homosexuals should love and not use; help and not hurt; be selfless and not selfish; and meet the responsibilities of commitment.[43]

(2) Lewis Williams-- who calls for a 'theology of engagement' to right the wrong of antihomosexual prejudice.[44]

(3) Del Martin and Phyllis Lyon-- who propose the criteria of encompassing commitment, personal communication and self-giving as a fitting test for authentic homosexual relationships.[45]

(4) Pierre-Claude Nappey-- who thinks that homosexual relationships can have a deep interpersonal dimension at the same time that they allow for more flexible moral rules.[46]

(5) James Nelson-- who correlates the rejection of homosexuality with male sexism and suggests that an openness to the former may lead to a transformation in the latter.[47]

(6) Morton Kelsey-- who urges that the Church provide spiritual direction and welcome to homosexuals who do not wish to change their sexual orientation.[48]

(7) Gregory Baum-- who focuses on mutuality as the key value in all sexual relationships and encourages gay Catholics to adopt a moderate and well-balanced minority position in order to keep

the issue alive within the ongoing life of the Church.[49]

I have included this full list of names to reassure those occasional readers of literature on homosexuality that their impression is indeed correct--that the traditional prohibition has been subjected to an onslaught of critical commentary. These radical revisionists of the first type all stress the moral neutrality of homosexuals acts. They also present various lists of values which should regulate all sexual conduct of whatever sort. Since they agree that logically homosexuals should not be excluded from full Church participation if all sexual orientations are capable of being lived responsibily, it follows that integration of heterosexual and homosexual Christians is a desirable goal. There are, however, other radical revisionists who think that the process of open fellowshipping is the first desirable step and that it should precede any ethical theorizing. To this group I will now turn.

(b) The Ecclesial Integrators--

The common ground for the representatives of this type of radical revisionism is a non-judgmental, fully participatory acceptance by the Christian churches of their homosexual members. The stress is on a shared discipleship which transcends any secondary division according to sexual preference. With a longer experience of equality of membership, the question of a homosexual ethic will surely be solvable. In the meantime, it is better to bracket that problem and get on with the support of the various dimensions of Church life.

The first of those who take this stance is Richard Woods, a Dominican priest, who has worked with the Dignity chapter in Chicago.[50] He considers homosexuality to be a <u>variation</u> in human sexuality which, for those who accept such identity, has a para-normative status. What such people need is both understanding and guidance

275

from the Church. But they also need to recognize their own spiritual resources. Because of their unique experience of reality, gays can perhaps open up some dimensions of prayer and liturgical expression that other people have yet to discover.

Woods glosses over the ethical question about homosexual acts with the comment that it is untenable to ask homosexuals to avoid each other's company. Instead, they should ban together in solidarity. But this should not lead to isolation, for their friendship patterns should also include heterosexuals. However, the primary challenge of gay Christians should be "the redemption of the gay world itself, by authentic witness and by creating alternatives to the morally destructive forces and structures of that world."[51]

The greatest asset of gays in this task may be a 'peculiar religious sensitivity.' To back up this point, Woods repeats the often whispered conjecture that "it is likely, though unproved, that a disproportionate number of ministers, priests, sisters, brothers, rabbis, sheiks and shamans are homosexual."[52] He then concludes by settling on the image of the clown as the best symbol for the creative dimensions of gay life. The clown is the embodiment of the artistic, prophetic and mystical components of human experience, always seen from a comic perspective. And if clowns can symbolize the best in the gay world, clowns are also Christ figures.

Woods attempt to capture a positive and reinforcing view of homosexual potentiality is a helpful antidote to the self-hatred and premature sterility of much of the gay world. Surely, there may be a peculiar giftedness possessed by some homosexuals which gives them an opportunity for special service in the Church. Insofar as this can be promoted, it should be. Yet a sheer stress on the good side cannot suppress the lingering doubts about the truthfulness of any radical change in the ethical position. Woods is standing

276

with a foot in two worlds simultaneously. On the one hand, he has found the traditional prohibition inapplicable to constitutional homosexuality. But he has played down the importance of the need for an immediate formal change in the teaching. On the other hand, he has encouraged homosexual affiliation within the Church, with the concomitant possibility of overt relationships developing. He is hopeful that such groupings in a Christian context might avoid some of the negative features of secular gay life. The problem of course is that it is not clear that the heterosexual component of the Christian community is prepared to live with this seeming contradiction between theory and practice.

In the final analysis, Woods' book is good in its comments on gay spirituality (especially when an implicit elitist attitude is avoided), but unhelpful in its peripheral discussion of sexual ethics.

Barbara Gittings presents a similar approach, but in an abbreviated form.[53] She isolates two main areas in which the Church should concentrate its efforts: supportive and integrative. At the supportive level, services of all kinds should be provided for homosexuals whether it be in alleviation of problems of a spiritual, emotional, personal or social sort. At the integrative level, bonded homosexual couples should be allowed to participate in activities designed for heterosexual married couples. In order to allow this to happen naturally, the Church should abstract for a while from the formal or ceremonial marriage of homosexuals. Finally, the Church should prepare its ministers to engage in ministry to gays by having homosexuals teach about the subject in seminaries and also provide special training for seminary teachers.

Gittings' reflections are more pastoral in focus than they are ethical, but she follows the same strategy as Woods when she suggests that sexually integrated living in the Church will

277

enable the ethical questions to be worked out in due time.

In a more recent proposal, Letha Scanzoni and Virginia Ramey Mollenkott castigate the Church for its bias in treating the homosexual as a pariah.[54] The Gospel standard, as they see it, is love of neighbor without regard to qualifying factors. "Jesus did not define the concept of 'neighbor' by geographical closeness, nor by race, nor by religion, but only by need."[55] A homosexual Christian is first of all a Christian and the matter of sexual identity should be allowed to disappear into irrelevance.

The authors acknowledge that there is a spectrum of opinion about homosexuality within the Christian community. But the very pluralism warns against a premature closure of the issue.

> The questions surrounding homo-
> sexuality in Christian perspective
> are far from settled. There is no
> uniform opinion among Christians
> and in fact a great deal of
> disagreement. . .a solid ground-
> work is being laid for creative
> rethinking on the theological/
> biblical/ethical level and for
> compassionate counsel on the
> practical/personal level.[56]

Once again ethical reflections is seen to flow out of concrete experience in the daily interaction of Church life. While the theoretical issue is being debated, the Church should create an open environment in its fellowship where all, without discrimination according to sexual preference can feel welcome.

The type of revisionism represented by these authors, what I have called Ecclesial Integration, is a theory for the interim. They sense a certain inevitability in the eventual recognition by the Church of a more radical ethic in its treatment of

278

homosexuality. But they are less concerned with arguing this point specifically than they are in encouraging homosexuals to take full part in Church life. The presumption is that the concrete experience of healthy homosexuals in the parish and in church organizations will win over the skeptical heterosexual majority.

The major problem with this approach is that it buys into the civil pattern of 'live and let live' too easily. The Church has a disciplinary task as well as a pastoral task if it would keep some semblance of integrity. A radical disjunction between theory and practice gradually calls into question the viablity of the teaching. As long as human actions and commitments make a difference (as I believe they do), then no amount of pretense will be able to counteract the existence of discrepant life-styles in the community of faith. What the Church cannot celebrate in a formal way will always have a marginal status. It may in fact be the case that regular contact between gay and straight Christians will lead to a new sexual ethic. But it may also be possible that a real exposure to the full spectrum of homosexual life may reinforce the present prohibition.

(c) The Sexual Anarchists--

In the radical literature of the gay liberation movement it is not uncommon to find devastating criticisms of the prevailing patterns of heterosexual relationship. In particular, the nuclear family with its monogamous roots is accused of being oppressive, sexist, and excessively narrow in focus. These gay liberationists envisage a new era in which men and women will be able to participate in a wide variety of sexual relationships, unfettered by social stigma and religious guilt. They urge homosexual people to avoid being forced into a one track conception of gay relationships, i.e., modeled on heterosexual marriage.

279

John Murphy is a good example of this non-theological anarchist approach.[57] He relates the story of his own gradual 'coming out' and his involvement in the gay activist movement. Then he limns the kind of change he expects to occur in the future. "We intend to restructure the most basic attitudes toward sexuality, the importance of the individual, the function of the family. We are going to make a total revolution."[58] Later on in his work he counters the usual accusations against homosexual propensities by saying,

> The traditional promiscuity of homosexuality, the numerous affairs and lovers that an 'average' homosexual supposedly experiences, all have a positive value. Once you realize that the standard values of a lifelong monogamous marriage are not necessary to a new kind of American culture or to your life and may, in fact, even be destructive, it is easy to see that having experiences with many people may strengthen you, rather than be a symptom of moral decay.[59]

Other voices from the movement repeat the same refrain. Carl Wittman describes heterosexuality as "a fear of people of the same sex, it is anti-homosexual, and it is fraught with frustrations."[60] He sees marriage as a social institution fraught with role playing. Paul Goodman, the popular essayist and novelist, defends his own behavior patterns with these words, "I have a hunch that homosexual promiscuity enriches more lives than it desensitizes."[61] And Linda Barufaldi and Emily Culpepper claim to shatter theological categories with their discovery of androgyny. With a strong sense of assurance, they say, "Over against the prevailing sense of reality, androgyny is anarchy. . .We are

280

leaving behind a primary paradigm for domination-subjugation relationships."[62]

While these spokespersons for an anarchistic view have no particular theological agenda, they are all aware of the influence of the Judaeo-Christian tradition on the civil law and on cultural attitudes in general. Therefore to attack the prevailing theological understanding of the man-woman relationship is to get at the source of prevailing sexual expectations. But there are starting to be Christian writers who speak in a language very similar to the sexual anarchists.

Bill Johnson, for example, the first openly gay clergy person ordained in the mainstream Protestant church in America, minces no words in his demand for a change.[63] The Church is, he says, the most patriarchal institution in the world. It is family oriented because of its heterosexual membership and because it is males who benefit from that state of affairs. "Heterosexual relationships and marriage as traditionally experienced are basically unhealthy. They are based on inequality resulting from the male dominance/control mentality."[64] True sexual fulfillment can be found in a variety of pairings (female/female, male/male, female/male) provided that responsible, honest love is present. It is not the structure that makes the relationship (as has been traditionally presupposed) but rather the openness and integrity of the participants.

A change in ethical teaching is long overdue, according to Johnson but it will require of gay people that they accept the androgynous (gynandrous) nature of human life. Once gays have a proper perspective on themselves, they will have the resources to take the Church in a new direction.

> We are called to share in
> the movement within the church
> that will serve to liberate the
> church from its homophobia and

281

sexism. . .It is particularly
important for Gay men in positions
of power. . .to be honest about
their Gayness and to expose the
absurdity of attitudes within the
church.[65]

Sally Gearhart is even more militant in her
impatience with the Church.[66] She declares that
lesbianism is a miracle of love because it must
resist all of the anti-female prejudice built into
Western culture by the Church. It is feminism
which draws women of various sexual persuasions
together in order to create a new order of sexual
liberation. Both inside and outside the Church a
heightened consciousness by women of their
inherent dignity and prerogatives will force a
reevaluation of the form of Church life. Gearhart
lambasts the Church in no uncertain terms.

The Christian church by its very
structure and by the very assumptions on which it is founded is
in direct, fundamental, and
irreconcilable conflict with
feminism. . .In both its structure
(Hierarchical, authoritarian, competitive) and its theology
(extreme and exclusive masculism)
the church is committed to the
annihilation of life-giving and
life-sustaining qualities and to
the subjugation of women and of
womanness.[67]

The alternative direction for the Church
which Gearhart proposes would entail a complete
and absolute rejection of what has gone before.
In her terms, it would be the 'lesbianization of
theology.' But she remains skeptical that most
Church members are ready for that step. If they
are not, the vanguard of the feminist movement
(along with gay men who are prepared to abandon
their masculine privileges) will rush out on its
own, embodying a continual challenge to "the very

282

existence of the women-hating hierarchical and exclusively masculist Judaeo-Christian tradition."[68]

While it should be obvious from my previous comments that I am not sympathetic with such radical challenges to the Christian teaching on homosexuality, they have in their favor that they lay out in stark and uncompromising fashion the true nature of the issue at stake. Unlike the perspective of the moderate revisionists who tend to concentrate on the acceptance of a limited percentage of homosexuals (namely, those who live in stable, exclusive relationships), the radical revisionists carry their argument all the way. For them, the whole spectrum of gay relationships may have a valid place, especially if they can offer the Church a new set of possibilities in expansive, egalitarian and self-liberating sexual expression.

The ethical libertarians base their revision on the moral neutrality of all sexual acts. The ecclesial integrators prescind from the ethical discussion altogether and promote a church in which sexual orientation has no first order relevance. The sexual anarchists call for an abandonment of the oppressive, sexist structure of heterosexual marriage. Among these three stances, I think that the anarchist one is at the heart of the homosexual dialectic.

III. Conclusion--

Christian ethical wisdom has a derivative status in the wider dispensation of things. Jesus Christ preached first of all about the religious truth of the Kingdom of God and only secondarily about the Way of Life which constituted the this-wordly foreshadowing of it. The Paschal mystery which concluded his mission was an event which broke through the sin-ruptured reality of the human condition and opened up the possibility of a grace-filled life of discipleship and obedience.

283

For a Christian who hears this history recounted the prior question is always--What is it that I believe, in whom do I place my trust? Yet the person of faith who accepts this Jesus as his or her Lord inevitably wished for moral guidance from this same source of life. And in a spirit of honest searching, he or she confronts the complexity of contemporary existence with the resources of the Gospel.

To live in the 20th Century is to be entrusted with a two milennia legacy of Christian teaching and reflection. The very variety of this theological heritage is enough to signal that simply passing on in an untainted fashion the kernels of previous formulation has never been considered sufficient. Great theology has achieved its treasured place because of the courage of thinkers who employed their creative gifts to speak about, and to, the challenges of the day. In the domain of the moral life, with all of the historical, social and cultural factors that must be taken into account, the need for constant reinterpretation of traditional teaching is even greater.

Among those dimensions of human life that have undergone the most change (in theory to be sure and to a large extent in practice), human sexual behavior is a prime candidate. For example, the privileged status of heterosexual marriage has been challenged by: (i) the numbers of young people who live together without a formalized commitment (ii) an increasing divorce and/or remarriage rate among all segments of the population (iii) the feminist critique of the familiar sex role patterning in marriage and (iv) mroe casual attitudes about extra-marital affairs. In addition, we have witnessed a revolution in child-bearing practices. In the Catholic world, the intramural debate about clerical celibacy has contributed to the prevailing opinion that sexual needs are so basic and unpredictable that to hinder their free expression is to border on the impossible.

It is in such a climate of sexual discussion that the debate about the morality of homosexual behavior has emerged. We are in the first or revisionist stage of discussion. As with so many other issues of ethical concern, a long-standing tradition is deemed unsuitable by some minority group within the Church. They proceed to develop a case by attaining the theoretical foundations of the established opinion. They suggest that a new ethical formulation is required. Some choose the moderate course of simply recommending slight modifications of the older theory. Others press for a wholesale rejection of the older approach. But the combined force of the two camps is enough to alert the wider Christian community to the presence of a serious split within the membership. The more respectable and capable that the revisionists seem to be the more disconcerting their very existence is to the majority.

For the duration of the revisionist period the concentration of labor is of the critical sort. We are told what seem to be the weaknesses and the liabilities of the previous methodology. Sometimes a few modest alternatives are proposed but overall a confidence is exuded that further research and experience will develop a more reliable approach. In the meantime, we are encouraged to rest content with the new pluralism where one method of analysis has been rejected without being replaced by another. The Church is a many-roomed mansion where there is plenty of space for contrary opinions to coexist.

The next step in the process of re-evaluation of traditional teaching is for the revisionist thesis to be subjected to the same quality of scrutiny that it has directed to the classic formulation. Flaws in historical analysis, unsubstantiated generalizations, premature conclusions, prejudicial rhetoric are all searched out by way of correcting the correctors. The participants in this level of discussion may be motivated by the deep conviction that the revisionists have not made their case. Or they

285

may consider the task of the scholar to be uncomfortable with any answer that goes unchallenged. Whatever the original spur, their contribution is to bring some balance and perspective into the discussion.

Finally, when the theorists have all had a chance to have their say, and when the mass of Christian people have been sufficiently alerted to the debate to express their own support or disagreement, a stage of working consensus is reached, not in some static once and forever sense, but as a matter of confident expression of a commonly held judgment.

Through this vastly simplified description of the process of moral debate within the Christian community, I want to suggest that we are presently at the tail end of the revisionist stage of development and that the time has come for a review and criticism of the revisionist approach. This book may be taken as one attempt toward that goal. In Chapter 9 I summarized the contemporary versions of non-revisionist theory. In this chapter I have looked at two types of revisionist position moderate and radical. Now I would like to offer my own formulation of an ethical judgment on homosexual behavior. It is a kind of non-revisionist position, but one which attempts to take seriously the valid criticisms of the traditional formulation. In order to ground my argument, I will develop the descriptive category 'the Christian Way of Life' and then contrast it with what I have already said about 'the Homosexual Way of Life.'

Footnotes to Chapter 10--

[1]Donald Goergen, _The Sexual Celibate_ (New York: Seabury, 1974), p. 77.

[2]_Ibid._, p. 189.

[3]_Ibid._, p. 195.

[4]Roger Shinn, "Homosexuality: Christian Conviction and Inquiry," in _The Same Sex_, edited by Roger Weltge (Philadelphia: United Church Press, 1969), pp. 43-54.

[5]_Ibid._, p. 50.

[6]Helmut Thielicke, _The Ethics of Sex_ (Grand Rapids: Baker, 1964), p. 282.

[7]_Ibid._, pp. 284-285.

[8]_Ibid._, p. 288.

[9]H. Kimball Jones, _Toward a Christian Understanding of the Homosexual_ (New York: Association, 1966).

[10]_Ibid._, p. 108.

[11]_Ibid._, p. 109.

[12]_Ibid._, p. 110.

[13]H. Kimball Jones, "Homosexuality--A Provisional Christian Stance," in _Is Gay Good?_, edited by W. Dwight Oberholtzer (Philadelphia: Westminster, 1971), p. 155.

[14]Charles Curran, _Catholic Moral Theory in Dialogue_ (Notre Dame: Fides, 1972), p. 217.

[15]Ralph Weltge, "The Paradox of Man and Woman," in _The Same Sex_, p. 64.

[16]Ibid., p. 66.

[17]John von Rohr, "Toward a Theology of Homosexuality," in Is Gay Good?, pp. 75-97; Theodore Jennings, "Homosexuality and Christian Faith: A Theological Reflection," in Homosexuality and the Christian Faith, edited by Harold Twiss (Valley Forge: Judson, 1978), pp. 57-68.

[18]Von Rohr, loc. cit., p. 93.

[19]Jennings, loc. cit., p. 61.

[20]Ibid., p. 67.

[21]D.S. Bailey, Homosexuality and the Western Christian Tradition (London: Longmans, Green and Co., 1955), pp. xi-xii.

[22]Ibid., p. 157.

[23]Ibid., p. 172-173.

[24]Ibid., p. 173.

[25]W. Dwight Oberholtzer, "Subduing the Cyclops--A Giant Step Toward Ethics," in Is Gay Good?, pp. 11-74.

[26]Norman Pittenger, Time for Consent: A Christian's Approach to Homosexuality (London: SCM Press, 1976).

[27]Ibid., pp. 31-32.

[28]Ibid., p. 92-96.

[29]Ibid., p. 78.

[30]Ibid., p. 98.

[31]John McNeill, The Church and the Homosexual (Kansas City: Sheed Andrews McMeel, 1976).

[32]Ibid., pp. 20-21.

[33]Ibid., p. 143.

[34]Ibid., p. 196.

[35]Anthony Kosnick, et. al., Human Sexuality (New York: Paulist, 1977).

[36]Ibid., pp. 200ff.

[37]Ibid., p. 214.

[38]Ibid., p. 218.

[39]Among the major problems of the book are the following: (i) it confuses ethical analysis with pastoral strategy. (ii) It obscures the fact-value controversy by placing an excessive confidence in the truth claims of the social sciences. (iii) It reviews the history of Christian teaching on sexuality in such a way that it becomes irrelevant for contemporary analysis. (iv) It continually describes the ethical alterna-tives by the use of typologies and then by choosing a 'middle way' it seems to come out on the side of moderation and reason. (v) It is unable to proscribe any kind of human sexual conduct in advance because of a misguided concept of openness. (vi) It makes the absence of 'negative moral absolutes' appear as a wholesale encouragement of all sexual possibilities. (vii) It presents a list of qualities of human related-ness which are drawn almost entirely from develop-mental psychology without any significant attempt to correlate them with Christian teaching and practice.

[40]Neale Secor, "A Brief for a New Homosexual Ethic," in The Same Sex, pp. 67-79.

[41]Ibid., pp. 78-79.

[42]Lewis Maddocks, "The Law and the Church vs. the Homosexual," in The Same Sex, pp. 95-110.

[43]Clinton Jones, <u>Homosexuality and Counseling</u> Philadelphia: Fortress, 1974), p. 15.

[44]Lewis Williams, "Walls of Ice-Theology and Social Policy," in <u>Is Gay Good?</u>, pp. 163-184.

[45]Del Martin and Phyllis Lyon, "A Lesbian Approach to Theology," in <u>Is Gay Good?</u>, pp. 213-220.

[46]Pierre Claude Nappey, "An Open Letter on Homosexuality," <u>Cross Currents</u>, 20, 1970, pp. 213-237.

[47]James Nelson, "Homosexuality and the Church," <u>Christianity and Crisis</u>, 37, 1977, pp. 63-69.

[48]Morton Kelsey, "The Homosexual and the Church," in <u>Sex: Thoughts for Contemporary Christians</u>, edited by Michael Taylor (Garden City: Doubleday, 1973), pp. 213-222.

[49]Gregory Baum, "Catholic Homosexuals," <u>Commonweal</u>, 100, 1974, pp. 479-482.

[50]Richard Woods, <u>Another Kind of Love: Homosexuality and Spirituality</u> (Garden City: Doubleday, 1978).

[51]<u>Ibid.</u>, p. 126.

[52]<u>Ibid.</u>, p. 148.

[53]Barbara Gitings, "The Homosexual and the Church," in <u>The Same Sex</u>, pp. 146-155.

[54]Letha Scanzoni and Virginia Ramey Mollenkott, <u>Is the Homosexual My Neighbor?</u> (New York: Harper & Row, 1978).

[55]<u>Ibid.</u>, p. 10.

[56]<u>Ibid.</u>, p. 132.

[57]John Murphy, Homosexual Liberation: A Personal View (New York: Praeger, 1971).

[58]Ibid., p. 41.

[59]Ibid., p. 178.

[60]Carl Wittman, "Refugees from Amerika: A Gay Manifesto," in The Homosexual Dialectic, edited by Joseph McCaffrey (Englewood Cliffs: Prentice-Hall, 1972), p. 159.

[61]Paul Goodman, "Memoirs of an Ancient Activist," in The Homosexual Dialectic, pp. 178-179.

[62]Linda Barufaldi and Emily Culpepper, "Androgyny and the Myth of Masculine/Feminine," Christianity & Crisis, 33, 1973, p. 71.

[63]Bill Johnson, "The Good News of Gay Liberation," in Loving Women/Loving Men, edited by Sally Gearhart and Bill Johnson (San Francisco: Glide, 1974), pp. 91-117.

[64]Ibid., p. 94.

[65]Ibid., p. 114.

[66]Sally Gearhart, "The Miracle of Lesbianism," in Loving Women/Loving Men, pp. 119-152.

[67]Ibid., p. 139.

[68]Ibid., p. 151.

Chapter 11

The Christian Way of Life

The Christian way of life is a product of
history.[1] It is made up of that specific configuration of moral values, norms, judgments and
practices that have recurred continuously in
Christian history. These components have seemed
so essential to its members that they have sought
to pass them on without error or misinterpretation
to the next generation. In a sense, by being born
or baptized into the Christian community, one is
immediately immersed into this way of life.
Amidst all of the diversity, and even serious disagreements, among the Christian churches there is
a basic level of commonality of perspective which
transcends all of the differences. The Christian
way of life is open to change and transformation;
it is not a static or closed system. Yet there is
a basic recognition of the need for loyalty to the
primordial and decisive event that was manifested
in Jesus the Christ.

There is no particular place that one can
point to where this way of life is described in
all of its fullness.[2] Even the Christian
Scriptures are far from adequate in this regard.
For the oral and written Gospel is first of all a
religious word, the glad tidings of the coming of
God's Kingdom. Only secondarily is it a form of
ethical teaching. Therefore, we must combine a
sensitive reading of Scripture with an awareness
of the many other sources that reveal how the
living Church sought to apply its deepest convictions to the concrete moral issues of everyday
life. Philosophy, law, theology, scientific
speculation and art are all important strata in
the search for evidence of how the Church did, and
does, form itself and educate and inspire its
members.

An adequate description of the Christian way
of life is beyond the scope of this chapter.
However, I will employ this analytical category as
a convenient method for opening up a different
approach to the problem of homosexual behavior.
This chapter will proceed in three stages. First,
I will give a brief sketch of some of the

294

essential components of the Christian way of life as I interpret it. Second, I will focus on the understanding of sexuality which I think is central to that way of life. Third, I will defend the conclusion that the Homosexual way of life, as described in the previous chapters, cannot be reconciled with the Christian way of life.

I. The Christian Way of Life

Before I attempt to describe some of the salient characteristics of the Christian way of life, I need to put the issue in some perspective. In contemporary theological ethics, there is a debate going on between those who think that there is no such thing as a distinctively Christian ethic and those who think there is. Since I include myself in the latter category, I must at least respond to the critics of this position. Thus, this section will be divided into two parts. First, I will argue the case for a distinctively Christian ethic relative to the contemporary discussion. Then, second, I will concentrate on the broader question of the nature of the Christian way of life.

(a) The Case for a Distinctively Christian Ethic-

Catholic moral theology has, since the time of St. Thomas Aquinas at least, employed a natural law methodology. The claim was made that this philosophical perspective provided a common frame of reference by which Christians and non-Christians could both communicate about, and arrive at, decisions affecting the social order. Although Catholic Christians surely accepted the importance of the Scriptures and of the teaching authority as sources of clarification and inspiration, there was a hesitancy to push the distinctive element too far lest the common frame of reference be lost. Protestant ethics, on the other hand, in its mainstream form has tended to want to preserve something distinctive for

295

Christian ethics. This sprang primarily from a more negative theological anthropology which highlighted the decisive impairment of the rational faculty as the result of sin. In the 20th century the influence of Karl Barth has been especially significant in this regard.

As a result of the severe criticisms levelled against the traditional natural law methodology, Catholic ethicists have had to reexamine the issue of the specificity of Christian ethics. The results of this discussion are far from conclusive. There seem to be two basic camps: those who deny the distinctiveness of Christian ethics and those who defend it, in one form or another.

(i) The Negative Position-- Those who claim nothing distinctive for Christian ethics tend to find in the common ethical wisdom of humankind the full basis (both in general orientation and in specific context) for a Christian moral life. While these thinkers surely recognize the inhibiting forces of sin and ignorance, they find that the Church must meet the same challenges in keeping alive its collective moral sensitivity as other participants in the human community. The promise of the presence of the Spirit in the community does not provide unmediated moral truth, but a confidence that Christians can recognize the truth wherever they might find it.

John Giles Milhaven, for example, claims that "any Christian ethic must rest on a secular base, man's experience in the world. . .All the values, responsibilities and obligations the Christian recognizes--except those pertaining to God, such as prayer--are forged first of all in this human experience."[3] And Willem Van der Marck operating out of a phenomenological background, arrives at the same conclusion. "Thus we speak of a Christian ethic not in order to indicate a conviction that there might be a non-Christian ethic as well, but simply in order to say that the human ethic is, in fact, Christian."[4] Finally, Charles

Curran, in a sustained defense of this position, contends that

> theological considerations of both the subject-pole and the object-pole of Christian existence, together with the historical and experiential data considered earlier, argue for the fact that there is not a strict dichotomy between Christian ethics and non-Christian ethics.[5]

In summary, then, those who take a negative position point to various factors in human experience which seem to relativize the claims for a distinctive Christian ethic. They turn the question into a challenge to those who disagree to prove their case on similar comparative grounds.

(ii) The Positive Position-- Catholic ethicists who defend the claim that the Christian ethic is unique develop their position by accentuating different factors. I will summarize the main ones.

(A) The Christian ethic has a distinctive orientation toward the future-- Herbert McCabe discerns a similarity between the task of the literary critic and the task of the ethicist.[6] In both cases, the specific material with which one works (e.g., for the ethicist a code of conduct) is less important than the vision or overall context within which one places it. The uniqueness of the Christian vision is that it has a revolutionary orientation toward the future, as portrayed in Jesus' preaching of the kingdom, which enables us to live with a hope, and to practice a way of life, which seems unreasonable to the contemporary world.

(B) The Christian Ethic is distinctive because it is developed within and nourished by, participation in the Christian community-- Basically, this position presupposes that the

297

institutional base which is the Church is both a carrier of tradition and a protection against individualism. For example, William E. May, while attracted to the many connections between Christian ethics, points out that "the mission of the Christian community. . .is, at least in part, to provide for all men the supportive context that will enable them to come to know what is human and to do this."[7] Enda McDonagh is even more explicit in his assertion that the Christian ethic is a community ethic; that is, it is given to human beings in community, understood in community, and designed for the building of community.[8] And finally, Norbert Rigali, after reacting negatively to the Rahnerian hypothesis of the 'anonymous Christian,' concentrates on what he calls the 'essential ethics of Christianity' which is a function of participation in the Church-community.

(C) The Christian ethic is distinctive because there is a specific Christian intentionality-- According to Josef Fuchs, only the Christian perceives the moral life in terms of a "personal, conscious, and freely-willed relation to the Father of Jesus Christ."[10] There are certain realities which the Christian alone recognizes and acknowledges. For instance, the crucifixion of Jesus Christ and the great stress on the centrality of love transform not only one's overall intention but also aid in the discernment of specific moral responsibilities. After surveying the variety of opinions on this issue, Richard McCormick ends up in substance agreeing with Fuchs. "It seems to me that if the light of the gospel can aid in the discovery of truly human solutions to our problems, then those who have the gospel have the source of knowledge which others not exposed to the gospel do not have."[11]

(D) The Christian ethic is distinctive because it provides a stimulus, a context and a motivation in the moral life-- In a provocative essay, Gerald Hughes rejects three theses which have been suggested as reasons for making claims of uniqueness for the Christian ethic: (i) that the teaching and example of Jesus is the key, (ii) that Christian revelation is a necessary supplement to natural truth and (iii) that God's will is the justification for any moral truth. Instead he proposes that while the Christian faith adds no substantive context it provides a stimulus, a context and a motivation.[12]

What these examples of positive and negative answers make clear is that prior concerns have affected significantly the way the evidence is interpreted. The negative group is willing to foresake a privileged position in order to keep open the ongoing dialogue with people of good will everywhere. The positive group thinks that being a Christian makes a difference in one's moral life, but they attempt to phrase their answer in such a way that it takes into account the existing disagreement and does not sound overly offensive to those outside the Christian community.

(iii) Conclusion-- I identify with the group of Catholic thinkers who argue that there is something distinctive about Christian ethics. Whether in some ideal, prelapsarian world this would have been true, I do not know. It is obvious that Christians hold many positions in common with other people of good will. This makes ordered life possible in a pluralistic society. But I believe that there is no guarantee that this will be the case in any particular social or cultural setting. And general agreement over the whole range of issues that Christians have thought important is even less likely to occur. I suspect that Christians in Western society have become complacent because so much of their cultural and legal tradition has been influenced by Christian sources. A quick trip into a non-Western culture, whether of a Marxist, Buddhist, Muslim or other type, can reveal the great discrepancy that exists over some fundamental issues. The United Nations and other international organizations are a reminder that the hope lives on that common ground can be found to formulate unified social policy on global problems. Yet the evidence is mixed at best as to the chances of success for such ventures.

There are many examples in our own time that suggest that Christians may find it progressively more difficult to reach an ethical consensus with those who do not share a similar faith stance. I say this cognizant of the fact that Christians have not always consistently applied their own ethical principles. Think, for example, of the various aspects of the dignity of human life question--abortion, infanticide, euthanasia, unjustified violence, revenge, nuclear war, terrorism, etc. Or ponder the equality of all people in the Lord vis-a-vis -- racism, sexism militant nationalism, and religious persecution. Finally, reflect on issues of economic justice--labor-management relations, immigration, distribution of scarce resources, monetary aid, and multi-national corporations. All of these questions are complex, but Christians may have to face the prospect of finding fewer other groups who even define the problems in the same general categories.

I hope that I am wrong. I hope that a wave of international cooperation and general benevolence will sweep the world. But from my point of view I think it is unlikely. With the breakup of the hegemony of Western culture, I suspect that more and more Christians will find themselves engaging in an ethical monologue in a more and more uncomprehending world. Karl Rahner's metaphor of the 'church of the diaspora' (small groups of dedicated Christians dispersed throughout a generally hostile culture) seems to capture the situation I envisage.

If my picture is at all true, and only the passage of time will tell for sure, I still have to detail what is distinctive about a Christian ethic. I consider the following characteristics to be peculiar to such an ethic. None of them individually is sufficient, but together they form a unique combination of qualities.

300

(1) <u>The Christian ethic is a Church-based ethic</u> -- The Christian never stands alone, as a solipsistic moral agent. Right from the start, the rite of baptism introduces the person into an historical community where status and honor accrue to those who effectively embody their faith convictions in concrete forms of service. Even the solitary mystic and the hermit pray to a threefold God whose very inner-life is a reminder of the interpersonal context of existence. This Church is held together by a common memory, a common task, and a common hope. When it structures itself in order to facilitate God's work in the world, it is unity of purpose and sharing of skill which enable it to be effective. Because the individual Christian is part of a Church, he or she can partake in a wisdom and a cumulative experience which transcends the bounds of any specific moral moment.

(2) <u>The Christian ethic is a self-consciously historical ethic</u> -- The Christian decision-maker of today does not start from scratch. To be a Christian is to have a fitting reverence for the previous manifestations of the life of the Spirit in the unfolding of the Church. It is to partake in a legacy or heritage, a shaping force, which enshrines the genius of many. In one sense, to be a peacemaker is to renounce the temptation to do harm to others where we are. But in a fuller sense, the Christian peacemaker is one who has absorbed the countless probings and questionings of the Christian past over the issue of violence in order to take into account both the complexity of the challenge of the moment and the purity of required response.

(3) <u>The Christian ethic is a creative ethic</u> --The Scriptures are silent on so many of the problems that plague modern life--vehicular safety, medical research, ecology, test tube babies, nuclear power, t.v. advertising. But this has always been a difficulty. The New Testament authors focused their energies on the issues of their day--the necessity for circumcision, food

301

sacrificed to idols, disunity in the community, treatment of the poor. And in the process, they modelled the style that subsequent reflection should take. What was less important than the specific problem at hand was the manner in which the teaching and witness of the Lord was used as the frame of reference for all analysis. There was no answer book available, no handy code that foresaw the solution to all problems. Instead there was stories, a narrative context, out of which each generation of Christians was to forge a creative response to the moral dilemmas of the present. So at the same time that there was continuity and consistency of teaching and practice in many areas of life, there was also to be a courageous willingness to face the unknown and the uncertain as well.

(4) The Christian ethic is a trans-temporal ethic -- The Christian views the world with an eye to that which lies beyond. The ambiguity of all human existence, the intermixture of success and failure, joy and sorrow, the wavering between utopian schemes and cynical indifference, are all reasons for wondering about the ultimate purpose behind our cumulative efforts. Those who believe in the transformative power of our participation in the victory of the risen Lord face such musings with a hope beyond all hope.

(5) The Christian ethic is a sacrificial ethic -- The Christian is privileged to walk in the steps of the Lord. The scandal of the cross lies close at hand for those who have experienced the relativity of all good things in this life. Fame and fortune, well-being and self-achievement, can be renounced only when the cause of God finds a deep resonance in our hearts. The patience of the spurned spouse, the tender care of the battle-field doctor, the struggle of the impoverished parent, these and thousands of other examples of Christian bearing-up under trial are the stuff of discipleship.

302

(6) The Christian ethic is a transformative ethic -- The Christian is called to participation in a process of personal metanoia. We are to be perfect even as our heavenly Father is perfect. There is to be no built in limit to our service or love or forgiveness. Yet, sin-fractured persons that we are, progress is slow and often contradictory. We know that the first step in effecting a better and more just society is the effort to become individuals of integrity in our lives.

(7) The Christian ethic is a heroic ethic -- From the time of the apostles and martyrs until the present, the Christian community has pointed to examples of flesh and blood, of saintly women and men of the past, to serve as models of the Christian life and as sources of inspiration for us today. The courage of conviction which faced the hostility of persecutors, the zeal for the discipline of prayer which lured thousands into the deserts and wilds, the steadfastness of the missionary journeyers and the fortitude of loving spouses and parents, all testify to the power of God at work among the humble lot of creatures like ourselves.

(8) The Christian ethic is an inclusive ethic --There is no aspect of human existence, no race or culture or sex, no economic political or social reality, which lies outside of the claim of the Christian ethic. The individual person on the labor force or in the market place is just as much under the sway of the sovereign Lord as in the solitude of a heart-felt prayer or the preparation for the moment of death. All of the natural order needs to be redeemed. But it is the God of creation who promises at the end of time a full reconciliation of all that has been so tragically ripped asunder.

(9) The Christian ethic is an active ethic -- We will be judged for what we do in the body. Life is not a charade played out before a benevolent divine dictator who will forgive us all in the end no matter what. The concreteness and

303

specificity of our unique stories as individuals
is a result of our capability for both good and
evil. There is a wide variety in the personal
configuration of the many factors that go to
making us a moral agent -- self-awareness,
experience, value commitments, discernment skill,
intelligence, good will. The projects we under-
take (those discrete bits of behavior which carry
our personal stamp) are the substance of whom we
are (and have become) manifested in the world.
They are our products and as such are signs that
we are neither angelic creatures of pure will nor
automations subject to complete manipulation by
external forces. To love our neighbor whom we can
see is the first step toward manifesting our love
of the God we cannot see.

(10) <u>The Christian ethic is a repentant ethic</u>
--Of ourselves alone we can do nothing, but with
God all things are possible. The self-righteous
and the saved have no need of the healing words of
salvation. In the midst of the euphoria of our
small successes in this life, we are continually
reminded of our hypocrisy, self-deception and
pride. The Christian ethic calls out to sinners
to turn from the path of evil and to return to the
path of life. All equivocation and weak-
heartedness must be left behind. It is as a
sinner justified by God that moral life becomes a
real possibility and grace reaches out to
reconcile an estanged human society.

This list is far from exhaustive, but it does capture a number of elements which I think make the
Christian ethic distinctive. I have pictured this
ethic as: Church-based, self-consciously historical, creative, trans-temporal, sacrificial, transformative, heroic, inclusive, active and
repentant. Once again, it is the combination of
all of these qualities which is important.
Together they form a context within which the content (the particular moral teachings) is learned
and subjected to further scrutiny. In the second
part of this first section of the chapter, I will

now describe some of the components of the Christian way of life.

II. The Nature of the Christian Way of Life

The Christian ethic has both form and content. In part one I have discussed some of its characteristics. Now I will concentrate on its content. But right from the start we are faced with a problem. Any ethic which is historical, creative and transformative will change and reinterpret itself with the passage of time. So what I am proposing is not some fixed, once-and-for-all content (at least not primarily) but rather a series of fundamental values which have been given normative status and enshrined in the determinative practices of the Christian community. A Christian is one who does what Christians do. If a person would belong to this voluntary and Spirit-filled group of believers, then his or her behavior should conform to the standards of the affiliated collectivity.

Rather than attempt an exhaustive description of the main rudiments of the Christian way of life, and before concentrating on its teaching of sexuality, I want to give three brief indications of what I am talking about. I will discuss them under the topics of: violence, money and worship.

(a) The Christian Way of Life and Violence -- Mahatma Gandhi has been quoted as saying that the Sermon on the Mount is the most beautiful teaching about the ethics of violence that has ever been devised; it is just too bad that Christians do not practice it. The advent of nuclear weaponry and the debacle of Vietnam have reminded contemporary Christians that there is a deep strain of pacifism in the Christian tradition that stands in judgment of all temptations to glorify violence or to retreat into attitudes of cynical realism.[13] Despite the aberration of the Crusades, the two main positions of Christians about war can be

305

interpreted as efforts to take the value of each human life with fitting seriousness.

The abhorrence of bloodshed and the high priority given to peace and reconciliation pervade the whole of the New Testament. Jesus glorifies the peacemakers, refuses to engage in a physical defense of his personhood, and cultivates a disposition of forgiveness for faults rendered. Paul pleads for unity in the community and prepares his converts for persecution. And as the Church grew within the Roman Empire, its members foresook participation in the army on religious grounds.

After Constantine and the radical shift in the relationship between the Church and the Empire, a just war theory was developed. But from Ambrose and Augustine to Ford and Ramsey, the criteria for a just war were a sophisticated and sincere attempt to highlight the value of human life in such a way that only a rare concatenation of factors could ever justify the destruction of life that comes with war.

But war is only one kind of violence. The Christian way of life has evolved in such a fashion that a whole series of related issues were seem to call for a related witnessing to the sacredness of life. Historically, the Christian is one who opposes: abortion, infanticide, euthanasia, revenge and terrorism. Even the allowance for war and capital punishment (in some instances) is done with the greatest reluctance and only after satisfying the believing community that some higher value is at stake.

It is not so much that Christians have an unspotted record of adherence to these central tenets. The pages of history, especially in Western society, are full of sinful and callous disregard of the priority of life. Yet the community has continually striven to teach its new members these values and the proper applications to life issues. The Christian way of life demands a firm renunciation of violence as a solution to

306

human problems or as an inevitable offshoot of the malevolence of the race. The prototypical Christian hero or heroine is not the warrior, the commander or the hangman, but the peacemaker, the unifier and the healer.

(b) The Christian Way of Life and Money -- Jesus himself seems to have expressed a general disregard of the economic sphere.[14] Surely, however, he recognized the idolatrous potential built into the pursuit of riches. And he gave high priority to meeting the needs of the poor and powerless. They were to have a special place in the Kingdom. Yet Jesus did nothing tangible to effect radical change in the economic system of the day and he left us no detailed plan for how to harmonize his relativizing of the importance of money (or its equivalents) with the necessity of work, of the dynamics of the marketplace, or of the equitable distribution of the world's goods.

From what we can tell the early Christian churches practiced a kind of primitive communism. With varying degrees of success, they balanced out the extremes of poverty and wealth not only in the local church, but even between different churches (cf. Paul in Jerusalem). Later as the Church attained a certain privileged place in the Empire, problems of social status among its members carried over into ecclesial affairs.

Christianity has existed within a wide variety of economic systems during the course of its history: from barter economy to feudalism to capitalism to socialism and communism. In each of these economic settings it has resisted the yoking of the Gospel to one particular range of alternatives. It condemned usury when that practice was inevitably bound to an abuse of the poor by the wealthy. It spoke out against class warfare when the proletariat and bourgeoisie were being pitted off against one another. Yet it has valued the dignity of work, the right of just compensation, the right of voluntary affiliation, and the right to protection in old age and

307

infirmity. It has pled for a managed economy, an international distribution of the goods of the earth, and just taxation. It has criticized self-serving policies of consumerism, hoarding, industrialization and technocratization.

The Christian way of life involves a recognition of the proper place of money or wealth in our existence in society. The first priority is the maximization of the just distribution of goods. Whatever particular economic structure of the present seems to offer the best chance to realize this goal should be supported for that reason. The Christian way of life refuses to allow the economic dimension of our life to shut out the fuller version of a complementary society where each will contribute as he or she is able, and each will receive as he or she stands in need.

(c) <u>The Christian Way of Life and Prayer</u> -- The Gospels picture Jesus as a man of prayer, who regularly withdrew from the crowd to commune wth his Father.[15] He prayed in the synagogue and encouraged his disciples to keep the Jewish forms of piety--prayer, almsgiving and fasting. After Pentecost, the local churches gathered together at the Lord's Supper to remember the deed Jesus had done and to celebrate their life in community.

During the course of Church history, the forms of prayer have been many -- from the lonely plaint of the isolated hermit to the Gregorian strains of the high liturgy at St. Peter's, from the rhapsodic dance of the African tribal to the somber restraint of the public penitential. But the priority of prayer in the Christian life has always been presupposed. The Christian is one who prays in time of trouble and public calamity, in moments of elation and triumph, at the turning points of life from birth to adulthood to death, and in situations of moral dilemma. And the Christian never prays alone, for even in relative ignorance of the individual's particular need, the Church prays as one.

308

The Christian way of life is impossible without prayer and worship. It is this imperative which keeps alive the sense of God's presence in the struggles and uncertainties of human activity.

What I have been suggesting by these three examples is that the Christian way of life has taken a certain shape in the course of its own evolution. Christians are known not only for certain doctrinal beliefs and moral teachings, but for concrete practices which witness to the centrality of certain moral values. It is this integral interaction between conviction and practice that makes the Christian way of life distinctive and unique.

Now I will turn to the particular area of concern of this book--the Christian teaching and practice in regards to human sexuality.

III. Sexuality and the Christian Way of Life

There are numerous studies available which review the history of the biblical, patristic and medieval teachings about sexuality.[16] In recent times, there has been a common strain of apology for what is taken to be the Hellenistic dualism, the celibate negativism, the canonical legalism, and the ascetic angelism in much of the post-Scriptural writing on the topic. St. Paul's misogynism, St. Augustine's retrospective regret for his own sexual escapades, and St. Thomas Aquinas' biologism have come under particular attack. At the same time, we are becoming aware of some controversial rejections of the sexual teaching articulated by leading Christian spokespersons and we are being reminded of the radical changes between the social context of the past and that which prevails today. Young people reach puberty earlier, live in an eroticized culture, are encouraged to value 'normalcy' as statistically determined, have 'perfection of technique' as a desired goal, put off marriage longer for reasons of career and economic security, often renounce the desire for children, and explore new conceptions of sexual roles and sexual identities. Amidst all of this confusion, some think that we should give up pretending that the Christian tradition has anything of value to say about sexuality.

On the contrary, what I want to suggest is that the Christian way of life has a positive orientation to distill and to represent the central elements of such an understanding. I will begin with a short preface, and then proceed to concentrate on three virtues which focus this interpretation, namely, chastity, love and faithfulness.

(a) _Preface_ -- Throughout the Scriptures marriage is seen as the paradigm sexual relationship. Since, as far as we know, all Jews married, this is not to be wondered at. In fact, the prophetic celibacy of Jeremiah and John the Baptist had a special power of witness because of the unusual situation in which they lived. It is said by some contemporary commentators that the Jews had a natural and healthy attitude toward sexuality that was quickly lost once Christianity spread into the Greco-Roman culture. This may be true to some extent but it easily degenerates into a romanticization of the distant past. The books of the Old Testament recount enough instances of sexual intrigue, adultery, jealousy and scandal to cool any over-enthusiasm for the idyllic experience of Jewish sexuality (not to speak of illiteracy, sexual subordination of women, work exhaustion and body odors).

The New Testament is relatively silent about sexuality as a topic. Jesus teaches about marriage and divorce and forgives the woman at the well and the woman taken in adultery. Paul gives instructions on marriage, celibacy and divorce, and castigates the man living with his step-mother and others who violate the prevailing norms. But there is no concerted effort to stress sexual conformity as the ultimate test of dutiful

310

discipleship. It is likely that the early age for marriage, the lack of anonymity, and the normal social pressures kept the majority of Christians from straying far from the accepted standards. Only in licentious Corinth or cosmopolitan Rome were the temptations to radical departures from the Christian ethic a subject of major concern.

Therefore, I think we should interpret the Scriptural teaching on sexuality in a thematic fashion rather than by concentrating on specific texts that make reference to sexual behavior. The four themes of creation, covenant, incarnation and resurrection seem to capture the most positive formulation of the Christian teaching on sexuality.

(b) Creation--

The two creation accounts in the book of Genesis picture sexual differentiation and the concomitant sexual attraction and complementarity as a part of the goodness of God's gift of cosmic existence.[17] Marriage is a divine institution in which two separate beings become 'one flesh.' While this sexual dimension of human experience has also been impaired by sin, it is still capable of contributing to the most profound expression of human community and solidarity. Unlike the divinity-controlled sacral understanding of sexuality that prevailed in other near-Eastern cultures, the Jews spoke of marriage as a secular reality, part of the goodness of creation. Furthermore, in the lyrical Song of Solomon they celebrated the beauty of erotic love in an appealing and joyful fashion. The Christian tradition has taken over this sexuality as a good gift of creation approach, contrary to all attempts (Gnostic, Manichean, Albigensian, Jansenist and Puritan) to make it the root of all evil or some inherently distorted human capacity.

311

(c) Covenant--

In the Bible the language of convenant is the preferred way of talking about mutuality, reciprocal responsibilities, and bondedness.[18] The Covenant that Yahweh makes with his people Israel (through Abraham, Moses and David) and the covenant of Christ with the Church (bursting into reality on Pentecost) are theological affirmations that search for an analogue. The most convenient one at hand, and also the most suitable, is found in the intimate relationship of a husband and wife in marriage. No other parallel, neither friendship nor participation in the body politic nor contract between agents of trade, is able to symbolize the same degree of personal involvement and intensity of purpose. Covenant language is also used to speak of infidelity to promise as in the relationship between Hosea and his adulterous wife Gomer, which serves as a sign of Israel's shattering of their obligations to their covenant partner Yahweh. Thus the Christian tradition has seen in the concept of convenant a fitting way to talk about promising and mutual obligation as well as fickleness and promiscuity in the context of sexual relationship.

(d) Incarnation--

The Son of God assumed the fullness of the human condition in the person of Jesus.[19] He was like us in all things but sin. As a result, he was a sexual being (of the male gender) who had to learn to integrate his sexual capabilities and desires into a mature sense of self. He was loved by many, including a number of women, and attained a reputation as teacher and practitioner of love. Yet he was a celibate who never married and who devoted himself selflessly to his public mission. Since sexuality was a part of the experience of the Jesus of history, it can never be alien to those who would follow in his steps. His celibate form of life was not an asexualization or a symbolic renunciation of an evil immersion in the flesh but rather a witness to a transcendent

312

willingness to foresake one of the goods of his world for a more complete dedication to the task at hand.

(d) Resurrection--

In the Kingdom of God there will be no marriage because the focus on the privileged context of love will be replaced by a more inclusive orientation of self.[20] That which was totally good in creation (sexuality) will be restored to its former harmony. Because of the hope that the promise of the Kingdom engenders, Christians in this life are freed from the necessity to marry. Now no form of sexual relatedness has an absolute value, but all are equally called as sexual beings (whether single, married or celibate) to recognize and proclaim the reality of the resurrection when their whole beings (including their bodies) will be accepted and transformed by the Lord.

This fourfold perspective of creation, covenant, incarnation and resurrection is the Christian antidote to either of the major alternatives in sexual conceptualization. Christians reject the implicit angelism of all attempts to make the human person into a spirit imprisoned in a bodily cage, a cage in which the sex drive is the everpresent reminder of the seduction of the higher by the lower. But, at the same time, Christians reject the ardent sensualism of those who portray the ecstasy of orgasm as the ultimate experience in the necessary movement to a total identification with our natural impulses. Neither by soaring to angelic reaches nor by descending to the world of instinct does the Christian expect to achieve a satisfactory integration of his or her sexual possibilities. Instead, it is by consciously assenting to the ambivalent human process of giving and receiving across time that two human persons know what they are capable of as human beings and how precarious is the realization of this possibility.

With this general background in mind, I will not turn to the three virtues which, in the sexual sphere, seem to be central to the Christian way of life--chastity, love and faithfulness.

(e) Chastity--

Chastity refers to the virtue which allows a person to live out his or her sexuality according to a value-oriented perspective. It presupposes a context of normativity which is supplied, in this instance, by participation in the Christian community. Like all virtues, it is regulated by the ancillary virtue of prudence, which determines the appropriateness of conduct for various ages and states of life. A chaste person is one who is capable of both exultation and celebration in the concreteness of a prized other and of discipline and restraint in the embodiment of the quality of a relationship.

Chastity has nothing to do with prudishness nor guilt-laden fear. It seeks no scapegoats and bears no malice. Chastity is not correlated with youth and innocence but with maturity and wisdom. Chastity is not virginity, especially in the sense of physical intactness, although it can be present in it. No degree of sexual failure eliminates the possibility of a chaste life, but it makes it proportionately more difficult. Chastity is that virtue which enables all people (of whatever sexual orientation, in whatever state in life) to achieve integrity of relatedness (to self, to other, and to God).

In the simple words of Bishop Mugavero, "Chastity is a virtue which liberates the human person. Chastity means simply that sexuality and its physical, genital expressions are seen as good for man and woman-good in so far as we make them serve life and love."[21] Or as expressed by Richard McCormick, "Mature chastity is really the sex instinct as educated to and dominated by altruism, or adult emotional responses."[22]

314

In the Christian frame of reference, chastity grows as the individual learns to move from the instinct of immediate self-gratification to a cultivated sense of delayed satisfaction. The precocious display of masculinity and femininity in the absence of the proper circumstantial factors is nothing more than conceit or a cover for deep-seated self-doubt. In the same way, the gestures of intimacy engaged in by those who are untutored in adult responsibility belie the groping and experimental character of the engagement. For every stage in life and for ever kind of relationship there is an appropriate form of chastity.

The chaste person in modern society attends to the minimal goal of acquainting him or herself with the biological facts of sexuality. Deliberate ignorance of bodily dynamics or psychological processes is no excuse for failure and disrepute. Yet the more demanding task involves a continual interaction with a variety of other humans as a unique sense of self emerges in the course of time. To be attracted and attractive, to be loved and rejected, to be sensitive and independent, all of these qualities of the self can only be discovered when one is capable of risking failure for the good that may be found.

For the Christian, chastity entails living as a sexual being within certain parameters. The single person is by definition unprepared or unwilling or incapable of the formal commitment of heterosexual marriage. In this light, the appropriate expression of affectivity must not include any symbolization which communicates a totality of self-donation and of reciprocal expectation. To do so would be a lie. And persons in a relationship who have ventured such expressions prematurely must return to a more realistic level of sexual communication. Otherwise, the partners become incapable of advancing any further in the maturity of their relationship.

315

The married person is freed from the need for sexual restraint with his or her spouse in the sense that all genuine expressions of love and affection can have their proper place. Yet, even here the well-being of the partner and the rhythm of human interaction require a sensitivity and concern for the other which can only be learned through experience. And further, the whole range of friendship and sharing outside of the marital bond take on a different complexion because of the preeminence of this bond. The monogramy of the partnership is the qualifier of all other potential sexual relationships.

The celibate person acknowledges the beauty and power of the sex donation of marriage, but foregoes this privilege in order to witness to and serve God's kingdom. Nevertheless, the celibate is fully a sexual being with the concomitant obligation to maintain a healthy degree of affectivity and warmth without succumbing to naive suitorship or to depersonalizing repression.

The widowed person, as well as the separated or divorced person, must learn a new skill of sexual relatedness. In the absence of an accustomed context for the expression of love and concern, a redefinition and reassessment of self is required. To prevent the anguish of loneliness and isolation, remembrance must be combined with sociability. For those fortunate enough to have children of their own, this may well be the place to begin.

Christian chastity is the informing virtue for each person in their life's journey as sexual beings. For the young, it may be understood only after developing the courage to stand apart from their subcultural mores. For the middle aged, it may require a reaffirmation of a previous willing-ness to choose one path among many as the test of one's truth. For the elderly, it may offer the opportunity to cap off the form of a life without hesitation or regret.

The Christian way of life sees chastity as the virtue of the sexual self whereby discipline is combined with heart-felt celebration, a sense of appropriateness with honesty of embodied communication. This virtue is the enemy of all forms of personal aggrandizement, of every irresponsible gesture of relatedness. It seeks for a fitting correspondence between intended meaning and act. It says that, though we are fully sexual beings, we are more besides and sexual expression must serve the purposes of the whole self before God.

(f) Love--

It is a commonplace of Christian analysis that the English language is impoverished when it comes to expressing the subtle distinctions among the forms of love.[23] Love is <u>libido</u> and <u>eros</u>, <u>philia</u> and <u>agape</u>. It is an instinctive drive, a relationship and a life-long calling. It is the most trivial and the most profound of all realities. It is the central Christian virtue and the form of all the other virtues. it is the nature of God and the source of all genuine society.

Yet for all of the complexity, there is hardly a Christian treatise on sexuality in which love does not play the critical role. Love, of course, need have nothing explicit to do with sexuality (as in 'washing feet,' 'serving the neighbor in need,' and 'laying down one's life for a friend') yet sexuality to be authentically realized must have something to do with love.

At the first level, love is about attraction and allurement. The sexual capability of the human person is actualized by another person. This may set off by the least significant of personal qualities, such as comeliness of body or a liveliness of spirit. It is not even necessary that the other be named. Often at a distance, giving free play to the imagination, a relatively unknown personage sums up the desired qualities

317

that are lacking in the real people we know. In
this initial stage, love is erratic and fickle,
the plaything of the emotions. Because there is
no experiential substance to the other party,
there can be no guarantee of the enduring nature
of the sexual possibility. Yet love must begin
somewhere, and in much of sexuality, love begins
with an instinctive attraction to the perceived
beauty of the other.

The second level in the sexual development of
love is more abiding delight in the unfolding of
the fullness of the other self. Physical
proximity and ease of communication enable the
pleasure in the other's company to grow and
blossom. The unfolding of two selves in interlocking ways has a sensuousness and a charm, a
lilting carefree air. The energy released finds a
ready focus in the rituals of music and dance.
Time together has an eternal quality as if the
whole world stood still for the duration. But,
despite the all-consuming passion of this form of
love, it still retains the undifferentiated
character of being in love with love. The other
is not yet known with the kind of specification
and depth that endures. The fading of beauty, the
revelation of a flaw, can divert the momentum and
leave one frustrated and distracted. Yet, for all
of this, the erotic stage of love can open out
into the kind of maturity of self-revelation and
other-acceptance that suits the capabilities of
adults.

Frienship builds on attraction and knowledge
to link two lovers in a common project. In such
cases, trust looms large as the key to further
growth. To trust the other is to give access to
the inner reaches of the mind and heart. It is to
open up one's dreams and fears to the sensitive
scrutiny of another agent. It is to no longer
defend oneself against imagined rebuke. Two
friends who trust can say words of contradictory
quality and still make sense, for as the character
of each breaks forth there exists a point of
reference which holds all things together.

Friends have character for each other because they believe that beyond the accidents of appearance and role there exists a unique other who can be loved, cherished and fostered. In a sense, the love of friendship need not speak the language of bodily gesture, yet in the kiss and the embrace it comfortably reaches out and says 'I care.' Part of the joy of friendship is the countless forms in which it comes. To build a circle of friends or to enspouse a friendship have equal validity and normally belong to the same dynamic of love.

The highest level of love is known first of all at a distance, as an act of humble reflection on our God hung on the cross. Because we have been so loved by God, we are empowered to love in return. This is the love of non-reciprocity, the love which gives without demanding anything in return. It is the love of dedicated self-sacrifice, of patient endurance in time of trial. It is the love which abides as the loved one changes. It risks all for the sake of the other. Of this love, we best speak in parable and story, for its achievement is arduous and many have faltered along the way. This love is stable, it structures a life. It comes from God and yet enhances our humanity. It is the love of community, for it demands a social base. It is the Church present in the particularity of the celebrative pair.

The Christian way of life is full of love in all its forms. And it preserves a sense of the progressive realization of the highest experiences of love. As sexual beings, we know love primarily through our interaction with prized others. And we strive to express that love in ways that are truthful and sincere. Ideally, the love of sexual passion and the love of permanent and exclusive commitment can cohere in a relationship. As in other areas of life, Christian couples should learn to be as good in their love-making as they are in their generous mutual service. Yet the maturing of love in space and time requires sufficient reserve and self-direction to allow the

319

other person to simply be so as to be known. Love
continually strives to say 'yes' with all of its
power, but it must also learn to say 'no' so that
the persons involved can learn the skills required
to love with all of their hearts.

(g) Faithfulness--

Throughout the long periods of Israel's
unfaithfulness to the covenant (shown by her
idolatry and social injustice), Yahweh ever
remained faithful and true. This same God
rejoices over the return of the one lost sheep.
And this is how it is to be with us. Our promise-
making is to be characterized by the same stead-
fast loyalty and perseverance to the end. It is a
violation of trust, a failure of freely chosen
responsibility, to renege on a promise, to go back
on a friend.

The Christian is called to be faithful in
relationship. Honesty, self-revelation and
maturity of judgment can prepare the way, but
finally there is a human leap where everything is
changed. Where formerly there was indeterminate-
ness and lack of specificity, now there is a life
with a texture and a purpose. It is in such
exercises of freedom that we transcend the
boundaries of a nebulous life and stand with
another to face the future together.

The Christian understanding of sexuality
attempts to combine a full acceptance of the
celebrative and integrative possibilities of
genital sexual expression with a seasoned realization of the ephemeral and fickle bondedness of the
relationship it calls into being. Fidelity is
more than gratuitous wish-fulfillment. It is a
painstaking, exasperating human activity.
Christians have looked for clues into the meaning
of loving faithfulness. In many instances they
have found them in adult couples of advancing
years who have raised a family and tested their
resolve through long years of mutual marital
support. It is not the period of courtship and

320

vow-taking that reveals the full dimensions of what will be required (even though it is an indispensable step). Rather it is contented survival though the exigencies of joint life (the sickness, hurts, disappointments, and stress) that render the words credible and give the partners the right to make similar demands of others.

Richard Roach captures the spirit of this interpretation when he says,

> I suggest that according to the Christian tradition sex primarily expresses exclusive fidelity, and exclusive fidelity ought to be one among other possible expressions of faithful love. . .It is the notion of exclusivity as modifying fidelity that reveals in sexuality the meaning in which Christian sexual restraint is grounded.[24]

Paul Ramsey in a rewording of a famous Niebuhrian aphorism describes Christian marriage in a similar fashion.

> Man's capacity for responsible fidelity to the being and well-being of another of opposite sex makes marriage possible. . .yet man's inclination toward unfaith-fulness and irresponsibility makes marriage necessary.[25]

Finally, Sidney Cornelia Callahan argues that fidelity to marital vows is a paradigm for other forms of sexual reciprocity.

> Mature persons open to the future and willing to accept responsibility for the care of others accept the continuity of promises and institutions as an enrichment of love. . .Verbal commitment, sexual commitment, and

social commitment given together
mutually help keep the inner and
outer man from divisions and build
up the human community.[26]

In the Christian way of life faithfulness to
promise begins, not in the exchange of mutual
affection between sexual partners, but in the
baptismal commitment to abide in response to God's
love. As baptized, we are continual witnesses to
the effective power of God's promise in the world.
And this enablement encompasses all dimensions of
human life in society. Having promised once from
the depths of our being, we are capable of further
articulations of the same basic investment of
self. As much as we should move slowly to the
point of readiness for such a challenge, it is the
Christian vision of hopeful assurance in the God
who can work wonders in our life that allows us to
say 'Yes, I do' and mean it with all the integrity
we can muster.

(h) Conclusion--

The Christian way of life inculcates three
virtues in the realm of sexuality: chastity
(disciplined determination of appropriate sexual
behavior according to the degree of relatedness of
the partners), love (intimate sharing of mutual
concern according to the natural stages of attraction, passion, friendship, and sacrificial
service), and faithfulness to promise (patient
perdurance in the voluntary exchange of reciprocal
commitment according to the community based
meaning of exclusivity and permanence). For all
of its history the Church has seen monogamous
marriage as the context which best promotes the
full realization of sexual expression while
preserving the priority of these values. Any
other pattern of sexual behavior which emerges in
human experience will be judged by the same
criteria. The Christian way of life has described
singleness and celibacy in such a way that they
can satisfy these tests. But, until recently, it
has never been suggested that the homosexual forms

322

of relatedness might also be a viable moral alternative in the Christian way of life.

IV. The Homosexual Way of Life and the Christian Way of Life

I have described homosexuality in such a way that it includes only adults who experience a steady and nearly exclusive erotic attraction to members of the same sex. I have suggested that the causes of homosexuality are uncertain, although there is a strong probability that it is based in environmental rather than biological factors. As such homosexuality is not a sign of mental illness even though a fairly high percentage of homosexuals may be suffering from one kind of personal impairment or another. The critical moral question is not--why are there homosexuals? or how can they be cured?, but, given the existence of a certain percentage of homosexual persons, can the Christian community celebrate, in any context of relatedness, the full expression of their sexual orientation through genital acts?

Traditionally, the tendency has been to look at homosexual behavior in terms of the meaning of the acts in the life of the particular person who engages in them. The negative judgments based upon biological finality and sexual symbolization, which were discussed in Chapter 9, both concentrate on the limiting circumstances that structure the possibilities of the individual homosexual perticipant. While these approaches are still valid in some of their articulations, I have chosen to take a different approach by reformulating the very question itself. In Chapter 7 I brought together a number of characteristics which I claimed constituted the homosexual way of life. In the previous sections of this chapter I have done the same for the Christian way of life. Now I would like to contrast them in order to argue their irreconcilability.

323

(a) Chastity and the Homosexual Way of Life--

I believe that the common denominator in the pattern of social organization of the homosexual sub-culture is a basic commitment to unrestricted personal sexual freedom. While factors of individual upbringing, taste, religious or philosophical conviction, or availability may influence the degree to which this freedom is exercised by a particular homosexual person, there is no generally accepted criterion (like unitive and procreative have been for heterosexuals) that can limit or restrict the form of this behavior.

Chastity is only possible when some value or interlocking set of values applicable to sexuality are proven to be promotive of human goodness and human flourishing. In the wide diversity of the social institutions of the homosexual world nearly every form of sexual possibility is explored and approbated. But it is not clear how they can be balanced off against each other in some evident hierarchy of appropriateness.

It is understandable why Christian theologians who wish to argue a case for the acceptability of some homosexual relationships have focused on the stable couple. It is the closest parallel to heterosexual marriage and it seems to at least offer a structured context for genital expression. Yet I have tried to show that the stable couple is not the typical arrangement in the homosexual way of life and that a number of homosexual spokespersons consider such a pairing to be inimical to the unrestricted exploration of the full homosexual possibility. Whether the number of stable homosexual partnerships would go up in a less repressive environment is impossible to prove in advance. I suspect that it would to some extent. But I also suspect that serial relationships, perhaps within the context of broad affiliation groups, would be closer to the norm.

While there is no doubt that an individual homosexual person can be chaste, I am not sure how habits of chastity are possible within the homosexual way of life. At most, some sub-groups may approximate a chaste ideal by encouraging a movement away from the more promiscuous, more anonymous, and more depersonalized forms of homosexual expression.

(b) <u>Love and the Homosexual Way of Life</u>--

Homosexuals are surely capable of intense and satisfying love. In its initial dynamics, the attraction and passion that drive two people to spend time together and to seek a higher quality of relatedness do not seem to vary according to sexual orientation. In fact, it is probably the case that some homosexual couples are more proficient in love-making (proficient in both level of communication and in genital pleasure inducement) than their heterosexual peers. To call someone a 'lover' in homosexual argot is both a sign of endearment and a proclamation of the desire for continued intimacy. But it is the handicaps to this progression in mutual revelation and discovery that are the cause for alarm.

Some homosexuals make deep friendships with other homosexuals. Yet it is not clear whether a sexual dimension to the relationship contributes to or inhibits such a development. The prevalent strains of jealousy and anger that creep into the lives of so many homosexual couples would seem to suggest that access to the privileged core of another person, which is the fruit of friendship, may also lead to a devastating caricature of that same person in fits of imagined or real slight. No doubt this also happens in the heterosexual world. But the shattering of the bond seems more irreparable when the mystery of sexual differentiation is not present to explain away the foundering of the relationship.

The most demanding form of love, the kind that directs itself to the well-being of the other without counting the cost to self, is difficult of achievement for any sexual being. No one can

325

claim that heterosexual marriage is any panacea for the selfish, the immature or the irresponsible. Yet the procreative context of such marriage provides the opportunity for the growth of a love which carries the partners beyond the original focus in each other to the wider dimensions of joyful and serious service of a broader community. Of this kind of structured love, the homosexual way of life seems to be tragically deficient. The preoccupation with sexual identity and freedom of expression seem to militate against a disinterested service of the neighbor, except for the overriding altruism of the individual homosexual.

I believe that the homosexual way of life confuses the sexual manifestation of love and artistry in the performance of pleasurable genital acts with the full range of the human capacity for love. Only with great difficulty does it allow for love-as-friendship to find a sexual focus. And even more regretably the inner direction of the homosexual group or couple has no pre-given forum (like the raising of children) in terms of which the individuals involved can let their experience of love overflow into the world around them.

(c) Faithfulness and the Homosexual Way of Life--

Silent strangers, habitues of gay baths and gay bars, and members of social cliques make no promises to each other. Participants in homophile organizations are committed to the cause but they are free to disengage at any time they wish. Even homosexual couples have no formal procedure for promise-making to each other (outside of the newly created rituals of some lesbian and church-oriented gay groups). As a result, it is not clear how faithfulness to promise can be considered an integral part of the homosexual way of life. At a minimum, we can say that friends and lovers should never violate the confidence of

326

cherished others or abandon them cruelly after the breakup of a relationship. But this is nothing more than decency or civility of response.

For some, faithfulness in a homosexual partnership is juxtaposed to the promiscuous pattern of the one-night stand. Better to promote the effort at permanence and exclusivity, even if the chances are slim, than to settle for the fragile and time-wrought ambience of the sexual dilletante. The logic of the argument is compelling, but more as a gesture of realism than as an honest portrayal of a viable alternative.

In promising-making, the form and the content of the promise must both ring true. In the homosexual way of life neither is adequate to a Christian interpretation of the sexual possibility. The form is deficient because neither Church nor civil society has seen fit to provide a social expectation within which such expressions of commitment have any binding force. In this instance, there is neither bond nor divorce, neither the public meshing of two lives nor its dissolution. Even if the state were to allow for such a public ritual, it could not guarantee that the general moral attitudes would grant it the same status as heterosexual promising.

The content of the promise is also deficient because no one knows for sure what the words should say. As soon as the concepts of 'permanence' or 'exclusivity' would be introduced, the disagreements within the homosexual community would be considerable. There is no active paradigm, no workable model of homosexual commitment. As long as this is the case, any words of promise are a vague assertion of a desire for stability and security in the midst of the tentativeness of a pleasurable relationship.

The evidence is not good that homosexual couples can overcome all of the obstacles against them and achieve a stable, loving and faithful bond. But even if this is possible for some, the clear majority of participants in the homosexual way of life are unaffected by such considerations. Faithfulness to self or to the homosexual liberation cause has a higher priority than private pacts between homosexual partners.

(d) Conclusion--

I am convinced that the homosexual way of life, as evolved in the social structures and practices of the homosexual sub-culture, is irreconcilable with the Christian way of life. It fails to adequately embody the normative Christian values of chastity, love and faithfulness to promise. Because it is centered in the pursuit of unrestricted sexual freedom, it can describe no limits to the function of sexuality in a life. As much as individual homosexuals may be chaste, loving and faithful, they achieve this integration despite, and not because of, the values of the homosexual world. In the days ahead, I suspect that the full import of homosexuality as a way of life will emerge from the public discussion that is being called for. This entails the acceptance of monogamous heterosexual marriage (and family life) as a sexist and oppressive institution and its replacement by some up to now untried forms of sexual institutionalization.

<u>Footnotes to Chapter 11</u>--

^{1}The metaphor of the 'Two Ways' as found in <u>The Didache</u> and <u>The Letter of Pseudo Barnabas</u> is a likely point of reference for the use of the term the 'Christian Way of Life.' Of course, John's Gospel speaks of those who walk in the darkness as opposed to the light and Paul contrasts 'the flesh and the spirit', 'this age and the age to come.' For a useful discussion of the ethical teaching of the first Christian centuries, see: Francis X. Murphy, <u>Moral Teaching in the Primitive Church</u> (Glen Rock: Paulist, 1968); Waldo Beach and H. Richard Niebuhr (eds.), <u>Christian Ethics</u> (New York: Ronald, 1955), pp. 46-57; Kenneth Kirk, <u>The Vision of God: the Christian Doctrine of the 'Summum Bonum'</u> (New York: Harper & Row, 1931); and R. Newton Flew, <u>The Idea of Perfection in Christian Theology</u> (Oxford: Clarendon, 1934).

^{2}Edward LeRoy Long, <u>A Survey of Christian Ethics</u> (New York: Oxford University Press, 1967); H. Richard Niebuhr, <u>Christ and Culture</u> (New York: Harper & Row, 1951); Ernst Troeltsch, <u>The Social Teaching of the Christian Churches</u> (New York: Macmillon, 1956); Kirk, <u>loc. cit.</u>; Flew, <u>loc. cit.</u>

^{3}John Giles Milhaven, <u>Toward a New Catholic Morality</u> (Garden City: Doubleday, 1970), p. 37.

^{4}Willem Van der Marck, <u>Towards a Christian Ethic</u> (Shannon: Ecclesia, 1969), p. 15.

^{5}Charles Curran, <u>Catholic Moral Theology in Dialogue</u> (Notre Dame: Fides, 1972), p. 19. It is interesting to note that in a later work, Curran somewhat modifies this view in the direction of speaking of a proper 'stance' or 'horizon' for Christian ethics based upon the Christian mysteries of creation, sin, incarnation, redemption and resurrection. <u>New Perspectives in Moral Theology</u> (Notre Dame: Fides, 1974), p. 56ff. A longer attempt to reconcile this discrepancy can be found in: <u>Ongoing Revision: Studies in Moral Theology</u> (Notre Dame: Fides, 1975), pp. 1-36.

[6]Herbert McCabe, What Is Ethics All About? (Washington: Corpus, 1969).

[7]William E. May, Becoming Human (Dayton: Pflaum, 1975), p. 21.

[8]Enda McDonagh, Invitation and Response (New York: Sheed & Ward, 1972), p. 38.

[9]Norbert and Rigali, "On Christian Ethics," Chicago Studies, 10, 1971, pp. 227-247.

[10]Josef Fuchs, Human Values and Christian Morality (Dublin: Gill and Macmillan, 1970), p. 124.

[11]Richard McCormick, "Notes on Moral Theology," Theological Studies, 32, 1972, p. 75.

[12]Gerard Hughes, "A Christian Basis for Ethics," Heythrop Journal, 13, 1972, pp. 27-43. In a followup article, Michael Simpson criticizes Hughes for not recognizing that the Christian faith also adds a "substantive content' to our moral knowledge, especially when Christ's death-resurrection and life of self-giving love are taken into account. "A Christian Basis for Ethics?," Heythrop Journal, 15, 1974, pp. 285-297.

[13]There is an extensive literature available on the history of Christian teaching on pacifism and just war theory. I have found the following works especially helpful: G.H.C. Macgregor, The New Testament Basis of Pacifism (New York: Fellowship, 1954); Roland Bainton, Christian Attitudes Toward War and Peace (New York: Abingdon, 1960); Ralph Potter, War and Moral Discourse (Richmond: John Knox, 1970); John Howard Yoder, The Politics of Jesus (Grand Rapids: Eerdmans, 1972); Thomas Merton, Faith and Violence (ND: University of Notre Dame Press, 1968); Stanley Windass, Christianity versus Violence (London: Sheed and Ward, 1964); LeRoy Walters, Five Classic Just War Theories (Yale dissertation,

330

1971); Frederick Russell, The Medieval Theories of Just War (Johns Hopkins dissertation, 1969); and James T. Johnson, Ideology, Reason and the Limitation of War (Princeton University Press, 1975).

[14]Ernst Troeltsch, The Social Teaching of the Christian Churches (New York: Macmillan, 1956); Max Weber, The Protestant Ethic and the Spirit of Capitalism (New York: Scribners, 1958); Joseph Gremillion, The Gospel of Peace and Justice (Maryknoll: Orbis, 1976); John A. Ryan, A Living Wage (New York: Macmillan, 1906); Robert Handy, The Social Gospel in America, 1870-1920 (New York: Oxford University, 1966).

[15]For two recent treatments of the function of prayer and liturgy in the moral life of the Christian see: James T. Burtchaell, Philemon's Problem (Chicago: ACTA, 1973), pp. 123-144; and Enda McDonagh, Invitation and Response: Essays in Christian Moral Theology (New York: Sheed and Ward, 1972), pp. 96-108.

[16]Cf., W. Cole, Sex and Love in the Bible (New York: Association, 1959); Helmut Thielicke, The Ethics of Sex (Grand Rapids: Baker, 1964); Joseph Blenkinsopp, Sexuality and the Christian Tradition (Dayton: Pflaum, 1969); Herbert Richardson, Nun, Witch, Playmate (New York: Harper & Row, 1971); Edward Schillebeeckx, Marriage: Human Reality and Saving Mystery (New York: Sheed & Ward, 1965); and Edward Schillebeeckx, Celibacy (New York: Sheed and Ward, 1968).

[17]Schillebeeckx, Sexuality and the Christian Tradition; Blenkinsopp, loc. cit.; Rosemary Haughton, The Theology of Marriage (ND: Fides, 1971).

[18]For a helpful presentation of the covenant theme in regards to sexuality see: Paul Ramsey, "A Christian Approach to the Question of Sexual Relations Outside of Marriage," Journal of Religion, 45, 1965, pp. 111-118.

331

[19]Cf., Blenkinsopp, loc. cit., pp. 81-101; Thomas Driver, "Sexuality and Jesus," in Sex: Thoughts for Contemporary Christians, edited by Michael Taylor (Garden City: Doubleday, 1973), pp. 43-56.

[20]Cf. Sidney Cornelia Callahan, Beyond Birth Control: The Christian Experience of Sex (New York: Sheed and Ward, 1968), pp. 17-58; and Rosemary Haughton, loc. cit., pp. 17-34.

[21]Bishop Francis Mugavero, "Sexuality--God's Gift: A Pastoral Letter," Catholic Mind, 74, May, 1976, p. 54.

[22]Richard McCormick, "The Priest and Teen-Age Sexuality," Homiletic and Pastoral Review, 65, 1965, p. 385.

[23]Victor Paul Furnish, The Love Command in the New Testament (New York: Abingdon, 1972); M.C. D'Arcy, The Mind and Heart of Love (New York: Meridan, 1947); Anders Nygren, Agape and Eros (New York: Harper & Row, 1939); Gene Outka, Agape--An Ethical Analysis (Yale U. Press, 1972); C.S. Lewis, Four Loves (New York: Harcourt, Brace and World, 1960); Daniel Day Williams, The Spirit and the Forms of Love (New York: Harper & Row, 1968).

[24]Richard Roach, "Sex in Christian Morality," The Way, 11, 1971, p. 156.

[25]Ramsey, loc. cit., p. 115.

[26]Callahan, loc. cit., pp. 127-128.

Chapter 12

The Church and the Homosexual

In the course of this book I have tried to develop an argument for the continuation of the Christian prohibition of homosexual genital acts by consenting adults. While the nature of the question is such that any argument will find its detractors, I would like to indicate in this final chapter how I propose to translate these ethical conclusions into pastoral practice in the ongoing life of the Church. This will require me to treat four problem areas: (i) homosexual marriages (ii) the ordination of professed homosexuals to ministry and priesthood (as well as entrance into the religious life) (iii) homosexual organizations in the Church or homosexual churches and (iv) pastoral counseling.

I. Homosexual Marriages-

The most convenient analogy in describing loving, committed homosexual couples for those theologians who advocate a change in Church teaching is heterosexual marriage. As I have indicated in previous chapters, the majority of revisionists envisage a future in which such social patterns would be the typical form of adult homosexual patterning. In fact, they hinge most of their expectation for a radical transformation in Christian attitudes on the feasibility of such a positive change. However, there is no agreement about whether the word 'marriage' is the proper term to capture the reality of the relationship.

The first problem is that civil law prohibits the validation of such unions. Even were Church representatives to witness the solemnization of an exchange of promises, it would have no formal status in the broader society. While some are pushing for a recognition of homosexual bonds by the State, it does not seem likely that this will by enacted in the immediate future. And even if a few of the more liberal states move in that direction, resistance in other sections of the country will probably be intense. A few homosexuals have resorted to name changes to mask their sexual

334

identity, but such subterfuges confuse the technical performance of the legal rite with the social approbation of the relationship.

A second problem is that it is not clear that the more militant spokespersons of the homophile movement consider this type of imitation of the patriarchal, oppressive, sexist institution of heterosexual marriage worthy of imitation. For them, the shattering of the old social presuppositions is a prerequisite for genuine liberation. Thus an influential component of gay liberationists attack the desirability of homosexual marriages as an accepted manner of celebration of partner commitment.

Third, the supportive context in the wider society is almost entirely missing for the homosexual pair. There are financial and legal issues to be sorted out in the penumbra of the established policies and legal interpretations. In the vast majority of instances, there are no children and therefore only one generation is involved. This raises problems in times of incapacitaion and old age. In those situations where one's family and/or friends are rejecting of the homosexual way of life, a deep sense of isolation may creep in. Thus, financial security, temporal continuity, and family concern may all be lacking.

But suppose the social and legal barriers to homosexual marriages are removed, what then? How should the Christian Church respond? Surprisingly, there are very few Christian theologians (even among the revisionists) who favor the extension of the liturgical rite of marriage to include homosexual couples. And this is true of both Catholics who consider marriage a sacrament, and Protestants who do not.

Philip Keane represents the mainstream of the Catholic tradition when he asserts,

> One way in which Church and
> society ought to witness this
> sense of ontic evil in homosexual
> acts is by refusing to permit
> homosexual marriages...The Church
> and society should be open to
> finding other ways of supporting
> stable homosexual unions, but
> these unions should not be equated
> with marriage.[1]

While not everyone who agrees with his conclusions
would employ the same analytical categories, they
would still vehementaly resist any change in this
regard. William Muehl, from a Protestant perspective, is less definitive, but equally resistant
when he says, "One needs to be very cautious about
sacramentalizing what may well be a ritual of
hatred or agression."[2]

Even among those who call for a reformation
of the Christian view of homosexuality, there is a
tendency to favor the development of another
ritual (perhaps of a paraliturgical status) which
would avoid confusion with the familiar marriage
ceremony. Norman Pittenger, for example, does not
support homosexual marriages in the Church.[3]
Instead he foresees the day when some sort of a
'service' with a blessing will be possible. And
James Nelson writes,

> But new rites can be created to
> meet legitimate needs unmet by
> existing symbols...A 'blessing of
> union' rite (by whatever name)
> could function in ways not identi-
> cal but parallel to marriage
> rites.[4]

In fact, the kind of ceremony that Pittenger
and Nelson picture is already being experimented
with in the Metropolitan Community Church. This
mainly homosexual denomination has instituted a
'Holy Union' in which public promises are
exchanged by homosexual couples.[5] The formula of

promise has been changed from the traditional one to 'be faithful as long as your love shall last.' According to the evolved interpretation, fidelity is taken to mean honesty rather than exclusivity.

Separate from this isolated instance of a denomination ratifying a formal ceremony for homosexual unions (and some clandestine ones by priests and ministers of the mainstream churches), there is no indication of strong support for such a move elsewhere. Elliott Wright sums up the contemporary situation in these words, "No confessional family or denomination has moved a single centimeter toward sanctioning marriage of members of the same sex, and probably none will in the near future."[6]

My own position is that homosexual marriage is an ontological impossibility, that is, the conditions necessary for a sacramental celebration of the relationship cannot be realized by a homosexual couple. The first of these conditions-loving fidelity-is capable of being debated. I have no doubt that some homosexual partners love each other deeply and manifest many admirable traits in their interpersonal lives. If fidelity is taken to mean permanent commitment to one other person in an exclusive and abiding way, I think the evidence is mixed. Many presentday homosexual couples would consider such a normative criterion to be alien to their own desires for self-development and self-fulfillment. Others might strive to be faithful, but with a low expectation for success. A few may achieve some semblance of, or an actual realization of, temporal continuity in the relationship. Relative to the many obstacles to such fidelity in our culture, this is an admirable achievement, especially in an age when the permanence of many heterosexual marriages leaves much to be desired. However, I suspect that there is something in the nature of the homosexual dynamism which prevents loving fidelity from being an integral component of many homosexual unions.

337

The second condition-procreative fruitful-
ness- is rendered impossible by the physiological
makeup of the participants. Even when lesbians
participate in artifical insemination procedures
or homosexuals of either sex adopt, the children
involved are only secondarily rooted in the sexual
bonding of the partners. It is true that the
instinctive drive toward generativity may be
equally strong in both heterosexuals and homosexuals, but its concrete expression in genital
acts in the homosexual partnership is incapable of
realization. Just as unmarried heterosexuals may
desire children of their own, even in the absence
of a sexual relationship, so may homosexuals. But
in the strict sense, neither group may have
children of their own.

Lest this view seem excessively biological
(as the ban on contraception has appeared to
many), I want to acknowledge that homosexual
couples may enhance the creativity in each other
and thus stimulate a cultural fruitfulness of a
kind. Perhaps this can explain the legitimate
achievements of famous homosexuals of all ages.
But I think this can be explained as a function of
friendship rather than procreativity. Loving
service of the neighbor is admirable whatever its
source. Yet there is no necessity for formalization of such friendship until this service
involves a helpless third party who must be protected from harm and raised to adulthood no matter
what degree of responsibility its parents desire
to assume. Friendships need nourishment and
support, but only the humanness of its offspring
(or potential offspring) in the committed heterosexual context entails a civic or ecclesial form
of public reinforcement.

The third condition-symbolic completion-is
also absent in the homosexual relationship. For a
Christian, the reconciliation and fusion of opposites is at the center of the mystery of God's
relationship to the Church. In the biblical
witness, the marriage bond between husband and
wife was chosen as the most fitting analogue

338

in human experience to this transcendant reality. Not only physically, but psychologically and expressively, the male-female dichotomy was understood to constitute one of the main polarities of the created order. While this interpretation was often employed in a prejudicial way to subordinate women in social, political and economic spheres, there does not seem to be any inherent reason why this should be the case. Differentness does not require overt discrimination according to sex. There are presently many indications even within the militant wings of the feminist movement that the denial of sexual differentiation was a false step and not promotive of genuine liberation.

The claim that only the male-female union can symbolize full sexual completion does not mean that male or female must take this step to be happy or valuable or normal. In the Christian tradition there is a strong assertion of the right of heterosexuals not to marry if that seems preferable. What it does mean is that no degree of personality or physical difference between individuals of the same sex can offer the same opportunity for complementary fulfillment. Male-male and female-female relationships are too closely based on similarties of orientation to encompass the utter givenness of the sexual other. This is why sexual compatibility and high levels of sexual communication between homosexual partners is no proof of the supiority of the relationship. On the contrary, it seems to lead to quick boredom and the endless pursuit of the ideal lover. While facility in sexual technique may often come easier to homosexual couples, it is the absence of mystery and the consequent waning of enthusiasm for the exploration of the depth of the other that explains the tragic recriminations that so easily creep into the best homosexual relationships. One can only be perpetually new and different if it springs from other than pose and role-playing.

A further dimension of the question of symbolic completion in homosexual unions is the function of the sex acts themselves. Most

339

evidence has shown that homosexuals engage in a variety of sexual practices. While anal intercourse has an inverted similarity to heterosexual intercourse, it is not the preferred technique. Rather oral intercourse and interfemoral intercourse are. Further, most homosexuals during the course of their lives (or of a particular relationship) alternate between playing the active and passive roles. What this suggests is that there is no correlation between phsysiological response and gender role definition. Homosexual actors do not simulate the male-female union as if the masculine nature of one and the feminine nature of the other were being brought to completion. Rather they potentially assume both sides of the gender defined spectrum. Their love-making may be sensually satisfying and communicative of a desire for reciprocal integration, but it can never symbolize the kind of fusion of opposites that heterosexual intercourse is capable of.

By way of conclusion, it is my conviction that the term 'homosexual marriage' is a misnomer because it refers to a reality which cannot exist. Homosexuals can be friends, lovers, and helpmates, but they cannot enter into a true marriage in the Christian sense. While some few may achieve loving fidelity in their relationship, they are incapable of realizing the values of procreative fruitfulness and symbolic completion. This is not a failure of good will or perseverance, but a function of the very givenness of the created order. Because there cannot be a homosexual marriage, the Church cannot celebrate such a reality in liturgical ritual. To do so is a mockery of the sacredness of the heterosexual union.

Yet, some have suggested, that even if no good case can be made for homosexual marriage, perhaps some other Church-focused ritual would be appropriate. My answer to this possibility is that the Church can only legitimately celebrate that which represents a genuine realization of a

value. Since I find the homosexual way of
life, including the most positive expression of it
(namely, stable couples) to involve the pursuit of
a disvalue, I do not see how the Church can pretend to give approbation to its continuance. Even
para-liturgical rites are an overt manifestation
of support and encouragement. Otherwise, why go
to all that bother. It is for this reason that
what may seem like a small, insignificant accommodation of the tradition to pastoral necessity may
create a climate of gradual acceptance. This is
surely part of the motivation of Christian theologians who propose it.

I am opposed to any change in Church practice
which would seem to legitimate, as an acceptable
form of the Christian life, stable homosexual
relationships. As much as such relationships may
need to be tolerated in pastoral practice, they
can never adequately represent the Christian
understanding of human sexuality.

II. Ordination of Homosexuals/Acceptance of Homosexuals to Religious Life

In 1051 Peter Damiani created quite a stir in
Catholic Europe when he published Liber
Gomorrhinus which castigated the prevailing decadence among the clergy, as seen in the spread of
homosexual practices. This even included, he
claimed, penitents confessing to the same priest
with whom they engaged in sexual relations. Much
of the reaction to Peter' book was negative and
Pope Leo IX quieted the controversy by rebuking
him for the harshness of his attitude. It is probable that Peter oversold the extremeness of the
situation. Yet there must have been enough truth
in his claims to make them credible.

Other than occasional outbreaks of prophetic
denunciation of clerical abuses, we have no way of
knowing to what extent homosexuality has been a
major problem among Catholic priests and
Protestant ministers. In the Catholic world, the

341

issue is further complicated by the celibate commitment of the priestly order. Where the unmarried minister in the Proestant denominations evokes considerable comment, sometimes taking the form of sexual innuendo, this does not necessarily occur with celibate priests. Only a characteristic effeminacy or a pattern of suggestive relationships is liable to raise the same questions about a particular priest.

In recent years, congregational reserve on the matter has been upset by the increasing militancy of gays within the Church. Autobiographies have been written by Church leaders admitting a homosexual lifestyle. In some instances criminal arrests have been made. And homosexuals in seminaries have gone public prior to ordination. What this has all meant is that conflicting evidence suggests either a large or a fragmentary gay presence in the ordained ministry of the Church. Thus there are really two questions being asked: (i) what is the present role of homosexuals in the Christian churches? and (ii) what should it be?

(a) The Presence of Homosexual Ministers and Priests in the Church-

Since a majority of Protestant ministers eventually marry, it would seem at first sight that this is sufficient proof tht homosexuality is not a major problem among them. But as we have seen this does not necessarily follow. Especially in professional jobs where appearances are important, some people enter marriage (either consciously or unconsciously) in order to keep up a proper image. Troy Perry, for instance, the founder of the gay-oriented Metropolitan Community Church, was married and had two sons before he came out as homosexual and began his proselytizing work. But whether they married or not, there seem to have always been homosexuals among the Protestant clergy. Tracy Early suggests that "Church officials were always aware that some homosexuals had been ordained; but generally it was considered a scandal whenever a case became public, and people preferred not to think about it."[7]   In more specific terms, Sally Gearhart and Bill Johnson have this to say about one denomination. "It is widely assumed in the gay community that there is a high proportion of closeted Gay men in the Episcopal priesthood...The propensity of Gay men to remain closeted seem especially acute within the patriarchal Episcopal church."[8]

As for the Catholic priesthood (whether in its secular or religious form), there is some suspicion that the percentage of homosexual oriented individuals is higher than in the general population. Richard Wood opts for the higher figure when he reports,

> a rather conservative estimate of the number of homosexual men and women in the Catholic priesthood and religious life, according to a consensus of priests and religious I surveyed at a recent workshop, falls around thirty percent. There seems to be a proportionate number in the Protestant ministry and the rabbinate as well.[9]

John Harvey, on the other hand, who has done extensive counseling of homosexual clergy and religious, phases it differently. He says,

> the data indicate that overt homosexuality is not greater among priests and religious than among the general population. The same data suggests that the incidence of latent homosexual conflicts is greater among seminarians and male religious.[10]

If, in fact, there are more homosexuals in the Catholic priesthood than statistical probabilities would lead us to expect, we can surely

343

ask why. The first reason would seem to be the limited range of ethical alternatives presented to the homosexual by the Catholic Church. A person who is required to remain celibate anyway might consider the celibate priesthood an enhancement of opportunity rather than a restriction. Better to assume a convenient, community-based form of service than to face the inevitable probing questions about the absence of an interest in marriage. And the conviction that religious work is a desirable form of sublimation of sexual energies can also lead in that direction.

A second reason would be the attraction of an all-male preparatory environment and a predominately male collaborative structure. The easy rapport with other men can counterbalance the strained inexperience in the world of women. It is not so much that a male environment provides seductive opportunities (although with some candidates this may be the case) but rather that it is familiar, comfortable, and relatively free of tension.

A third reson would be the old axiom that 'like attracts like.' There are some indications that particular dioceses or religious communities have been willing to admit homosexual candidates on a par with heterosexual candidates. As a result, a higher percentage of members have this particular disposition and the nature of the common life assumes certain characteristics that in turn attract more such candidates.

While it is undoubtedly true that the churches, both Protestant and Catholic, have always had closeted gays in their ministries, we will never know for sure how significant their presence has been. In fact, it only becomes an imperative question when sexual orientation also become a matter of public acknowledgement and overt expression. In the confidential setting of spiritual direction or of formal evaluation of candidates for ordination, it is proper that those entrusted with the good of the community probe the

344

significance of a person's sexual attitude and
behaviors. And, of course, the same is true of
those applying for acceptance into seminary
programs. But, having met the standards of moral
and professional competence for ordination, a
minister or priest who is homosexually-oriented
(and capable of living a celibate life) might well
consider the question a private matter that he (or
she) is free to communicate or not as seems
opportune.

(b) On the Ordination of Publically-Professed
Homosexuals-

It is the advent of the gay liberation movement which has created the social ferment which
today overflows into the life of the Church and
confronts it with a major policy decision. The
first dimension of the issue is whether a self-
conscious homosexual identity in a candidate for
ordination is sufficient grounds for disqualifica-
tion. The second dimension is whether openness to
overt homosexual relationships in such candidates
(at the present time or in the future) is an
ethical issue or a political issue. Let us look
at each of these dimensions in turn.

(1) Homosexual Identity and Ordination-This
particular dimension of the problem is only a concern to those denominations which rule out the
possibility of morally responsible homosexual
relationships. In these cases, the most important
question is why an individual wishes to make his
or her sexual orientation a matter of public
record. The most likely explanation is as a means
of identification with the struggle for gay rights
within the Church. Or perhaps a particular person
wants to avoid a sense of personal hypocrisy or
duplicity. The desire for an honest response to
seminary interrogation can be respected in its own
terms. Yet in a Church-setting where both morally
and emotionally the majority of members are
hostile to such propensities it can be legitimately wondered whether the price is too high to
warrant the practice.

345

In the Catholic context, where a formal celibate commitment is required for ordination, this celibate form of sexual proclamation should be sufficient to invest the ordinandus with the proper credentials. In a sense, one's sexual orientation is only important if it affects one's ability to faithfully live a celibate life. To present oneself as a homosexual candidate is to make too much of the sexual experience of self out of which the willingness to be a non-genital sexual being has emerged. It also shortcircuits one's ability to serve the whole Church. I think it is proper for the bishop and/or the seminary authorities to refuse to ordain Catholic seminarians who insist on manifesting publically their homosexual orientation. While this need not be a situation of scandal (since there is nothing morally objectionable in simply being a homosexual), it is a matter of communication of a vision of celibate ministry in the Church. At this moment in Church history, the political and social meaning of such attestations is too ambiguous to be acceptable.

(2) Homosexual Relationships and Ordination- For those denominations of a more liberal bent, where there is no definitive policy on the morality of homosexual behavior, there is the further question of whether homosexual and heterosexual candidates for ordination should be treated on a par. If gays intend to abide by the kind of relatedness criteria suggested by the revisionist theologians, should not the denomination be open to their sense of ministerial vocation? In a number of instances, these candidates have excelled in their academic and pastoral training. The only thing that seems to be holding them back is an unwillingness on the part of Church authorities to accept their requests for ordination.

The climate has changed drastically in the more progressive interdominational seminaries. For example, there are gay seminarian caucuses with official recognition at Berkely, Boston,

346

Chicago and New York.[11] A number of places invite representatives of militant gay groups to address the student body. And courses in ethics often teach the material on homosexual ethics with a strong revisionist slant. But as so often happens in liberal Protestantism (and in liberal Catholicism for that matter) the seminaries have probably lost touch with the local churches. It is not at all clear that, even in the most pluralistic settings, ordained homosexuals have much hireability. In 1972, for instance, Bill Johnson, an open homosexual, was ordained by the United Church of Christ after some delay and much acrimonious debate. But even that denomination has proceeded slowly since its ability to absorb professed gay ministers is limited.

A sampling of opinion from the Protestant mainstream would tend to reinforce this hesitance. For instance, Don Williams (a Presbyterian) and Ruth Tiffany Barnhouse (an Episcopalian) oppose the ordination of active homosexuals.[12] The Christian Century magainze in an editorial on the question has this to say about the United Methodist church.

> If we read the present church climate correctly, the young leaders of the Council on Youth Ministry may be reaching too far at this time in asking the church to grant the privileges of full ordination to homosexuals. A church has the right and the responsibility to establish criteria for its ordained leaders...In evaluating the rights of homosexuals to receive ordination, arguments will have to begin at the point of whether homosexuality is a natural pattern of sexual adjustment for some persons or an aberration.[13]

Despite these words of caution, there are some spokespersons who argue for ordination provided that a proper selection process and training program is undertaken. In this spirit James Nelson reviews the discussion in his own denomination as moving toward a gradual change of policy.

> The ordination question continues to be difficult...The recommendation made by the United Church's Executive Council in 1973, if difficult to implement, is the appropriate stance: 'It (the Executive Council) recommends to assocaition that in the instance of considering a stated homosexuals candidacy for ordination the issue should not be his/her homosexuality and his/her understanding of the morality of its use.' This, indeed, is the logic of full acceptance.[14]

Two other writers take the tack of sexual rights within the Church as the grounds for admission to ordination. Lewis Maddocks argues that "the church should not exclude homosexuals as a class from membership, ordination, seminaries, or as employees within local parishes, juridictional entities, or in positions of national leadership."[15] On somewhat the same grounds, Tracy Early speaks of the failure to witness to the principle of equality in a pluralistic society. "If churches criticize government or other institutions for discriminating against homosexuals and themselves continue to discriminate in employment, they may find critics charging them with inconsistency."[16]

By way of conclusion, I would suggest that the ordination of active homosexuals has already taken place on a small scale. It has not won widespread support, even in the more liberal denominations. But since the barrier has been broken down, it is likely that a steady supply of homosexual candidates will present themselves for ordination. This will cause an ecumenical problem for those denominations, such as Roman Catholicism, which oppose such a move on ethical grounds. The retrospective revelation of homosexual identity and behavior patterns by priests and ministers does not have the same import as a conscious choice by a particular denomination to overturn its long standing ban. We are all accustomed to failure in commitment by those who experiene their own weakness and sin. What is not so familiar, and what I oppose as improper, is the trivializing of sexual conduct so that it has no decisive influence on a person's qualifications for ordination.

(3) <u>Homosexuals in the Religious Life</u>-The communal character of congregations of male and female religious is one of their chief attractions. For homosexual persons, who often have known first-hand the depths of isolation and personal shame, the desire for an extended-family living context can be very strong. To be accepted <u>as one is</u>, with whatever range of talents and interests, and to be supported by a mutual sense of purpose, is a comforting prospect. And there is the added advantage of being able to embrace a celibate option in a typical and well-established fashion rather than by way of seeming idiosyncrasy and misanthropy.

In the pre-Vatican II formative regime for religious life there were many practices, rootedin age-old experience, which prompted a deliberate reserve in same-sex relationships. Particularly for the young religious, when his or her sexual drive was presumed to be strong, the danger of passionate friendships and compromising situations was stressed and certain ascetical practices were engendered. This controlled milieu no doubt kept some percentage of prospects from homosexual encounters that would have been the only interpersonal sexual outlet in a unisexual situation. It also, as a side effect, often communicated an

349

excessively negative view of the importance of friendship and affective relationships for celibate religious.

Whatever we may think about this previous era of religious community life, the changes initiated by the Council have brought many issues to the surface which formerly could be suppressed. One of the most controversial is the admission of homosexual candidates to the religious life. The main source of tension are two: (i) can such persons lead healthy celibate lives? (ii) does the percentage of homosexual religious in a particular congregation affect in any drastic way the nature and quality of the common life?

In regards to the prospects for healthy celibate adjustment by homosexual religious, there seem to be no certain answers. John Harvey, who has written more explicitly about this matter than most, comes to this conclusion. "The fact of the tendency is not in itself a disqualifying condition, unless it is associated with other disorders or neuroses."[17] John Cavanaugh, who like Harvey has counseled many homosexual religious, says, "There are no hard-and-fast rules concerning the entry of the homosexually--oriented individual into the religious life. We cannot expect grace to work like magic. *Gratia* perficit naturam."[18]

One of the difficulties in giving an effective answer to this question is the active encouragement of homosexual friendships among celibates by some professional counselors.[19] In an era when liquor and mild drugs are readily available and sometimes form an integral part of social events, the stimulus to act out genitally, without fear of public censure, is a disturbing development. The creation of a homosexual subculture within a particular community house is sometimes the unfortunate side-effect of such clandestine or isolated encounters.

It seems to me that the following rules of thumb are a reasonable approach to the issue.

350

(i) All candidates for the religious life should be subjected to the same intense screening process. As far as I know, there is no definitive way to ascertain a homosexual orientation except through the self-revelation of the candidate. Neither written testing nor oral interviews can screen out homosexuals (as such), but they can improve the probabilities that those homosexuals who are admitted will not exhibit pathological traits.

(ii) If a candidate admits to a homosexual orientation, efforts should be made to pursue his or her general sexual history. In some instances, such a judgment may be premature or a function of some guilt-laden experiences of the past. In other cases, there may be an extensive pattern of acting out. And of course, there is a whole range of possibilities in the middle. A prudent estimate then should be made by the community (or by a spiritual director if this emerges later on) of the candidates chances of success as a celibate religious.

(iii) Instances of homosexual behavior during the time of preparation for final admission to the community should be treated with the seriousness they desire, but with no special rancor or condemnatory air. A prime consideration should be the context in which such acts took place and their probable meaning in a personal life history. Situations of public scandal and the breaking of the incest taboo within the community itself are usually more significant than other types of behavior. Mitigating factors might be the relative youth or inexperience of one of the participants. Every effort must be made to avoid the appearance of indifference or condonation toward the offenses. As far as possible there should be a symmetry between the treatment of homosexual and heterosexual violations by celibate religious.

(iv) Homosexual religious should not be entrusted with the task of supervising the formation of new members unless they have

351

exhibited a consistent and long-term pattern of responsible behavior. Otherwise, the potential for abuse of privilege is too great to risk the young persons involved.

If these procedures are followed, I believe that it is acceptable to admit homosexually-oriented persons to the religious life. I personal by know a number of exemplary religous who are homosexual and who have witnessed to their ability to lead healthy celibate lives. And others who have written on this topic have said the same.

However, I still must address the second part of the question, that is, is there a limit to the percentage of homosexuals that a given community can absorb without affecting the nature and quality of their life together? As far as I know, no one has chosen to even formulate this question in print, no less to answer it. Therefore, I will have to rely on my own tentative probing of the issue.

I suspect that at the present moment of church history, there is a wide variation from one community or province to another in the percentage of their homosexual membership. This is probably a function of a number of factors: the origins of the community; the quality of its leadership; the standards for admission; the nature of its work; the structure of governance, etc. At some point in the evolution of a community's identity it seems likely that a group with a fairly high per-cent of homosexuals will take on some of the characteristics of the homosexual subculture. This would entail in men's communities some of the following: an intense curiosity in social dynamics; a prevalence of gossip and rumor; strains in the supervisory-obediential structure; a manifest desire for affective reassurance; and a stress on solidarity of performance.

In addition to an evident shift in the inter-personal context of community life, those

communities with a significant homosexual
membership will find, their heterosexual celibate
members tending to overcompensate in the other
direction. In male communities this would
normally involve an intense concern for 'macho' or
culturally-approved ways of reinforcing one's
masculine identity. Furthermore, a conscious
attempt to avoid those individuals who give off
the wrong signals in this regard may develop.

In the long run, each community of religious
must evaluate for itself whether, in an age which
is saturated by consciousness of sexuality and in
which the celibate life is looked upon by many as
a quaint and curious, if outdated, tradition, it
is possible to project a vital and attractive
community image to heterosexual candidates if the
homosexual issue is neglected. It is not just a
matter of survival, but of carrying on a healthy
and diversified witness to the beauty of embracing
the celibate life for the sake of the kingdom.

III. Homosexual Churches and Homosexual Church
Church Organizations-

The majority of gays who are active in homophile organizations seem to have written off the
Christian Church as an inherently oppressive
institution. Because of the long tradition of
condemnation of homosexual behavior, the Church is
seen as the source of many of the difficulties
experienced by gays rather than as a source of
comfort and acceptance. In order to counteract
this impression, a number of attempts have been
made in recent years to mobilize Christian
resources for effective ministry to gay persons
and groups.

The most noteworthy of these efforts has been
the establishment of the Universal Fellowship of
Metropolitan Community Churches (MCC) by Rev. Troy
Perry.[20] On October 6, 1968 Perry, who came from
a Pentecostal background, began the first services
of the MCC in Los Angeles. Twelve people showed

up. After a period of rapid growth the first church building was dedicated in 1971. However, on January 27, 1973 a fire heavily damaged the structure. Later that year Perry stepped down as pastor in order to devote his energies to the now burgeoning denomination.

Since that time there have been signs of strain within the denomination. The personality of the local minister seems to be the prime determinant of the vitality of the individual MCC church. Perry himself has never pretended to be an intellectual. His services combined elements of various liturgical traditions, from the informality and humor of the country chapel to the symbolism and panoply of the solemn mass. Since his parishioners came from different church backgrounds, Perry attempted to provide something for everyone.

One of the directions of the MCC has been gay evangelism. This has included visits to gay bars and restaurants, letter-writing programs for gay prisoners and maintenance of hot-lines for crisis intervention. In addition, it has issued a series of publications and tracts. In order to prepare for a future expansion of their ministry, they have opened Good Samaritan Seminary, the first exclusively gay seminary in history. Another first has been the establishment of the 'Lavender Ladies', a society for transvestite church members.

Following the lead of the MCC, the first homosexual synogogue was founded in Los Angeles in 1972 and called the Metropolitan Community Temple (MCT). Since then other synogogues of similar affiliation have been founded.

There is also a small scale presence of gay priests with a tenuous affiliation with the Eastern Orthodox Church who operate out of San Francisco. These individuals seem to be attracted by the opportunity for involved displays of liturgical gamesmanship rather than by the desire to

354

found viable church groups. In their short history as gay hierarchs, these isolated self-proclaimed priests and bishops have concentrated on the bizarre and the unusual, including continual schisms, so that no one takes them too seriously.

In the Catholic context, the most evident organization dealing with gays is called Dignity. It was founded in 1969 in San Diego by Rev. Pat Nidorf, an Augustinian priest. Since that time, it has established chapters in most of the major cities of the country and it has won some degree of support from a number of Catholic bishops. The quality and style of interaction in the local groups seems to hinge to a great extent on the local leadership. Dignity holds an annual convention and periodic regional meetings.

The reaction to Dignity by interested observers has been a function of which dimension of their work was perceived as most indicative. For some, it is a belated attempt by the Church to overcome a long history of discrimination and neglect. For others, it is a focal point for reasoned debate of the Christian significance of the gay life-style. But there remains a group of critics who see this organization as a contradictory presence in the Church's life, since they suspect that it is a convenient front for a concrete effort to undermine the integrity of Christian ethical norms.

It is my opinion that Dignity can serve a useful function in the Catholic Church. I say 'can' because it is not always clear that its promise has been realized in fact. As a gathering place for homosexuals seeking mutual counsel and support within a Christian faith stance it is to be applauded. As a place for liturgical celebration and Christian community service it is equally to be commended. Even as a forum for exploring the ethical alternatives relative to sexuality in a serious and creative way, it can contribute to the quality of moral discourse in

355

the Church. But at times _Dignity_ has settled for being a place of refuge where all styles of accommodation to the homosexual way of life were tolerated indiscriminately. In those instances, it has ceased to represent a specifically Catholic perspective.

For the future, we can expect that all of the major denominations will have something comparable to _Dignity_ (and many of them already do). It is likely that such groups will be at the forefront of the calls for a change in the ethical teaching about homosexuality. How much influence they have on the wider denominational membership will depend on the astuteness of their leadership and the credibility of their witness. I think they normally serve a useful purpose as an instrument of pastoral concern. But they are also capable of being mobilized into pockets of hostility which have no realistic connection with the mainstream church. From our vantage point, it is hard to say which of these potential courses will actually be taken.

IV. Pastoral Response to the Homosexual-

In the logical order our ethical stance about homosexual behavior precedes our concrete judgments about what pastoral response to a particular homosexual person is appropriate. But, in actuality, most heterosexual counselors only develop a keen interest in the ethical problem because of their pastoral involvement in the lives of homosexual Christians. Without attempting a full-scale discussion of pastoral strategy, I would like to offer some general propositions as the beginning point for a humane and compassionate response to the plight of the homosexual Christian.

(1) Because the homosexual way of life is irreconcilable with the Christian way of life, the Church must continue to preserve the integrity of its teaching office- It is incorrect to say that

356

the Church should remain silent in a time of moral controversy. Instead, it should provide two things. First, it should clearly spell out the nature and form of the arguments against homosexual behavior. In moral catechesis it should positively relate the condemnation of homosexuality to the values and virtues to be sought in Christian sexuality. Second, it should provide a forum in which professional theologians, and other people with particular competence, can debate the revisionist proposals. In this setting there should be full freedom of expression. Yet the majority of Christians should not confuse the existence of diversity of opinion on the matter as a sign that this represents the working consensus of the living Church. Theologians are trained to disagree and to challenge established positions. Only over a significant period of time does the full range of issues emerge. As much as the teaching Church is dependent on the labors of theologians and other experts, it is different from a mere reporting of the state of the discussion at a particular moment. In regards to the homosexuality question, the traditional position (in one form of another) is supported by the majority of Catholic theologians and probably by a majority of Protestant theologians as well. Now that the revisionists are being challenged on their own grounds, the quality of the discussion is sure to improve.

(2) The Christian Way of Life encompasses every dimension of human existence; sexuality is only one facet of the self and must not be allowed to usurp the primary place- One of the tragic results of the contemporary movement toward gay liberation is that both homosexuals and heterosexuals have been led to make too much of the importance of sexual identity. While the Freudian revolution has helped us to appreciate that sexuality is an integral part of our conscious and unconscious self from birth to death, I believe that Ernest Becker is right in stressing the problem of death as the central human dilemma. All of us are sexual beings, but we are also

357

economic beings, political beings, cultural beings and social beings. The relative silence of the New Testament on matters of sexuality is a good warning to us to avoid the overemphasis on genital integration as the source of all happiness or pain. To serve our neighbor in distress, to be responsible citizens, to treat the innocent and the feeble with respect, to nourish human life and all the created world, these are all challenges which each person must face, whatever degree of sexual harmony has been achieved.

(3) Among the forms of sexual offense, homosexual behavior is not necessarily of the greatest gravity- The meaning of homosexual activity in the lives of individuals is a function of a great many factors in their personal history. Age, family environment, sexual experience, degree of relatedness, self-consciousness, extenuating circumstances, etc., can all determine whether a specific instance of sexual engagement is expressive of a person's character and moral orientation or is a bit of discrete behavior only peripherally connected to the evolution of an existential standpoint. In most instances, the repetition of a pattern of sexual responsiveness will indicate more about the individual than any one act can. Especially troublesome are homosexual patterns which reveal a tendency toward violence, coercion, anonymity, seduction of the young, impersonality and promiscuity.

(4) Some forms of the Homosexual Way of Life are more destructive than others- Among the structural components of the Homosexual way of life that I described in Chapter 4, the only three that seem to have positive features connected with them are: social cliques, couples and homphile organizations. In each there is some degree of self-revelation and reciprocal expectation for personal investment in the other(s). Social cliques can provide some sense of communal arrangement whereby the worst feature of the sexual marketplaces of the tea houses, baths and bars can be avoided. It is possible for

tenderness, solicitude and criticism to be shared in these contexts. It gives the individual homosexual a place to stand, a sense of belongingness. This is especially important as advancing age takes its toll on one's sexual prospects. But social cliques provide no ethical guidelines whereby the choices of its members are regulated. There is acceptance, but no judgment, and as a result the ultimate levels of commitment and promise-making are always inappropriate.

As far as homophile organizations are concerned, they create no moral problem as such, but since usually they advocate a complete freedom of homosexual exploration, the connection between theory and practice must inevitably be raised. I suspect it is difficult for a Christian homosexual (separate from Church-based groups) to participate for long in militant homophile organizations and maintain any allegiance to the Christian way of life.

(5) Homosexual couples, consciously committed to a permanent and exclusive relationship, offer the best hope for the preservation of Christian values by active homosexuals-As I have continually argued, the Christian church has not, cannot, and should not, celebrate a rite of marriage for homosexual couples. But, as a number of theologians have reasoned, for those homosexuals incapable of living a celibate life, such a private arrangement is surely preferable to the other alternatives of Christian homosexuals who are capable of such a commitment. Especially among those who have been sexually active for a long period of time, the odds are against them. Yet, there is some evidence that a small percentage have successfully moved in that direction.

It is my opinion that clergy persons should avoid all involvement in the public formalization of such close-coupled commitments. Whether prudence would dictate other forms of pastoral support for the couple cannot be decided in advance.

359

(6) The celibate option for Christian homosexuals should continue to be presented as the
most consistent response to the Christian ethical
judgment- By celibate I do not mean sexless,
friendless or loveless. A Christian homosexual
has the same needs for understanding, affection
and support that any other person does. By a
tragic combination of circumstances, certain
sexual outlets are ethically unacceptable. Yet
there is a whole range of types of relatedness
with both men and women, including deep friendships, which can make a healthy and satisfying
existence possible. Normally, a homosexual makes
no formal promise to live a celibate life.
Rather, he or she is in a position comparable to
an unmarried heterosexual (comparable except for
the absence of an acceptable context for full
genital expression).

There is no denying the strains that can
accompany such a restrictive ethical understanding. In an era when self-development and
self-fulfillment are the watchwords of the day,
any limitation on human freedom can seem harsh and
negativistic. Yet we have no reason to believe
that homosexuals have any greater sex drive than
heterosexuals. And we we have encouraged heterosexuals to live chaste lives as unmarried, as
widows/widowers, and as divorced persons. The
Christian community has a stake in preserving the
symmetry of the ethical demand in the situation of
both heterosexuals and homosexuals.

Any failure to totally realize this celibate
criteria does not negate the possibility of future
success. We are all sinners who violate our own
best moral convictions, but we can be healed and
forgiven. It is not so much some standard of physical virginity that counts (although this is
important for the young person struggling with
homosexual way of life). Masturbatory fantasies,
crushes, and physical expressions of affection may
trouble a celibate homosexual without a turning
point in sexual normativity being effected.

360

(7) __Christian__ homosexual persons should
strive to __develop__ __friendships__ with __Christian__
__heterosexuals-__ One of the great dangers of the
homosexual way of life is that it can isolate gays
from any intimate and sustained contact with
heterosexual social life. This tendency toward
exclusivity is understandable since all low status
groups are inclined to shut out the hostile world
from their places and moments of leisure and
recreation. But such separation from the mainstream of Christian social life can be fatal for
those who already feel alienated from the Church.
One dimension of such friendships can sometimes be
the availability of a non-gay person who can
accept the revelation of a person's homosexual
orientation without fear or censure. It is a
common phenomenon in friendships between gays and
non-gays that the ultimate test of the depth of
the relationship is the ability to accept, nourish
and love each other despite the difference of
sexual identity. This should not be done prematurely or in situations where the risks are too
high. All of us have interlocking circles of
friends, each circle allowing one side of our
personalities to be revealed. Yet that it is
appropriate with some friends, and that it is a
decisive step for many homosexuals, is borne out
by the experience of many.

(8) __Many__ __pastoral__ __issues__ __related__ to homo-
__sexuality__ __are__ __best__ __discussed__ __under__ __another__ rubric-
Homosexuals are subject to all of the problems
that other human beings are (but sometimes in
higher percentages). Whatever counseling
strategies have proven effective in other contexts
should be tried here also. Thus, difficulties
with alcohol and drug addiction, depression,
venereal disease, violent tendencies, family
antagonisms, etc. should be treated with whatever
combination of therapies offer the best prognosis
for success. Homosexuals in heterosexual marriages need long-range counseling to examine their
alternatives. Homosexuals contemplating heterosexual marriage as a solution to their problem
should be discussed from going through with it.

361

Perhaps the single most imperative need today is for the assistance of dedicated Christian homosexuals who have striven to keep the Christian ethical standard and who can help other homosexuals to do the same. Out of their collective experience hopefully we may develop a more comprehensive pastoral strategy that will really make this contingent of the Christian community feel respected and wanted.

V. Conclusion-

The Christian Way of Life is an all-encompassing expression in the lives of the disciples of Jesus Christ of the seriousness with which they wish to translate their faith into action. Countless men and women have had the audacity to believe that, despite their fallibility and sinfulness, they coul be so taken by the Spirit of God that they could make this high call into a reality. In line with these convictions, the Christian community has, from the very beginning, laid expectations on its members in regards to their sexual expression. These standards have never been easy, and in imitation of their Master and Lord, the best Pastors have always looked with compassion and forgiveness on those who have failed. Yet the Church as teacher and guide has collectively reaffirmed the importance of preserving a distinctive Christian sense of the values at stake in all sexual relationships.

In our time we struggle with a mixed witness on this issue in the wider Christian community. This should not be taken as an excuse for losing heart or failing to educate ourselves as to the key matters of dispute. This book is one contribution to a needed reexamination of the ethical teaching on homosexuality. It is not the last word, but I trust it has been a helpful word.

In the final analysis, I have been unable to reconcile the homosexual way of life with the Christian way of life.

Footnotes to Chapter 12-

¹Philip Keane, Sexual Morality: A Catholic Perspective (New York: Paulist, 1977), p. 89.

²William Muehl, "Some Words of Caution," in Homosexuality and the Christian Faith: A Symposium, edited by Harold Twiss (Valley Forge: Judson, 1978), p. 86.

³Norman Pittenger, Time for Consent: A Christian's Approach to Homosexuality (London: SCM Press, 1976), p. 78.

⁴James Nelson, "Homosexualtiy and the Church," Christianity & Crisis, 37, 1977, p. 69.

⁵Cf., Ronald Enroth and Gerald Jamison, The Gay Church (Grand Rapids: Eerdmans, 1974, pp. 85ff.

⁶Elliott Wright, "The Church and Gay Liberation," Christian Century 88, 1971, p. 284.

⁷Tracy Early, "The Struggle in the Denominations: Shall Gays Be Ordained?" Christianity & Crisis, 37, 1977, p. 118.

⁸Sally Gearhart and Bill Johnson, "The Gay Movement in the Church, in Loving Women/Loving Men, edited by Sally Gearhart and Bill Johnson (San Francisco: Glide, 1974), p. 76.

⁹Richard Woods, Another Kind of Love: Homosexuality and Spirituality (Garden City: Doubleday, 1978), p. 103.

¹⁰John Harvey, "Homosexuality and Vocations," American Ecclesiastical Review, 164, 1971, p. 44.

¹¹Gearhart and Johnson, loc. cit., p. 77.

[12]Don Williams, *The Bond That Breaks: Will Homosexuality Split the Church?* (Los Angeles: BIM, 1978), p. 130; Ruth Tiffany Barnhouse, *Homosexuality: A Symbolic Confusion* (New York: Seabury, 1977), p. 177.

[13]Editorial, *Christian Century*, 92, 1975, p. 243.

[14]James Nelson, *loc. cit.*, p. 69.

[15]Lewis Maddocks, "The Law and the Church versus the Homosexual," in *The Same Sex*, edited by Ralph Weltge (Philadelphia: United Church Press, 1969), pp. 105-106.

[16]Early, *loc. cit.*, p. 107.

[17]Harvey, *loc. cit.*, p. 55.

[18]John Cavanaugh, *Counseling the Homosexual* (Huntington: Our Sunday Visitor, 1977), p. 164.

[19]Cf. Donald Goergen, *The Sexual Celibate* (New York: Seabury, 1974), pp. 188-196.

[20]For this material, I am drawing primarily on the book by Ronald Enroth and Gerald Jamison called *The Gay Church* (Grand Rapids: Eerdmans, 1974). It is basically a journalistic descriptive endeavor but it does cover the main points of recent developments.